Main Idea Activities
for English Language Learners
and Special-Needs Students
with Answer Key

HOLT

World History
The Human Journey
Modern Era

HOLT, RINEHART AND WINSTON
A Harcourt Education Company
Austin • Orlando • Chicago • New York • Toronto • London • San Diego

Contents

Main Idea Activities

Contents

Main Idea Activities

Contents

Contents

Main Idea Activities

CHAPTER **1**   Main Idea Activities 1.1
                                    Prehistoric Peoples

VOCABULARY Some terms to understand:

• **conclusions (7):** the results of a reasoning process

• **receding (7):** moving or backing away; slanting backward

• **bison (8):** buffalo

• **harpoons (9):** spears used for hunting

• **antlers (9):** solid bones protruding from the head of a member of the deer family

• **canoes (9):** light narrow boats with sharp ends and curved sides

• **millet (10):** small-seeded grasses grown for grain or hay

• **furrows (10):** trenches in the ground made by a plow

ORGANIZING INFORMATION Fill in the Venn diagram by placing the items listed below in the correct parts of the diagram: Neanderthals, Cro-Magnons, and Both.

• lived about 35,000 to 130,000 years ago   • buried their dead

• *Homo sapiens*   • made their own tools

• spear-throwing made them good hunters   • believed in an afterlife

• artwork found on cave walls shows bulls and horses

• appeared in Europe about 35,000 years ago

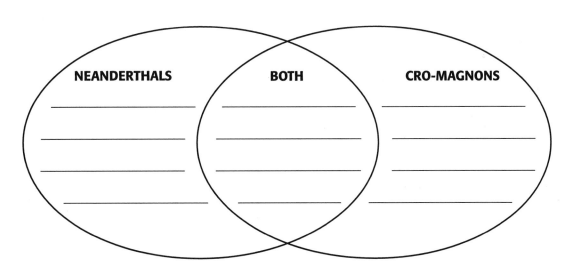

EVALUATING INFORMATION Mark each statement *T* if it is true or *F* if it is false.

_____ **1.** One reason for studying the remains of hominid skeletons is to find out how long the hominids lived.

_____ **2.** Initially, the early humans were nomads.

Name _____ Class _____ Date _____

_____ **3.** The reason that early humans moved from Africa to Asia was to search for food.

_____ **4.** Most people who are alive today are *Homo sapiens*.

_____ **5.** Because the Cro-Magnon people buried meat and tools with their dead, scientists think the Cro-Magnons believed in life after death.

REVIEWING FACTS Choose the correct items from the following list to complete the statements below.

anthropologists	archaeologists	fire	Cro-Magnon
Stone Age	Donald Johanson	Neanderthal	Middle
New	agricultural revolution		

1. Scientists called _____ study the remains of skeletons.

2. Scientists who dig into the earth to find ancient artifacts are called

_____.

3. In Ethiopia, _____ discovered the remains of a female hominid skeleton.

4. The period of prehistory that begins with the development of stone tools is called

the _____.

5. Only when humans learned to make _____ could they begin to live in colder areas of the world.

6. No one is sure why the _____ people disappeared from the Earth.

7. The _____ people looked similar to how we look today.

8. During the Mesolithic, or _____ Stone Age, people learned to make canoes.

9. People began to settle in permanent villages during the Neolithic or

_____ Stone Age.

10. The Neolithic _____ marked a long period of time in which people moved from food gathering to food producing.

CHAPTER 1 — Main Idea Activities 1.2

The Foundations of Civilization

VOCABULARY Some terms to understand:

- **unsuitable (11):** not proper or appropriate
- **climate (11):** average weather conditions at a place over a period of time
- **canals (12):** an artificial waterway for boats or irrigation
- **dikes (12):** barriers built to control or confine water
- **cooperation (12):** the act of working with others
- **skilled (12):** able to make good use of knowledge in doing something
- **phase (13):** a particular appearance in a repeating series of changes, for example, phases of the moon; a stage in a process

ORGANIZING INFORMATION List the appropriate characteristic of civilization associated with each drawing.

- People have the ability to produce food.
- People build large towns or cities and set up a form of government.
- People perform different jobs.
- People develop a calendar and some form of writing.

Characteristics of a Civilization

_____

_____

_____

_____

Chapter 1, Main Idea Activities 1.2, continued

EVALUATING INFORMATION Mark each statement *T* if it is true or *F* if it is false.

_____ **1.** By the end of the New Stone Age, all people lived in permanent settlements.

_____ **2.** The Nile, Tigris and Euphrates, Indus, and Huang River valleys had floods after periods of heavy rain.

_____ **3.** As farmers improved their ways of growing food, the population began to decrease.

_____ **4.** The first governments were formed to help new societies run more smoothly.

_____ **5.** Because of the division of labor, fewer people had to be farmers.

_____ **6.** Cultural diffusion is the spread of ideas and other aspects of culture from one area to another.

_____ **7.** Bronze is a mixture of copper and gold.

_____ **8.** The invention of bronze tools marked the end of the Iron Age.

UNDERSTANDING MAIN IDEAS For each of the following, write the letter of the best choice in the space provided.

_____ **1.** Which of the following was NOT one of the first four permanent settlements?
   a. the Nile River valley
   b. the valley of the Tigris and Euphrates
   c. the Indus River valley
   d. the Seine River valley

_____ **2.** Which of these caused farmers to develop methods of irrigation?
   a. long periods without rain
   b. wildfires
   c. the development of cities
   d. laws made by the government

_____ **3.** Calendars were developed so that
   a. traders could plan their travel routes.
   b. people would know when the yearly floods would stop and start.
   c. sacrifices could be planned for the gods and goddesses.
   d. cultural festivals could take place.

_____ **4.** Because written language developed, people in ancient civilizations were able to
   a. begin writing novels.
   b. keep a record of their culture.
   c. stop speaking to one another.
   d. track the phases of the moon.

CHAPTER (2)   Main Idea Activities 2.1
Ancient Kingdoms of the Nile

VOCABULARY Some terms to understand:

- **domesticated animals (18):** animals that are tamed for food or work
- **delta (21):** a broad flat valley where a river empties into the sea
- **isthmus (21):** a thin strip of land with water on either side
- **prevailing winds (21):** winds that blow continually from one direction
- **annual cycle (21):** patterns that happen every year
- **fertile soil (21):** land that is good for farming
- **eyewitness accounts (22):** stories about life and history from real people
- **absolute power (22) (24):** the right to make laws and control everyone in a country
- **internal strife (23):** hard times and fighting within a country
- **imperial power (25):** a government that has power over many lands or groups of people

ORGANIZING INFORMATION Write Old Kingdom, Middle Kingdom, or New Kingdom to identify the period associated with the following symbols of Ancient Egypt.

The chariot was introduced by the Hyksos, foreigners from Asia.	The Sphinx was built alongside the Great Pyramids.	Hatshepsut was the first female pharaoh.
_____	_____	_____

Chapter 2, Main Idea Activities 2.1, continued

EVALUATING INFORMATION Mark each statement *T* if it is true or *F* if it is false.

_____ **1.** The Nile River dominates the geography of Egypt.

_____ **2.** Ancient Egyptian civilization was born between the Nile's first great cataract and the delta.

_____ **3.** Farmers were the first people who moved to the Nile Valley.

_____ **4.** Egyptians discovered how to produce bronze by mixing copper and tin.

_____ **5.** The flooding of the Nile took away valuable soil from farms.

_____ **6.** Ancient Egyptians believed their pharaohs were gods.

_____ **7.** The army limited the pharaoh's power.

_____ **8.** Society in the Old Kingdom was divided into the upper and lower classes.

REVIEWING FACTS Choose the correct items from the following list to complete the statements below.

| Menes | polytheism | Rosetta Stone | papyrus |
| Hatshepsut | pharaoh | Ramses II | hieroglyphics |

1. An Egyptian form of writing that used pictures, signs, and symbols to represent

words and ideas is called _____.

2. _____ was the first female pharaoh and the first female ruler in ancient history.

3. The word _____ means "great house."

4. Scholars discovered the key to understanding Egyptian writing in the

_____.

5. The belief in many gods is called _____.

6. The Egyptians wrote on _____, a kind of paper made from the stem of a plant that grew along the Nile.

7. In about 3200 B.C., _____ united Egypt and ruled as the head of a great Egyptian dynasty.

8. The last great pharaoh was _____.

Main Idea Activities 2.2

Egyptian Life and Culture

VOCABULARY Some terms to understand:

- **geographic isolation (26):** when a place is set apart by mountains, deserts, or seas
- **ramps (26):** sloping walkways connecting a lower and a higher place
- **lever (26):** a bar that rests on a support and lifts a heavy object when one end is pushed down
- **elite group (27):** a group with special privileges
- **played a major role (27):** was the cause; was important
- **afterlife (28):** life after death
- **sacred (27):** having to do with religion; holy or highly respected
- **sally forth (29):** go gladly forward

REVIEWING FACTS Choose the correct items from the following list to complete the statements below.

Giza	decimal	Osiris	mummification
Great Pyramid	Amon-Re	scarab beetles	herbs

1. The best known pyramids are found at _____.

2. The _____ is built of more than two million blocks of stone.

3. The Egyptian number system is similar to our _____ system today.

4. Egyptian healers used magic spells, medicines, and _____ to cure diseases.

5. The most important Egyptian god was _____, the god of the sun.

6. The god _____ judged people after death.

7. The Egyptians considered bulls, crocodiles, cats, and _____ sacred.

8. To make life after death possible, ancient Egyptians preserved the body in a process called _____.

EVALUATING INFORMATION Mark each statement *T* if it is true or *F* if it is false.

_____ **1.** Because the Nile protected it from invasions, Egypt was able to create a rich culture.

_____ **2.** The building of the pyramids did not require great skill.

_____ **3.** Egyptians believed that both humans and animals had an afterlife.

_____ **4.** Women in ancient Egypt had no legal rights and ranked lower than their husbands.

_____ **5.** Egyptians placed tools and food in tombs so people in the future could study their culture.

_____ **6.** Ancient Egyptian traders traveled in caravans for safety.

UNDERSTANDING MAIN IDEAS For each of the following, write the letter of the best choice in the space provided.

_____ **1.** Which of the pictures is an Egyptian symbol meaning life?

a.   **c.**

b.   **d.**

_____ **2.** Egyptians mummified their dead because
   a. they believed everyone was a god or goddess.
   b. they thought it was artistic to decorate tombs.
   c. they believed people's bodies were needed in the afterlife.
   d. they believed mummified people would come back to life.

_____ **3.** Egyptian scholars invented a more exact calendar with 365 days and 12 months based on the
   a. phases of the moon.
   b. flooding of the Nile.
   c. rising of a bright star.
   d. five days of their holidays.

_____ **4.** Osiris was associated with the Nile because
   a. the sun warms the Nile.
   b. when the Nile flooded, it brought death to many families.
   c. the river flooding and receding was like Osiris's death and rebirth.
   d. Osiris judged people after death.

Name _____ Class _____ Date _____

Sumerian Civilization

VOCABULARY Some terms to understand:

• **cradle of civilization (30):** spot where organized human communities began

• **barren (31):** having no life

• **dikes (31):** barriers built to control or confine water

• **migration (31):** movement of people into a region

• **nomadic people (31):** people who move frequently from place to place

• **vaults (32):** high ceilings made by building a series of arches

• **tardiness (34):** lateness

ORGANIZING INFORMATION Fill in the Venn diagram by placing the items listed below in the correct parts of the diagram: Sumerian Civilization, Egyptian Civilization, and Both.

• was geographically isolated

• built ziggurats

• was often invaded by wandering tribes

• practiced polytheism

• had a system of writing

• believed in an afterlife

• did not believe in rewards after death

• built pyramids

Comparing Ancient Cultures

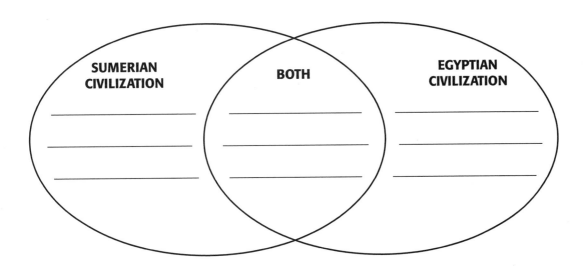

Chapter 2, Main Idea Activities 2.3, continued

REVIEWING FACTS Choose the correct items from the following list to complete the statements below.

ziggurats	circle	stylus
arch	flood control	wheel

1. Society in the Fertile Crescent was built around cooperation for

_____ and irrigation.

2. Sumerian pictographs were made with a wedge-shaped tool called a(n)

_____ .

3. The Sumerians built rounded roofs in the shape of vaults or domes after they

invented the _____ .

4. The most striking Sumerian buildings were temples known as

_____ .

5. The Sumerians may have been the first to use the _____ .

6. The Sumerian mathematical system is based on the division of the

_____ into 360 degrees.

UNDERSTANDING MAIN IDEAS For each of the following, write the letter of the best choice in the space provided.

_____ **1.** The Tigris-Euphrates Valley supported early civilization because
    a. the Fertile Crescent was ideal for farming.
    b. invaders brought new cultures to the region.
    c. the Sumerians developed a system of writing.
    d. the Babylonian class system was efficient.

_____ **2.** Because the rivers flooded without warning, early Sumerian people viewed nature and the gods as
    a. unimportant to their lives.
    b. kind and merciful because farming was easy.
    c. harsh and unpredictable.
    d. harsh because there was frequent drought.

_____ **3.** Which of these phrases describes the history of the Fertile Crescent?
    a. a series of easy changes between rulers
    b. continual peace
    c. constant invasion and conquest
    d. a slow and steady cultural growth

Empires of the Fertile Crescent

VOCABULARY Some terms to understand:

• **related languages (35):** languages that share an original source

• **to adopt a culture (37):** to take on the beliefs or customs of a culture that is not your own

• **smelt (37):** to melt metal; refine

• **epic (38):** a long narrative poem that tells the story of a hero

• **eclipse (38):** the hiding of the sun by the moon; a shadow on the moon created by the Earth

• **secret agents (39):** spies

• **held in check (39):** made to behave

• **universal struggle (40):** a struggle that is common to all people

ORGANIZING INFORMATION Fill in the chart by writing the correct item in the space provided.

• Akkadian
• Babylonian
• Hittite

• Assyrian
• Chaldean
• Persian

Empires of the Fertile Crescent	
Important Events	**Empires**
Sargon's great empire extended as far as the Mediterranean.	
Hammurabi wrote his code of laws concerning all aspects of life.	
People began to smelt iron.	
The cavalry—soldiers on horseback—was used for the first time.	
Nebuchadnezzar rebuilt Babylon into a magnificent city with Hanging Gardens.	
Conquered peoples were allowed to keep their own religions and laws.	

Chapter 2, Main Idea Activities 2.4, continued

EVALUATING INFORMATION Mark each statement *T* if it is true or *F* if it is false.

_____ **1.** Under the code of Hammurabi, punishment was extremely harsh.

_____ **2.** Under Hittite law, even minor crimes received the death penalty.

_____ **3.** The Assyrians enslaved the people they conquered.

_____ **4.** Of all the empires, only the Chaldeans did not make advances in astronomy and mathematics.

_____ **5.** Trade in Babylon prospered because of the city's impressive roads.

_____ **6.** Secret agents known as the "King's Eyes and Ears" first appeared during the rule of Cyrus the Great.

REVIEWING FACTS Choose the correct items from the following list to complete the statements below.

Alexander the Great	Royal Road	Nineveh
Zoroastrianism	Semitic	Seven Wonders of the World
Epic of Gilgamesh	Assyrian	

1. The Akkadians spoke a _____ language.

2. The city of _____ was the heart of the Assyrian civilization in the Fertile Crescent.

3. Nebuchadnezzar built the Hanging Gardens of Babylon for his wife, and the Greeks

regarded them as one of the _____.

4. The _____ king had absolute power and was answerable only to the god Ashur.

5. One of the oldest works of literature kept by Assyrian scholars is the

_____.

6. The Persian Empire built the _____ to connect its cities and expand trade.

7. _____, which centered on the struggle between good and evil, may have influenced Jewish and Christian thought.

8. _____, a Greek, conquered the Persian Empire in 331 B.C.

Main Idea Activities 2.5

The Phoenicians and the Lydians

VOCABULARY Some terms to understand:

- **colonies (42):** lands that are ruled by a distant country
- **exports (42):** goods sent from one country for sale in another
- **winning the favor (42):** working to please
- **natural disaster (42):** a disaster caused by nature, such as a flood, fire, or earthquake
- **commerce (42):** the buying and selling of goods; trade
- **cultural diffusion (42):** the mixing of customs, skills, languages, and beliefs
- **goods (43):** things made to be sold
- **services (43):** work done for others

ORGANIZING INFORMATION Fill in the chart by placing the items listed below in the correct section: The Phoenicians or The Lydians.

- invented the alphabet
- invented the art of glassblowing
- developed a money economy
- once lived in what is now Turkey
- may have sailed as far as Britain
- first to use coins for exchange
- greatest traders in the ancient world
- well known for their prized purple cloth

The Phoenicians and the Lydians	
The Phoenicians	**The Lydians**
_____	_____
_____	_____
_____	_____
_____	_____
_____	_____

Chapter 2, Main Idea Activities 2.5, continued

EVALUATING INFORMATION Mark each statement *T* if it is true or *F* if it is false.

_____ **1.** Phoenicia was a loose union of city-states under one king.

_____ **2.** Lumber from the Lebanon Mountains was an important natural resource for Phoenicians.

_____ **3.** Phoenicians tried to win the favor of all the gods they worshipped.

_____ **4.** Our alphabet can be traced back to the Phoenicians.

_____ **5.** The first coins used by Lydians were made of gold and silver and were shaped like beans.

_____ **6.** Like the Phoenicians, the Lydians ruled an empire.

REVIEWING FACTS Choose the correct items from the following list to complete the statements below.

barter	Greece	murex	Asia Minor
Babylon	Tyre	Sicily	Carthage

1. Phoenicians made the cities of Sidon and _____ not only world famous, but also centers of the dyeing trade.

2. The color purple was produced from a shellfish called _____.

3. In North Africa, Phoenicians established the city of _____.

4. Phoenicians had colonies on the islands of Sardinia, Malta, and

_____.

5. The Phoenician government was modeled on those of Egypt and

_____.

6. The Phoenician alphabet came to us through ancient _____ and Rome.

7. In ancient times, the western portion of _____ was called Lydia.

8. Before the Lydians invented coins, traders relied on _____, the exchange of one good or service for another.

CHAPTER **2** Main Idea Activities 2.6

The Origins of Judaism

VOCABULARY Some terms to understand:

- **heritage (44):** something handed down from ancestors
- **moral (45):** having to do with right and wrong
- **hardened (45):** tough
- **reached the height (46):** became as powerful as they would become
- **prophecy (46):** religious prediction
- **idols (46):** false gods
- **ethical (46):** behaving decently and respectfully
- **lived in the hearts of (47):** was loved by

ORGANIZING INFORMATION Fill in the graphic organizer by writing the remaining items in the correct order.

- After wandering in the desert, the Hebrews reached the "promised land."
- The Egyptians enslaved the Hebrews for 400 years.
- King Saul united the 12 tribes of Israel.
- The Hebrew Kingdom was split into two, Israel and Judah.
- Moses brought the Ten Commandments to the Hebrews.

Sequence of Events

1. Abraham's descendants traveled west to Egypt.	2.	3. Moses led the Hebrews out of slavery.	4.
5.	6. The Hebrews conquered the Canaanites.	7.	8.

Chapter 2, Main Idea Activities 2.6, continued

EVALUATING INFORMATION Mark each statement *T* if it is true or *F* if it is false.

_____ **1.** Abraham's descendants left Canaan to go to Egypt probably to escape drought and famine.

_____ **2.** It was only Moses, not the Hebrews, who made a covenant with Yahweh to follow the Ten Commandments.

_____ **3.** Hebrew judges enforced the law and settled disputes.

_____ **4.** Prophets appeared sometimes to warn the people of God's punishment.

_____ **5.** To the early Hebrews, Yahweh was a god to love, not to fear.

_____ **6.** The Hebrews believed that Yahweh allowed them to choose between good and evil.

_____ **7.** Yahweh was both a human and spiritual force.

_____ **8.** Political rulers among the Hebrews are not representatives of Yahweh.

_____ **9.** The first four of the Ten Commandments establish man's relationship with Yahweh.

_____ **10.** The Hebrew religion emphasizes fear for elders, not proper conduct.

REVIEWING FACTS Choose the correct leader's name from the following list to complete each statement below.

Solomon   Moses   Abraham   David

1. Modern Jews trace their heritage as far back as _____.

2. Under the leadership of _____, the Hebrews made a covenant with Yahweh.

3. King _____ made Jerusalem the religious capital.

4. The kingdom of Israel reached the height of its size and power under King

_____.

Main Idea Activities 3.1

Indus River Valley Civilization

VOCABULARY Some expressions to understand:

- **archaeological digs (53):** place where archaeologists dig up old buildings or ruins
- **ritual immersion (54):** dipping someone in water for a religious purpose

Other terms:

- **subcontinent (52):** a large landmass that is smaller than a continent
- **plain (52):** a flat stretch of land
- **inhabitants (52):** people who live in a place
- **sparse (52):** very little; scanty
- **podium (54):** a raised platform or area
- **pictographs (55):** pictures used as signs for forms of writing

ORGANIZING INFORMATION Complete the chart about the physical geography and climate of the Indian subcontinent by writing each item below where it belongs.

- mid-June through October
- Himalayas
- Indo-Gangetic Plain
- Deccan
- Western Ghats
- Ganges and Indus
- monsoons
- November through March

Physical Geography and Climate of Indian Subcontinent	
Physical Geography	**Climate**
1. separates north of India from the rest of Asia _____	**5.** winds that mark the seasons in India _____
2. two great rivers of the Indian subcontinent _____	**6.** time of little rainfall in India _____
3. high plateau that makes up much of interior of the subcontinent _____	**7.** time of heavy rainfall in India _____
4. mountains that rise from a coastal plain on the Arabian Sea _____	**8.** very high temperatures in summer _____

Chapter 3, Main Idea Activities 3.1, *continued*

EVALUATING INFORMATION Mark each statement *T* if it is true or *F* if it is false.

_____ **1.** Geography and climate played important roles in the development of civilization on the Indian subcontinent.

_____ **2.** The Ganges and the Indus are the two great rivers that flow across the Indian subcontinent.

_____ **3.** The monsoon winds come from east to west in November.

_____ **4.** The timing of the monsoons does not have a great effect on agriculture.

_____ **5.** There are no ruins left of the Harappan civilization in the Indus River valley

_____ **6.** Each city in the Harappan civilization had a citadel, or a strong central fortress.

_____ **7.** Some Harappan craft workers made goods for trade.

_____ **8.** The Indus River valley civilization may have disappeared because of a disastrous event such as an invasion, earthquake, or flood.

UNDERSTANDING MAIN IDEAS For each of the following, write the letter of the best choice in the space provided.

_____ **1.** The first civilization developed in the Indus River valley about
  a. 1,000 years ago.
  b. 4,500 years ago.
  c. 6,000 years ago.
  d. 10,000 years ago.

_____ **2.** The region drained by the Indus and Ganges rivers is called the
  a. Indo-European Delta.
  b. Ganges-Harappan Plain.
  c. Himalayan Flatlands.
  d. Indo-Gangetic Plain.

_____ **3.** The ability of the Harappan leaders to store and distribute surplus food showed that they were able to make
  a. good choices.
  b. crop-destroying floods.
  c. careful, long-range plans.
  d. invaders retreat.

_____ **4.** The early people in the Indus River valley developed a written language as shown by
  a. letters from leaders to their subjects.
  b. religious writings.
  c. pictographs dating from 2300 B.C.
  d. connections between pictographs and other written languages.

VOCABULARY An expression to understand:

- **system of social orders (57):** a set of rules relating to how people live in a society

Some terms to understand:

- **nomadic (56):** living without a fixed home or location; moving from place to place
- **immortality (11):** living forever
- **sonar (58):** device for finding objects by using sound waves
- **barter (58):** to trade goods without exchanging money
- **diverse (59):** different
- **hunter-gatherers (59):** people who get their food by hunting animals or gathering food in the wild

ORGANIZING INFORMATION Complete the graphic organizer about different parts of Indo-Aryan life. Write each item on the line in the correct section.

- Sanskrit
- Vedas
- Brahmins
- farming
- bartering
- irrigation

Indo-Aryan Life	
Religion	**Economy**
• _____	• _____
• _____	• _____
• _____	• _____

Chapter 3, Main Idea Activities 3.2, continued

EVALUATING INFORMATION Mark each statement *T* if it is true or *F* if it is false.

_____ **1.** The nomadic people who crosssed the Hindu Kush Mountains beginning in 1750 B.C. were called the Indo-Europeans.

_____ **2.** The Vedas are great works of religious literature.

_____ **3.** Sanskrit is the language of the Indo-Aryans.

_____ **4.** The earliest gods in the Vedas were drawn from nature.

_____ **5.** There were many temples in early Vedic religion.

_____ **6.** Vedic religious rituals became very complicated.

_____ **7.** The development of southern India was affected by the same forces as the development of northern India.

_____ **8.** The Indo-Aryan migrants had a large impact on northern India.

REVIEWING FACTS Choose the correct item from the following list to complete the statements below.

Vedas	Sanskrit	Indo-Aryan
"That One"	Brahmins	raja

1. The chief of a state or territory was called a _____.

2. The term for the Vedic god who created order in the universe is

_____.

3. Special priests, called _____, knew the proper forms and rules for Vedic religious rituals.

4. The _____ are the Indo-Aryans' great works of religious literature.

5. The _____ word for war means "a desire for more cows."

6. Vedas were written in _____.

Hinduism and Buddhism

VOCABULARY Some terms to understand:

- **authority (60):** power; right to control
- **role models (60):** people whose way of living influences other people to live in the same way
- **transformed (61):** changed
- **illusion (61):** a false impression or belief
- **sacred (62):** connected with a god or religion; holy
- **arose (63):** began
- **ventured (63):** went
- **vowed (63):** pledged; stated one's intention
- **virtue (65):** good

ORGANIZING INFORMATION On the pyramid, list the different classes of people that made up the caste system. List the classes in order of importance from greatest to least.

- merchants, traders, farmers
- peasants
- untouchables
- Brahmins
- rulers and warriors

THE CASTE SYSTEM

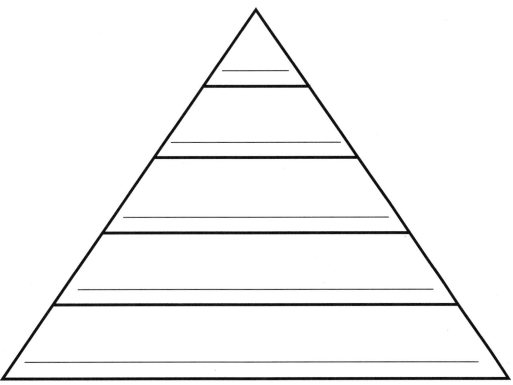

Chapter 3, Main Idea Activities 3.3, continued

EVALUATING INFORMATION Mark each statement *T* if it is true or *F* if it is false.

_____ **1.** Two of the world's greatest religions, Hinduism and Buddhism, developed in India.

_____ **2.** The Upanishads were written explanations of the Vedic religion.

_____ **3.** Indian epics were short poems about religious ideas.

_____ **4.** Two important developments that transformed Indian society between 1500 B.C. and A.D. 500 were the caste system and Hinduism.

_____ **5.** According to the Hindu idea of karma, a person's actions have no impact on his or her life.

_____ **6.** Siddhartha Gautama was the son of a prince in a wealthy family.

_____ **7.** The Buddha taught that desire of any kind causes suffering.

_____ **8.** Buddhism has remained a very popular religion in India.

REVIEWING FACTS Choose the correct item from the following list to complete the statements below.

Eightfold Path	Right Intentions	varnas	Ramayana
Nirvana	reincarnation	Four Noble Truths	maya

1. The _____ teach how desire leads to suffering.

2. The state of perfect peace is called _____.

3. One of the most famous Indian religious stories is called the

_____.

4. According to Buddhist teaching, following the _____ can lead to salvation.

5. In Buddhism, living a life of good will is called _____.

6. Hindus believe that the world we see is an illusion, or _____.

7. The caste system was divided into four _____, or social classes.

8. _____ is the belief that souls are reborn.

Main Idea Activities 3.4

Ancient Indian Dynasties and Empires

VOCABULARY An expression to understand:

• **appeared on the scene (66):** became known; took over power

Some terms to understand:

• **standardized (67):** made the same
• **missionary (67):** person sent on a religious mission or journey
• **flourished (68):** did very well
• **dominant (68):** had the most members or held control

ORGANIZING INFORMATION On the chart, list the items that go with each of the Indian rulers. There should be two items for each ruler.

• golden age of Indian civilization
• became a Buddhist
• Hinduism became the most popular religion in India
• had an army of 600,000 soldiers with chariots and elephants
• ordered an end to killing and conquest
• standardized weights and measures

Rulers of Ancient India		
Chandragupta Maurya c 320 B.C.	**Aśoka** 270 B.C.	**Chandra Gupta II** A.D. 374
• _____ _____ • _____ _____	• _____ _____ • _____ _____	• _____ _____ • _____ _____

EVALUATING INFORMATION Mark each statement *T* if it is true or *F* if it is false.

_____ **1.** Chandragupta Maurya's rule was recorded by a Hindu soldier.

_____ **2.** Mauryan rulers took one-fourth of each harvest in taxes.

_____ **3.** Aśoka's laws were carved on stones in public places

_____ **4.** During Aśoka's rule, living conditions improved.

_____ **5.** The Gupta family expanded their territory by spreading Buddhism.

_____ **6.** The early years of the Gupta rule are called the golden age.

_____ **7.** The Gupta rulers gave power to local leaders.

_____ **8.** In the Gupta period, people watched dramas in theaters.

UNDERSTANDING MAIN IDEAS For each of the following, write the letter of the best choice in the space provided.

_____ **1.** The rulers of the Magadha kingdom were the first to
    a. unify the whole subcontinent of India.
    b. try to unify much of India.
    c. establish Buddhism as a religion.
    d. set up trade routes with Europe.

_____ **2.** Chandragupta's grandson, Aśoka,
    a. was a weak and powerless ruler.
    b. spread the Buddhist religion outside of India.
    c. was a well-known Hindu holy man.
    d. had no interest in helping the common people of India.

_____ **3.** One of the actions that Aśoka took was to
    a. set up a rigid bureacracy to carry out his commands.
    b. continue conquering other lands until he died.
    c. provide rest houses on trade routes.
    d. place a ban on all artistic activity.

_____ **4.** During the reign of Chandra Gupta II,
    a. the Indian people never stopped fighting wars.
    b. civilization in India declined.
    c. great progress was made in the arts.
    d. local rulers did not have much power.

 **CHAPTER 3**

Main Idea Activities 3.5

Ancient Indian Life and Culture

VOCABULARY An expression to understand:

- **barely got by (69):** had just enough to live and no more

Some terms to understand:

- **prohibited (69):** did not allow
- **adaptability (70):** able to change when needed
- **determination (70):** having a fixed and firm purpose
- **quadratic equations (71):** equation in algebra with no higher powers than the square of an unknown quantity or quantities.
- **disinfected (71):** killed or destroyed germs

ORGANIZING INFORMATION Complete the table of advances in science, medicine, and mathematics that took place in ancient India by listing the following items in the appropriate box.

- inoculation
- quadratic equations
- identified seven planets
- astronomy
- bone setting
- concept of zero

Advances in Ancient India in Science, Medicine, and Mathematics	
1. Science	• _____ • _____
2. Medicine	• _____ • _____
3. Mathematics	• _____ • _____

EVALUATING INFORMATION Mark each statement *T* if it is true or *F* if it is false.

_____ **1.** Under Hindu law, women had the same rights as men.

_____ **2.** Women in ancient India could not own property or study sacred writings.

_____ **3.** Men in ancient India were allowed to have more than one wife.

_____ **4.** Ancient Indian cave paintings tell us about their daily life.

_____ **5.** There was little or no education for anyone in ancient India.

_____ **6.** Indian scientists were not highly skilled.

_____ **7.** Indian doctors were advanced but did not understand the spinal cord.

_____ **8.** Indian doctors figured out how to prevent smallpox long before anyone in Europe was able to do so.

REVIEWING FACTS Choose the correct item from the following list to complete the statements below.

suttee	Laws of Manu	polygyny
stupa	Nalanda	*Panchatantra*

1. The practice of having more than one wife is called _____.

2. A _____ is a dome-shaped Buddhist shrine.

3. The _____ stated that widows were to obey their sons.

4. The practice of _____ meant that widows committed suicide by throwing themselves on their husband's funeral pyre.

5. Many ancient Indians were educated at _____, a Buddhist university.

6. Fables from the Gupta period are found in the _____.

CHAPTER **4**   Main Idea Activities 4.1

Geographic and Cultural Influences

VOCABULARY Some terms to understand:

- **geographic variety (76):** many different landforms
- **plateau (76):** a broad stretch of high, flat, level land
- **extreme temperatures (76):** the hottest and coldest temperatures
- **political sections (76):** regions ruled by separate governments
- **prone to (78):** likely to
- **barbarians (79):** savages or people lacking refinement
- **infrequent (22):** not often

ORGANIZING INFORMATION Fill in the chart by writing each *effect* opposite to its *cause* in the chart.

- The river began to flow more slowly.
- Chinese nicknamed the Huang River "The Yellow River."
- China did not adopt many outside skills or ideas.
- Chinese nicknamed the Huang River "China's Sorrow."

Links Between Geography and Culture

Cause	Effect
The Huang River is tinted by fertile yellow soil.	_____
Huang River floods killed many families.	_____
Farmers built dikes to protect their crops.	_____
Mountains and deserts isolate China from other cultures.	_____

Chapter 4, Main Idea Activities 4.1, continued

EVALUATING INFORMATION Mark each statement *T* if it is true or *F* if it is false.

_____ **1.** The region we call China has always been ruled by one government.

_____ **2.** China Proper is surrounded by three great river systems.

_____ **3.** After Chinese farmers built the dikes, floods did not happen again.

_____ **4.** The climate of southern China is best for growing crops.

_____ **5.** In many places, the Huang River is much higher than the land around it.

_____ **6.** The Xi River is an important transportation route.

_____ **7.** The ancient Chinese recognized many civilizations besides their own.

_____ **8.** The Chinese believed China was the center of the world.

UNDERSTANDING MAIN IDEAS For each of the following, write the letter of the best choice in the space provided.

_____ **1.** China's isolation was caused by
   a. mountains and deserts.
   b. flooding of its many rivers.
   c. extreme temperatures.
   d. its many political sections.

_____ **2.** Because of the frequent flooding of the Huang River, the ancient Chinese
   a. were able to farm fertile yellow soil.
   b. built China Proper on a high mountain.
   c. nicknamed the river "China's Sorrow."
   d. planted several different crops.

_____ **3.** China's river systems gave the Chinese people
   a. the ability to reduce the flooding on their farms.
   b. fertile soil and commercial waterways.
   c. a very rich and different culture.
   d. enough foreign goods during floods.

_____ **4.** Its geography helped China
   a. develop a culture all its own.
   b. invade other countries.
   c. lose its identity.
   d. get ideas from other cultures.

CHAPTER 4   Main Idea Activities 4.2

The Shang Dynasty

VOCABULARY An expression to understand:

- **eat my words (81):** take back what I said

Some terms to understand:

- **mythological (80):** relating to stories that explain nature, practices, or beliefs
- **complex (81):** not simple
- **durable (82):** able to exist for a long time
- **human destiny (82):** what people's lives are meant to be
- **ideograph (83):** a picture or symbol that represents not the object pictured but an idea it suggests

ORGANIZING INFORMATION Fill in the chart by writing each fact or legend in the correct column.

- Priests saw the future in oracle bones.
- Yu drained the floodwaters so people could live in China.
- Markings on oracle bones had helped scholars.
- An all-powerful and friendly dragon lived in the seas.
- Pangu awoke from 18,000 years of sleep to create the universe.
- The moon told the people when to plant.
- Each Chinese pictograph represents a single word.
- A Chinese king was popular if he could predict the harvest.

Fact and Legend in the Shang Dynasty	
Fact	**Legend**
_____	_____
_____	_____
_____	_____
_____	_____

EVALUATING INFORMATION Mark each statement *T* if it is true or *F* if it is false.

_____ **1.** The Shang rulers were respected because they taught flood control.

_____ **2.** The Shang dynasty had a well-organized government.

_____ **3.** The Chinese developed the earliest alphabet.

_____ **4.** Most Chinese practiced monotheism.

_____ **5.** There is only one dialect in the Chinese language.

_____ **6.** The Chinese discovered how to make silk threads.

_____ **7.** Not all Chinese under the Shang rulers were farmers.

_____ **8.** Ceramic art, as we know it today, began in the Shang Dynasty.

MATCHING Match the following terms with the sentence that defines them.

_____ **1.** animism   **a.** 600 Chinese drawings represented words.

_____ **2.** oracle bones   **b.** This was important for planning the harvest.

_____ **3.** bureaucracy   **c.** You might visit this person to learn your future.

_____ **4.** calligraphy   **d.** Artisans made fine carvings from this bone.

_____ **5.** pictographs   **e.** This fine writing was done with ink and a brush.

_____ **6.** ivory   **f.** A government gives tasks to levels of workers.

_____ **7.** kaolin   **g.** Chinese believed that even stones have a spirit.

_____ **8.** lunar calendar   **h.** Artisans made fine pottery from this white clay.

_____ **9.** Shangdi   **i.** This great god controlled humans and nature.

_____ **10.** priest   **j.** Cattle shoulder bones might predict the future.

CHAPTER **4**   Main Idea Activities 4.3

The Zhou, Qin, and Han Dynasties

VOCABULARY Some terms to understand:

- **tribute (84):** something given to show respect; a forced payment
- **mandate (84):** an order or command
- **candidate (85):** a person who seeks an office or position
- **economic policy (87):** a set of rules and practices for the management of money
- **surpluses (88):** more than what is needed
- **unify (88):** to make into one

ORGANIZING INFORMATION Fill in the chart by placing the items listed below in the column next to the dynasty during which they occurred.

- Rulers divided powers between family members.
- Laborers were forced to build the Great Wall.
- Chinese today call themselves people of this dynasty.
- The word "China" was taken from this dynasty's name.
- Right to rule came from heaven.
- Trade prospered along the Silk Road.

Comparing Dynasties	
1. Zhou	• _____ • _____
2. Qin	• _____ • _____
3. Han	• _____ • _____

Chapter 4, Main Idea Activities 4.3, continued

REVIEWING FACTS Choose the correct item from the following list to complete the statements below.

paper	Silk	scholars
Wu Ti	Liu Bang	leveling

1. The Qin emperor suppressed criticism from _____.

2. _____, a commoner, founded the Han dynasty.

3. Liu Che, the longest ruling Han emperor, is also known as

_____.

4. The _____ program worked because the government stored grain for the lean years.

5. _____, a Chinese invention, is still used for writing today.

6. The _____ Road from China crossed Central Asia and reached the Mediterranean region.

UNDERSTANDING MAIN IDEAS For each of the following, write the letter of the best choice in the space provided.

_____ **1.** The Qin took power only when it won after
   a. the Zhou passed power to their sons.
   b. centuries of fighting among the Warring States.
   c. fifteen years of fighting.
   d. a long period of relative peace.

_____ **2.** During the 15-year rule of the Qin dynasty,
   a. scholars were not made to work.
   b. many changes happened in Chinese life.
   c. critics were heard.
   d. many Chinese left for other places.

_____ **3.** The Han dynasty ruled over its great empire
   a. by putting into place a civil service system.
   b. by dividing China into managed territories.
   c. with a cruel and harsh army.
   d. by training poor farmers to work for the government.

_____ **4.** The Silk Road was important because
   a. traders brought the Chinese silk and jade.
   b. trading brought in gold, silver, and wool.
   c. the Chinese were eager for ideas from the outside world.
   d. it connected regions to China Proper.

CHAPTER **4**   Main Idea Activities 4.4

Philosophies of Ancient China

VOCABULARY Some terms to understand:

- **at the root of (89):** the cause of
- **welfare (90):** well-being
- **shunned (91):** pushed away; rejected
- **spontaneity (91):** the condition of acting in a free or natural way
- **missionaries (92):** traveling teachers who spread religious views in other countries
- **compassion (92):** caring for others

EVALUATING INFORMATION Mark each statement *T* if it is true or *F* if it is false.

_____ **1.** The concept of yin and yang helped people accept constant changes in government.

_____ **2.** If you listened to Confucius, you would obey your parents.

_____ **3.** According to Confucius, an ideal government would care only about the welfare of its people.

_____ **4.** According to Mencius, individuals need government controls to behave ethically.

_____ **5.** Laozi taught people to be humble, quiet, and thoughtful.

_____ **6.** Legalism and Daoism were the key philosophies in Chinese society.

_____ **7.** Buddhism became popular in China during a time of war and insecurity.

_____ **8.** Buddhism was especially popular among the upper classes.

_____ **9.** Chinese society became divided between believers in Confucianism, Buddhism, and Daoism.

_____ **10.** The *Dao De Jing* explains how to live simply.

Chapter 4, Main Idea Activities 4.4, continued

UNDERSTANDING MAIN IDEAS For each of the following pictures, write the letter of the best choice in the space provided.

_____ 1.
   a. represents the dualism of nature
   b. shows the passive side of yin
   c. represents political disorder
   d. shows "The Way"

_____ 2.
   a. thought people should show compassion for everyone
   b. thought people should return to nature
   c. thought people were naturally selfish and untrustworthy
   d. thought ethics, morals, and respect of family was of greatest importance

_____ 3.
   a. spoke about the importance of duty
   b. was the source of many temples and ceremonies
   c. believed in severe punishments for breaking laws
   d. taught that the Dao was the governing force of nature

_____ 4.
   a. taught kindness, peace, and escape from misery
   b. influenced Mencius
   c. taught the proper use of violence against harsh governments
   d. emphasized a respect for one's parents

REVIEWING FACTS Choose the correct items from the following list to complete the statements below.

   Analects   The Way   compassion
   Mahayana   legalists

1. Confucius' teachings are collected in the _____.

2. Another name for the Dao is _____.

3. The form of Buddhism popular in China is called _____.

4. The _____ believed in strong harsh laws.

5. The Buddhist idea of _____ toward other people was a new idea in China.

CHAPTER **4** Main Idea Activities 4.5

Chinese Life and Culture

VOCABULARY Some terms to understand:

- **figure (as in family figure) (93):** a person thought of in a certain way
- **property rights (93):** the right to own land and buildings
- **ox-drawn plows (94):** a tool for tilling a field, pulled by an ox
- **standardized (94):** make the same in form, quality, or size
- **classics (94):** a book or piece of art that is famous for its excellence
- **calculations (95):** answers found by adding, subtracting, etc.
- **sunspots (95):** dark spots on the sun's surface
- **stemmed from (95):** grew out of
- **anesthetic (43):** pain reliever

ORGANIZING INFORMATION Fill in the chart by placing the items listed below in the correct section: Men, Women, or Both.

- honored for strength
- honored for gentleness
- held elders in great respect
- ruled the family
- accepted decisions from their superiors
- lived with relatives in one house
- had no property rights
- had more power after giving birth to a son
- chose careers for the sons

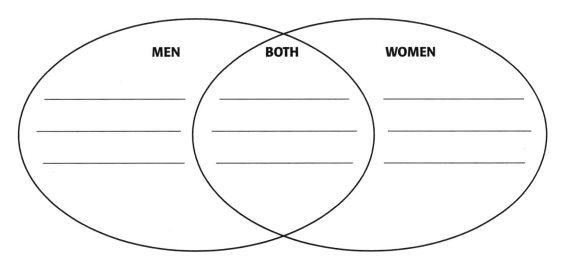

Chinese Family Roles

MEN   BOTH   WOMEN

Chapter 4, Main Idea Activities 4.5, continued

EVALUATING INFORMATION Mark each statement *T* if it is true or *F* if it is false.

_____ **1.** In ancient China, the family was the most important social structure.

_____ **2.** Most people in ancient China worked in the government.

_____ **3.** Farmers were required to build government road and canals.

_____ **4.** Books were a common link for people throughout China.

_____ **5.** An educated Chinese man had studied the philosophy of Confucius.

_____ **6.** Chinese astronomers tracked the movement of the planets.

_____ **7.** The Chinese learned to make paper from the Egyptians.

_____ **8.** Chinese medicine was based on the idea of a life force.

REVIEWING FACTS Choose the correct items from the following list to complete the statements below.

seismograph	sundial	acupuncture
measures	hemp	genealogy

1. The first _____ dropped metal balls when there was a small earthquake.

2. Chinese doctors use needles in a healing process called _____.

3. The Chinese invented the _____ in order to tell time.

4. Chinese paper was made from fishnets, old rags, bark, and

_____.

5. Studying _____ is important to people who honor their ancestors.

6. The Chinese standardized the system of weights and _____.

CHAPTER 5   Main Idea Activities 5.1

Early Greeks and the Rise of City-States

VOCABULARY Some terms to understand:

• **peninsula (106):** a long piece of land almost completely surrounded by water

• **mainland (106):** a body of land that makes up the main part of a continent

• **clan (107):** a group of family members who share common interests

• **fort-like (108):** similar to the strong, protected place used as an army post

• **issues (109):** important, but unsettled matters

ORGANIZING INFORMATION Fill in the graphic organizer by writing the events in the correct sequence.

• The Greeks formed independent city-states.

• Minoans traded throughout the Aegean Sea.

• Legendary King Minos built a great civilization.

• Mycenaeans conquered central Crete.

A Growing Civilization

```
┌─────────────────────────────────────┐
│                                     │
│                                     │
└─────────────────────────────────────┘
                  │
                  ▼
┌─────────────────────────────────────┐
│                                     │
│                                     │
└─────────────────────────────────────┘
                  │
                  ▼
┌─────────────────────────────────────┐
│                                     │
│                                     │
└─────────────────────────────────────┘
                  │
                  ▼
┌─────────────────────────────────────┐
│                                     │
│                                     │
└─────────────────────────────────────┘
```

Chapter 5, Main Idea Activities 5.1, continued

EVALUATING INFORMATION Mark each statement *T* if it is true or *F* if it is false.

_____ **1.** Their geographic location made it easy for the Greeks to establish a central government.

_____ **2.** The Greeks depended upon the sea for transportation, food, and business.

_____ **3.** We learned about Minoan culture by studying the frescoes of Minoan artists.

_____ **4.** Crete's rich soil provided the Minoans with abundant food.

_____ **5.** The Greek word *polis* referred to a fort, a city, and the farming lands around it.

_____ **6.** The Greek city-states were united under one economy and government.

_____ **7.** In a polis, only a small group of free males were considered citizens.

_____ **8.** In the agora, people bought food and discussed important ideas.

_____ **9.** People in the Greek city-states spoke several languages.

_____ **10.** Greeks built each polis around a fort on an acropolis.

CLASSIFYING Decide whether each item refers to the Greek, Minoan, or Mycenaean culture. In the space provided, write *Mi* for Minoan, *My* for Mycenaean, and *Gr* for Greek.

_____ **1.** This was the first Greek civilization.

_____ **2.** They adopted the Minoan system of writing.

_____ **3.** People were identified by the polis in which they lived.

_____ **4.** A volcanic eruption and tidal waves weakened this civilization.

_____ **5.** These people founded Athens and Sparta.

_____ **6.** The palace and the homes of nobles had running water.

_____ **7.** They built the fort-like city of Peloponnesus.

_____ **8.** They valued political independence.

 **CHAPTER 5**

Main Idea Activities 5.2

Greek Government and Society

VOCABULARY Some terms to understand:

- **javelin (111):** a light spear
- **discus (111):** a heavy disk of metal and wood
- **fortress (111):** a large and permanent fortification
- **stadium (111):** a place for outdoor games with rising seats around a field
- **commoner (112):** someone who is not a member of the noble class
- **infantry (112):** soldiers trained to fight on foot

ORGANIZING INFORMATION Place each item in the correct category of the web.

- ruler of Mount Olympus, king of the gods
- god of poetry, music, and light, a son of Zeus
- the god of wine and fertility, another son of Zeus
- goddess of wisdom and womanly goodness, a daughter of Zeus
- Mycenaean king who was the hero of Homer's epic poem

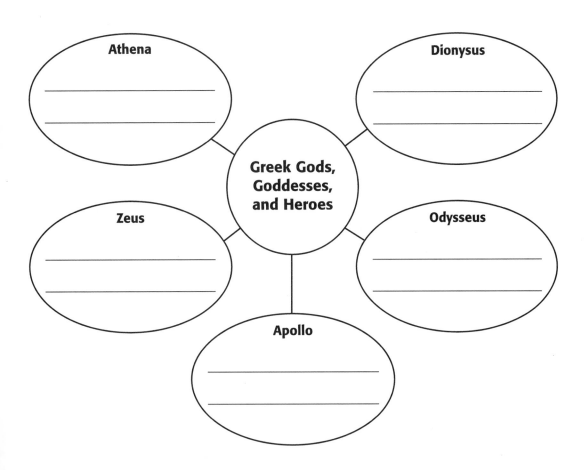

Chapter 5, Main Idea Activities 5.2, continued

REVIEWING FACTS Choose the correct items from the following list to complete the statements below.

myths	epics	oracle	*Iliad*	Homer
Athens	*Odyssey*	Helen	Zeus	aristocracies

1. The Greeks created _____ about gods, goddesses, and heroes.

2. The blind poet _____ is said to have written two long poems about Greek history.

3. Long poems about heroes and great events are called _____.

4. The _____ tells about the events of the Trojan War.

5. The Trojan War was an attempt to rescue the Mycenaean queen,

_____.

6. The _____ tells what happens after the Trojan War.

7. _____ was named after the goddess of wisdom.

8. The Olympic Games were organized as a tribute to _____.

9. Greek nobles controlled special city-states called _____.

10. In ancient Greece, an _____ might tell you about the future.

EVALUATING INFORMATION Mark each statement *T* if it is true or *F* if it is false.

_____ **1.** It took Odysseus ten years to get home after the Trojan War.

_____ **2.** Greeks turned to religion to explain why people sometimes lost self-control.

_____ **3.** Greeks expected their religion to save them from sin.

_____ **4.** Women and slaves had political rights in ancient Greece.

_____ **5.** When a tyrant became brutal, people pressed for election.

_____ **6.** Democracy began in some city-states.

Sparta and Athens

VOCABULARY Some terms to understand:

- **militarize (113):** to build up armed forces; to have a warlike spirit
- **systematically (113):** in an organized way
- **citizens (114):** people who have the right to vote and own property
- **barracks (114):** buildings where soldiers live
- **stimulated (115):** made more active
- **debtors (115):** people who owe money
- **creditors (115):** people who lend money
- **jurors (115):** group of people who listen to evidence, then reach a decision; judges

ORGANIZING INFORMATION Complete the Venn diagram by listing the items below in the correct section: Athens or Sparta.

- recognized citizens, metics, and slaves
- completely controlled citizens' lives
- became a completely military society
- created the first real democracy

Comparing City-States

Athens
- _____
- _____
- _____
- _____

Both
- important Greek *polis*
- women had no part in government

Sparta
- _____
- _____
- _____

EVALUATING INFORMATION Mark each statement *T* if it is true or *F* if it is false.

_____ **1.** Men in Sparta were forced to give their entire lives to the military.

_____ **2.** The Spartans enslaved the helots.

_____ **3.** Wealthy women became citizens in Ancient Greece.

_____ **4.** Boys and girls in Sparta studied music to learn discipline and coordination.

_____ **5.** Metics could own land in Athens.

_____ **6.** Cleisthenes believed the aristocrats should be powerful.

_____ **7.** The first written laws of the Athenians that Draco created were harsh and severe.

_____ **8.** Ideas for American democracy began in ancient Athens.

UNDERSTANDING MAIN IDEAS For each of the following, write the letter of the best choice in the space provided.

_____ **1.** The Spartans used force to control the helots because
   a. they were hard to teach.
   b. there were many more Spartans than there were helots.
   c. the helots outnumbered the Spartans.
   d. they were half-citizens and could not vote.

_____ **2.** Sparta had a strong government and an unbeatable army but
   a. their women were weak.
   b. young Spartans were undisciplined.
   c. they had no income.
   d. they did not advance in the arts and sciences.

_____ **3.** Solon, a ruler in Athens elected for a one-year term, did one of the following:
   a. outlawed slavery due to a debt.
   b. wrote many laws.
   c. led the army.
   d. made owning a slave legal.

_____ **4.** Athens had a direct democracy in which
   a. laws were passed by a council of male citizens.
   b. all citizens passed laws.
   c. citizens participated directly in decision making.
   d. citizens were allowed to live in the city.

CHAPTER **5**

Main Idea Activities 5.4

Daily Life in Athens

VOCABULARY Some terms to understand:

- **mainstay (118):** the main support
- **ode (119):** a poem that honors something or someone
- **ideal (120):** a perfect model
- **sound mind (120):** a normal and healthy mind
- **flanks (120):** troops on the side of an army

ORGANIZING INFORMATION Fill in the chart by placing each item under the correct category of education.

- reading, writing, and grammar
- mathematics and rhetoric
- military skills
- manners
- poetry, music, and gymnastics
- government and ethics

Athenian Education

Pedagogue	• _____
Elementary School	• _____
	• _____
Sophist School	• _____
	• _____
Military Training	• _____

Chapter 5, Main Idea Activities 5.4, continued

EVALUATING INFORMATION Mark each statement *T* if it is true or *F* if it is false.

_____ **1.** The Athenian economy was based on overseas colonies and trade.

_____ **2.** Most Athenian trade was done by travelers on ancient roads.

_____ **3.** Athenians believed money should be spent on private homes.

_____ **4.** Athenian homes were simple one-story brick buildings.

_____ **5.** Women and girls were considered inferior to men and boys.

_____ **6.** It was impossible for an Athenian girl to get an education.

_____ **7.** Mothers took care of all the children until they were six years old.

_____ **8.** Athenian education was based on a sound mind and a healthy body.

REVIEWING FACTS Choose the correct items from the following list to complete the statements below.

Sophist	rhetoric	hoplites	agora
Black	terraced	ethics	olive oil

1. Athenians grew olives, grapes, and figs on _____ hillsides.

2. The Greek colonies were along the Mediterranean, Aegean, and

_____ Seas.

3. Athenian families got water from a fountain near the _____.

4. Lamps in Athenian homes burned _____.

5. The name _____ is taken from a Greek word meaning "wise."

6. The study of _____ deals with what is good and bad.

7. _____ was the study of oratory.

8. The _____ formed the center of the military.

CHAPTER 5 — Main Idea Activities 5.5

The Expansion of Greece

VOCABULARY Some terms to understand:

- **outnumbered (121):** to be met by greater numbers than one's own forces
- **fleet (121):** a group of warships
- **odds (121):** chances
- **strait (122):** a narrow water passage
- **league (123):** a group of people who join together for a common reason
- **orator (124):** someone who speaks in public
- **tyranny (124):** rule by force
- **siege (125):** the surrounding of a city or fort by an enemy army
- **politically unstable (125):** having a weak government

ORGANIZING INFORMATION Fill in the sequence chart with the events of the Persian Wars. Write the following events in the order in which they happened.

- Athenians and Spartans defeated the Persians.
- The Persians marched towards Athens.
- The Greeks sank much of the Persian fleet.

- the Battle of Marathon
- Persians invaded Greece.
- the Battle of Thermopylae

The Persian Wars

1. In about 500 B.C., Greeks in Asia Minor rebelled against the Persians.

2.

3.

4.

5.

6.

7.

8. The Persian Wars ended.

EVALUATING INFORMATION Mark each statement *T* if it is true or *F* if it is false.

_____ **1.** The Spartans showed great courage at the Battle of Thermopylae.

_____ **2.** The Persian War ended the threat of Persian invasion.

_____ **3.** The Delian League was an alliance of 140 city-states led by Athens.

_____ **4.** Pericles standardized the system of weights and measures in Greece.

_____ **5.** As Athens became powerful under Pericles, the Delian League became more independent.

_____ **6.** Young men of Athens and Sparta were eager to fight in the Peloponnesian War.

UNDERSTANDING MAIN IDEAS For each of the following, write the letter of the best choice in the space provided.

_____ **1.** Why was Pericles's leadership so important?
   a. He extended the empire.
   b. He helped Athens achieve the most complete democracy in history.
   c. He brought stability and prosperity to the Mediterranean region.
   d. All of the above.

_____ **2.** The Peloponnesian War
   a. broke out when Greece was united under Pericles.
   b. was the result of the plague.
   c. began because older Spartans wanted to return to fighting.
   d. began with quarrels over trade.

_____ **3.** During the war, the Spartans forced the Athenians
   a. to depend upon their navy for fighting.
   b. to live behind city walls for years.
   c. to become friends with the city-state of Syracuse.
   d. to join forces against Syracuse.

_____ **4.** Why were the Athenians forced to surrender to Sparta?
   a. They were starving.
   b. The war continued for 27 years.
   c. The aristocrats seized power.
   d. The plague killed Pericles.

Name _____ Class _____ Date _____

VOCABULARY Some terms to understand:

- **sculpture (130):** the process of carving, modeling, or welding a hard material into a work of art

- **proportion (130):** harmonious relations of parts to each other or the whole

- **impressed (131):** dazzled; affected deeply

- **contour (131):** the outline of something, or a line to show the outline

- **grace (132):** beauty of form and movement

UNDERSTANDING MAIN IDEAS For each of the following pictures, write the letter of the best choice.

_____ 1. Why do people admire this building?
   a. It represents the finest gymnasiums.
   b. It has perfectly balanced proportions.
   c. It shows light and shade.
   d. It represents the grace of the human body.

_____ 2. Greek vase paintings illustrated scenes from
   a. buildings.
   b. wars.
   c. Olympic games.
   d. everyday life.

_____ 3. Why was this stele created?
   a. to commemorate Hegeso after she died
   b. to commemorate Hegeso's servant
   c. to show an example of Greek painting
   d. to honor Athena

_____ 4. What human traits does this sculpture show?
   a. beauty and grace
   b. strength and athletic ability
   c. pride
   d. all of the above

Chapter 6, Main Idea Activities 6.1, continued

EVALUATING INFORMATION Mark each statement *T* if it is true or *F* if it is false.

_____ **1.** The Parthenon on the Acropolis in Athens showed the people's love for Athena.

_____ **2.** People admired the Parthenon for its view of the city.

_____ **3.** Vase painters used light and shade on pottery to show color.

_____ **4.** Greek vases show the best-preserved examples of Greek painting.

_____ **5.** Greek sculptors used mathematics to create their art.

_____ **6.** Greek art mirrored how the Greeks looked at the world and themselves.

_____ **7.** Greek art glorified human beings.

_____ **8.** Most Greek art had no other purpose than to be admired.

REVIEWING FACTS Choose the correct items from the following list to complete the statements below.

architecture	moderation	colonnade	restraint
Phidias	usefulness	golden age	Egyptian

1. In the 400s B.C. Greece entered an era of artistic achievement called the

_____.

2. To this day the Parthenon is considered a fine example of Greek

_____.

3. Greek sculpture shows the influence of _____ art.

4. The series of columns around the Parthenon is called the

_____.

5. The 40-foot statue of Zeus at the Temple of Olympia was sculpted by

_____.

6. Greek art expressed beliefs in harmony, balance, order, and

_____.

7. Moderation in Greek art means simplicity and _____.

8. In Greek art, beauty and _____ are combined.

CHAPTER **6**   Main Idea Activities 6.2

Philosophers and Writers of the Golden Age

VOCABULARY Some terms to understand:

- **logic (133):** the science of proof by reasoning
- **perfect (134):** being entirely without flaw or defect
- **dialogue (134):** a conversation between two or more persons
- **superstition (135):** a belief or practice resulting from fear of the unknown
- **exaggerated (136):** enlarged beyond the truth
- **pride (137):** conceit or self-love

ORGANIZING INFORMATION Complete the chart by putting each item in the correct category of Greek Drama.

- Some force always defeats the main character.
- Plays made fun of ideas and people.
- Heroes are punished for displaying hubris.
- Main characters solved their problems.

Greek Drama	
Tragedies	**Comedies**
_____	_____
_____	_____
_____	_____
_____	_____

Chapter 6, Main Idea Activities 6.2, continued

REVIEWING FACTS Choose the correct items from the following list to complete the statements below.

Aristotle   Pythagorean theorem   Father of History
Thales of Miletus Hippocrates   philosopher
Plato   Socratic Method

1. The word _____ means lover of wisdom.

2. The first philosopher, _____, wanted to understand the universe.

3. When students try to think for themselves instead of memorizing facts, they are

following the _____.

4. _____ thought that things around us are copies of ideas or "forms."

5. _____ believed that every field of knowledge should be studied in a systematic way.

6. If the lengths of the two shorter sides of a triangle are known, you can figure out the

length of its longest side by using the _____.

7. The founder of medical science is _____.

8. Herodotus is called the _____ because he recorded his opinions about the places and people he saw in his travels.

EVALUATING INFORMATION Mark each statement *T* if it is true or *F* if it is false.

_____ **1.** Philosophy is one of the Greeks' greatest achievements.

_____ **2.** Plato believed that an ideal ruler is chosen for his wealth.

_____ **3.** Egyptians believed that natural events are the works of the gods while the Greeks thought that such events could be explained.

_____ **4.** Most Greek philosophers specialized in one field of knowledge.

_____ **5.** Hippocrates used a method of healing that is based on magic.

_____ **6.** Thucydides, a historian, believed that studying the past helps us understand human nature.

Alexander the Great

VOCABULARY Some terms to understand:

- **undermine (138):** to injure or weaken in a slow and sneaky way
- **era (138):** a period of history
- **assassinated (139):** killed for political reasons
- **loyalty (140):** being faithful
- **efficiently (141):** done in a way that brings about a desired effect

ORGANIZING INFORMATION Fill in the chart by listing the items below in the correct section: Philip II of Macedon, or Alexander the Great

- defeated Thebes and Athens at the Battle of Chaeronea and united Greece
- trained in the army and educated by Aristotle
- conquered the huge Persian territory by 331 B.C.
- borrowed the Greek idea of the phalanx
- his reign spread a new Hellenistic culture
- restored order in Macedon

Two Macedonian Kings	
Philip II of Macedon	_____ _____ _____
Alexander the Great	_____ _____ _____

EVALUATING INFORMATION Mark each statement *T* if it is true or *F* if it is false.

_____ **1.** Philip II of Macedon learned about the Greek army as a student in Thebes.

_____ **2.** When Philip II of Macedon became king, he organized the best-disciplined army to conquer Athens.

Chapter 6, Main Idea Activities 6.3, continued

_____ **3.** Philip II of Macedon was satisfied to rule Greece.

_____ **4.** The fiery speeches of Demosthenes inspired the Athenians to fight Philip.

_____ **5.** As a military commander, Alexander was less skillful than his father.

_____ **6.** Alexander died at age 33 in the Persian city of Susa.

_____ **7.** Macedonian generals married Persian women, following the lead of Alexander.

_____ **8.** Alexander's troops were loyal to him because they admired his courage.

UNDERSTANDING MAIN IDEAS For each of the following, write the letter of the best choice in the space provided.

_____ **1.** Which statement is NOT true about Philip II of Macedon?
   a. He admired Greek ways.
   b. He organized a well-disciplined army.
   c. Some Greeks saw him as a savior.
   d. He was threatened by Demosthenes.

_____ **2.** Demosthenes attacked Philip
   a. with phalanxes.
   b. by organizing the city-states.
   c. with a series of speeches.
   d. by training a young Athenian army.

_____ **3.** Why was the new culture called *Hellenistic*?
   a. Alexander's generals married women of the Persian royal family.
   b. It combined Hellenic, or Greek, ideas with Asian ideas.
   c. It was based on the ideas of Helen of Troy.
   d. It was entirely Greek.

_____ **4.** When he died, Alexander's empire stretched as far as
   a. the Persian Gulf.
   b. Persia and China.
   c. Asia Minor, Syria, Egypt, and India.
   d. Asia Minor, Syria, Egypt, and Mesopotamia.

The Spread of Hellenistic Culture

VOCABULARY Some terms to understand:

- **prosperous (142):** rich
- **complaint (143):** expression of grief or pain
- **peace of mind (143):** a feeling of being secure or safe
- **compound pulley (143):** a series of small wheels with grooves in the rims, used with ropes to pull or lift heavy objects
- **surgery (145):** an operation performed to cure a disease

ORGANIZING INFORMATION Match the effects of the Hellenistic culture with their causes. Use the items below to fill in the chart.

- The middle ranks thrived.
- People turned to new religions and philosophies.
- New values changed people's lifestyles.
- Four schools of philosophy became popular.
- People felt more unity, security, and personal worth.
- More people could afford an education.

Effects of Hellenistic Culture	
Cause	**Effect**
• Trade increased in the Hellenistic world.	
• More people became prosperous.	
• People learned Greek values.	
• As cities grew larger, the Greek concept of the polis declined.	
• New cults introduced worshippers to mysteries.	
• Many people turned to philosophy for understanding.	

Chapter 6, Main Idea Activities 6.4, continued

EVALUATING INFORMATION Mark each statement *T* if it is true or *F* if it is false.

_____ **1.** Women stayed at home in Hellenistic culture.

_____ **2.** Alexandria, Egypt, became the center of Hellenistic trade and learning.

_____ **3.** Hellenistic scientists used simple instruments to learn about the world.

_____ **4.** Euclid's ideas about geometry have been proven false.

_____ **5.** We learned about the value of the pi (π) from Archimedes, a great mathematician.

_____ **6.** Archimedes experimented on the compound pulley, but it did not work.

_____ **7.** Hellenistic scientists concluded that the brain is the center of the nervous system.

_____ **8.** Aristarchus convinced people that the Earth moves around the sun.

_____ **9.** Hipparchus predicted eclipses.

_____ **10.** Hellenistic geographers knew that the Earth was round.

CLASSIFYING INFORMATION In the space provided for each item, write *C* for Cynicism, *Sc* for Scepticism, *St* for Stoicism, or *E* for Epicurism.

_____ **1.** Diogenes

_____ **2.** Pyrrho

_____ **3.** Zeno

_____ **4.** Epicurus

_____ **5.** People should live simply without regard to pleasure and wealth.

_____ **6.** The universe is changing, so knowledge is uncertain.

_____ **7.** People can be happy if they follow the spark of divine reason.

_____ **8.** People should seek pleasure and avoid pain.

Founding the Roman Republic

VOCABULARY Some terms to understand:

- **quarrelsome (151):** apt to pick a fight
- **emergency (151):** an urgent need for help
- **dramatically (151):** in a manner that has a striking effect
- **safeguards (152):** safety devices; protections
- **appointed (152):** named officially
- **morale (153):** courage and confidence to keep one's spirits up when facing hardships

ORGANIZING INFORMATION Fill in the graphic organizer by writing the functions of each group of citizens in the early Roman Republic.

- controlled public funds
- had power over the actions of the Senate and other public officials
- oversaw the conduct of citizens
- commanded the army; had power to veto
- decided on foreign policy
- oversaw the moral conduct of citizens

GOVERNING BODIES OF THE ROMAN REPUBLIC

Senate

_____

_____

Magistrates

_____

_____

_____

Assemblies

_____

EVALUATING INFORMATION Mark each statement *T* if it is true or *F* if it is false.

_____ **1.** Italy's geography enabled it to control regions to its north and south.

_____ **2.** Rome's location helped protect it from invasion by sea.

_____ **3.** Citizens in assemblies did not have real power.

_____ **4.** The plebeians gained more power through demands and strikes.

_____ **5.** The Roman Republic was mostly a time of peace.

_____ **6.** Every landowning citizen was required to serve in the Roman army.

_____ **7.** Only wealthy nobles could afford to hold a Roman office.

_____ **8.** Even partial citizens in distant cities could vote in Roman elections.

REVIEWING FACTS Choose the correct items from the following list to complete the statements below.

Apennine	Tiber	Twelve Tables	legionnaires
checks and balances	plebeians	Conflict of the Orders	
Senate	Etruscans	patricians	

1. The _____ Mountains run the length of the Italian peninsula.

2. The earliest city dwellers in Rome were called the _____.

3. Rome was built on seven hills along the _____ River.

4. The most influential and powerful of Rome's governing bodies was the

_____.

5. The division of power among the magistrates was called _____.

6. The struggles between plebeians and patricians were called the

_____.

7. The _____ were mainly farmers and workers.

8. The _____ were powerful landowners who controlled the government.

9. The engraved Roman laws were called the _____.

10. Citizens in the major unit of the army were called _____.

Main Idea Activities 7.2

Rome Expands Its Borders

VOCABULARY Some terms to understand:

- **tactics (155):** ways of employing forces in combat
- **stampeded (155):** surged as a group
- **revenge (157):** the act of getting even with an enemy
- **livestock (157):** animals kept or raised on farms

ORGANIZING INFORMATION Fill in the graphic organizer by using the following items.

- captured a Carthaginian ship
- built "boarding bridges" inside the ships
- used an army trained in land warfare
- army stampeded across the bridge

- ship rammed into enemy ship
- army captured the enemy
- used the captured ship as model

HOW ROME FOUGHT AT SEA

_____
↓
_____
↓
_____
↓
_____
↓
_____
↓
_____

pick up spot art from WH03PE Pg 155

EVALUATING INFORMATION Mark each statement *T* if it is true or *F* if it is false.

_____ **1.** Fear over loss of power caused the Punic Wars.

_____ **2.** *Punic* is a Greek word describing Phoenicia.

_____ **3.** In the second Punic War, Hannibal led a huge army across the Alps to Italy.

_____ **4.** Hannibal won allies outside of Rome.

_____ **5.** After the war, the Senate gained total control of the army.

_____ **6.** Roman soldiers returning home found their farms unharmed.

_____ **7.** The government fed some farmers who moved to the cities.

_____ **8.** Rome's new empire created a rich class of business people.

UNDERSTANDING MAIN IDEAS For each of the following, write the letter of the best choice in the space provided.

_____ **1.** The Romans greatly expanded the lands under their control
　　　a. by building markets along the southern coast.
　　　b. when the Carthaginian navy lost.
　　　c. before it had a navy.
　　　d. through warfare and alliances.

_____ **2.** Rome's navy became a force equal to the Carthaginian fleet because
　　　a. it employed land warfare tactics at sea.
　　　b. Carthage paid a large sum of money.
　　　c. Hannibal's army was too strong.
　　　d. it captured a Carthaginian ship.

_____ **3.** Why did Rome attack Macedonia?
　　　a. Macedonia offered land to Carthage.
　　　b. Macedonia traded goods in Sicily.
　　　c. Macedonia joined Carthage in the Second Punic War.
　　　d. Macedonia was gaining power throughout the Mediterranean.

_____ **4.** What happened in the Roman Republic after the Punic Wars?
　　　a. The gap between the rich and the poor grew.
　　　b. People from other provinces became citizens.
　　　c. Soldiers were farming in their vineyards.
　　　d. The nobles lost their power to the governors.

CHAPTER **7**

Main Idea Activities 7.3

The Birth of the Roman Empire

VOCABULARY Some terms to understand:

• **numbered (158):** restricted to a definite number

• **crisis (158):** a situation that has reached a serious phase

• **restore (159):** to bring back to or put back into a former state

• **conspirators (160):** people who plot or plan to do something

• **frontier (160):** the line or border between two countries

• **insane (160):** crazy or mentally ill

ORGANIZING INFORMATION Match the groups of rulers to the name of their era. Fill in the graphic organizer using the items below.

• Julio-Claudian Emperors   • First Triumvirate

• Second Triumvirate   • Flavian Emperors

• Five Good Emperors

RULERS OF THE ROMAN EMPIRE

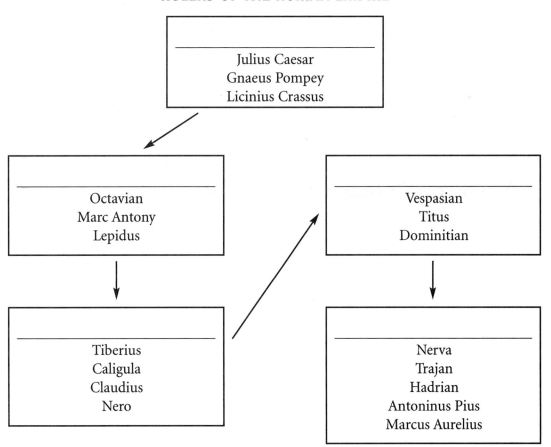

Chapter 7, Main Idea Activities 7.3, continued

EVALUATING INFORMATION Mark each statement *T* if it is true or *F* if it is false.

_____ **1.** Concern for the poor caused the death of the Gracchi brothers.

_____ **2.** Sulla took command of the military primarily to gain fame and fortune.

_____ **3.** When Pompey asked him to, Julius Caesar gave up his army.

_____ **4.** During Caesar's time, the Senate grew in both number and power.

_____ **5.** Octavian captured Marc Antony and Cleopatra in a naval battle in Actium.

_____ **6.** The Roman Empire began with Augustus Caesar's reign.

_____ **7.** Britain became part of the Roman Empire under Claudius.

_____ **8.** Hadrian built a wall from Britain to Rome along the frontier to protect Roman boundaries.

MATCHING Place the letters of the descriptions next to the appropriate names and terms.

_____ **1.** Hadrian

_____ **2.** Cleopatra

_____ **3.** Julius Caesar

_____ **4.** Nero

_____ **5.** Social War

_____ **6.** Marcus Aurelius

_____ **7.** Gaius Gracchus

_____ **8.** Marcus Brutus

_____ **9.** Triumvirate

_____ **10.** Pax Romana

a. tribune who used public funds to buy grain to sell to the poor at low prices

b. ally rebellion also known as the bloodiest in Roman history

c. rule of three

d. dictator for life

e. Caesar's friend who turned traitor and killed him

f. ally in Egypt who joined Mark Antony to rule the Roman world in the east

g. period of peace that lasted for 200 years

h. emperor blamed for a big fire in Rome

i. emperor from Spain who tried to Romanize the provinces

j. emperor who preferred Stoic philosophy to wars

 **CHAPTER 7** Main Idea Activities 7.4

Roman Society and Culture

VOCABULARY Some terms to understand:

- **reinforcements (163):** extra troops
- **recreation (164):** activities a person does when on vacation or relaxing
- **dormice (164):** European animals like small squirrels
- **fungi (164):** growth on a tree, related to mushrooms
- **hearth (165):** the stone or brick floor of a fireplace
- **satires (165):** writings in which humor is used to make fun of something bad or foolish
- **mimes (165):** actors who perform without speaking

ORGANIZING INFORMATION Fill in the chart by placing each item under the correct category.

- taught their children at home
- helped entertain guests
- could accept inheritances
- made all the important family decisions
- conducted religious ceremonies
- managed the households
- taught daughters to manage the household
- could own property
- taught sons the duties of citizenship

FAMILY ROLES IN ANCIENT ROME

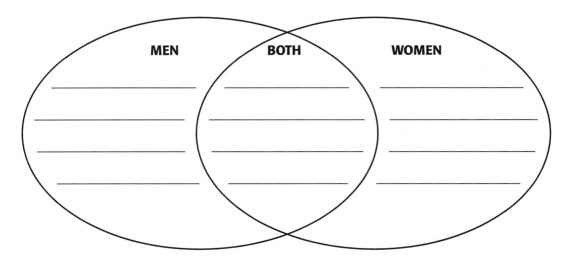

EVALUATING INFORMATION Mark each statement *T* if it is true or *F* if it is false.

_____ **1.** To match the needs of the huge empire, the Romans changed the laws.

_____ **2.** Well-constructed road systems promoted trade and made the army more efficient.

_____ **3.** The army was not always successful in crushing rebels.

_____ **4.** All Romans, including the rich, ate simple meals of bread, cheese, and fruit.

_____ **5.** If you had slaves in the Roman Empire, you lost respect.

_____ **6.** Early Romans worshipped ancestral spirits.

CLASSIFYING INFORMATION These are among the most important legacies of the Roman Empire. In the space provided, mark the letter of the correct category.

A. Law and Government
B. Engineering
C. Science
D. Architecture
E. Literature
F. Languages
G. Recreation

_____ **1.** the Colosseum, the great arena in Rome

_____ **2.** twenty-three letters of the alphabet

_____ **3.** *Aeneid* by Virgil, *Metamorphoses* by Ovid, *Annals* by Tacitus

_____ **4.** Galen's summary of all medical knowledge

_____ **5.** aqueducts or bridge-like structures that carried water

_____ **6.** code of Twelve Tables

_____ **7.** the Ptolemaic system

_____ **8.** the use of concrete, arch, and vaulted dome

_____ **9.** basic principles that should apply to all humans

_____ **10.** *Parallel Lives,* Greek and Roman biographies by Plutarch

_____ **11.** Italian, French, Spanish, Portuguese, and Romanian

_____ **12.** gladiators, chariot racing

CHAPTER 7

Main Idea Activities 7.5

The Rise of Christianity

VOCABULARY Some terms to understand:

- **violate (168):** to treat something sacred disrespectfully
- **sacked (168):** robbed and looted a captured city
- **hitherto (168):** before this time
- **exclude (169):** to leave out
- **ascend (169):** to rise up
- **penalties (169):** punishments for breaking a law
- **sect (170):** religious faction

ORGANIZING INFORMATION Fill in the sequence chart with the events leading to the rise of Christianity. Write events from the list in the order in which they happened.

- Rome outlawed Christianity.
- Romans feared Jesus would lead an uprising.
- Jesus of Nazareth began teaching in communities outside the city.
- Jesus was arrested, tried before Pontius Pilate, then crucified.
- Romans believed that followers of Jesus were attacking Roman religion and law.

THE RISE OF CHRISTIANITY

• Hadrian banned all Jews from Jerusalem.

↓

↓

↓

↓

↓

↓

• Romans turned to Christianity for hope during violence and unrest in the A.D. 200s.

EVALUATING INFORMATION Mark each statement *T* if it is true or *F* if it is false.

_____ **1.** Judaea was a Roman province in A.D. 6.

_____ **2.** Zealots rebelled against the Romans because they wanted independence.

_____ **3.** The destruction of Jerusalem strengthened the role of priests.

_____ **4.** At first, in the villages he visited no one wanted to listen to Jesus.

_____ **5.** Because Jesus was teaching about love, the Romans did not think he was an enemy of the state.

_____ **6.** The resurrection of Jesus became the central event of Christianity.

_____ **7.** Theodosius declared Christianity the official religion of Rome.

_____ **8.** Jesus was the first pope.

UNDERSTANDING MAIN IDEAS For each of the following, write the letter of the best choice in the space provided.

_____ **1.** What happened to the Jewish religion after the Romans sacked Jerusalem?
  a. Rabbis or scholars became the leaders.
  b. The priests built other temples.
  c. The Jews worshipped near the wall.
  d. The Jews wrote their history.

_____ **2.** How did Rome recognize that Christians were different?
  a. Their numbers became so large in a very short time.
  b. They failed to stop the spread of Christianity.
  c. They tried to influence others to disobey Roman law.
  d. They opposed the idea of worshipping more than one god.

_____ **3.** How did Christians become martyrs?
  a. They were put to death because of their beliefs.
  b. They obeyed Roman law but practiced their own religion.
  c. They attacked the fact that Romans worshipped too many gods.
  d. They converted many Romans to their point of view.

_____ **4.** When did Roman law accept Christianity as a religion?
  a. during the era of the Five Good Emperors
  b. when the Christian church had become very large
  c. before Christian property was seized
  d. soon after they were allowed not to worship the emperor

CHAPTER **7** Main Idea Activities 7.6

The Fall of the Western Empire

VOCABULARY Some terms to understand:

- **sole (173):** only
- **inefficient (173):** wasting time, energy, or materials
- **plundering (175):** robbing or taking by force
- **triggered (175):** set off; started
- **corrupt (176):** evil, dishonest, and rotten

ORGANIZING INFORMATION How did Emperor Diocletian try to solve the empire's problems? Fill in the chart using three of the following solutions. One problem has two solutions.

- He tried to control prices and wages.
- He collected more taxes.
- He appointed a co-emperor and two assistants.
- He drove out invading barbarians.

Problem	Solution
The empire had grown too large.	_____ _____
There was lawlessness within the empire.	_____ _____
The economy was in crisis.	_____ _____

EVALUATING INFORMATION Mark each statement *T* if it is true or *F* if it is false.

_____ **1.** By granting citizenship to all free people of the empire, the government gained more taxpayers.

_____ **2.** Because wealth continued to flow into the empire, there was a shortage of silver for coins.

_____ **3.** The efforts of Diocletian and Constantine slowed the empire's decline.

_____ **4.** Diocletian was successful in improving the economy by controlling prices and wages.

_____ **5.** Constantine banned Christianity throughout the empire.

_____ **6.** The Germans who invaded the West set up a united empire.

_____ **7.** Because of the German invasions, knowledge of the world and the past declined.

_____ **8.** A government designed for a small city-state effectively controlled a vast empire.

REVIEWING FACTS Choose the correct items from the following list to complete the statements below.

Constantinople	inflation	Germans
transportation	Mediterranean	Attila

1. When the prices of goods increased but the value of the silver coin decreased, Rome experienced _____.

2. _____, Rome's capital city in the East, served as a base from which to defend the eastern empire.

3. When _____, the Hun, overthrew Romulus Augustulus, the Roman Empire ended.

4. The most troublesome of Rome's invaders were the _____.

5. Among the many causes of the decline of the Roman Empire was growing too fast in an age of slow _____.

6. Rome governed the entire _____ with a system designed for a city-state.

VOCABULARY Some terms to understand:

- **rapids (182):** a dangerous stretch of a river where water moves rapidly and with force
- **sparse (182):** few and scattered
- **depressions (184):** low areas
- **similarity (185):** likeness
- **up-to-date (185):** timely or current
- **staple crops (185):** produced regularly or in large amounts, such as wheat and rice
- **vital (186):** of utmost importance

ORGANIZING INFORMATION Fill in the web by writing items in the correct section.

- covers one-fourth of the African continent
- areas of jungle
- vast stretches of dry grasslands
- from the Arabic word for "shore"

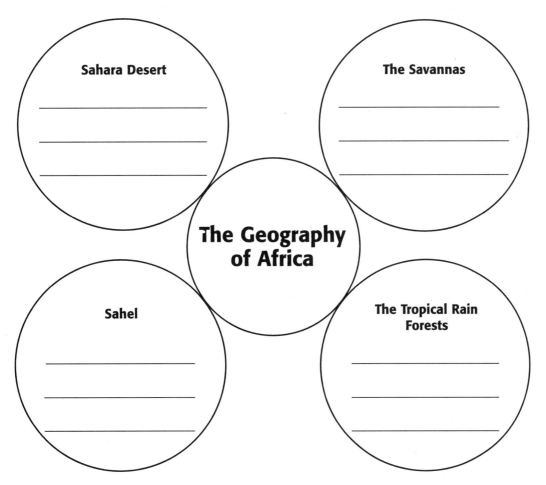

Chapter 8, Main Idea Activities 8.1, continued

EVALUATING INFORMATION Mark each statement *T* if it is true or *F* if it is false.

_____ **1.** Natural harbors and rivers once made travel and trade among Africans easy.

_____ **2.** Many lakes and mountains lie along the eastern edge of the African plateau.

_____ **3.** Understanding African history is hard because ancient people spoke Bantu.

_____ **4.** Stories of African history have been passed down in the oral tradition.

_____ **5.** Africans had little or no contact with Asia for thousands of years.

_____ **6.** Many early Sub-Saharan cultures were complex, well organized, and wealthy.

_____ **7.** Women played a crucial role in African families and the economy.

_____ **8.** In many parts of Africa, village elders had authority over life and work.

_____ **9.** Villages in Africa set their pace by the cycles of planting and harvesting.

REVIEWING FACTS Choose the correct items from the following list to complete the statements below.

Great Rift Valley	Bantu	Lake Victoria	plateau
Mount Kilimanjaro	Asia	Kalahari	griots

1. Much of sub-Saharan Africa is a _____.

2. The Namib and _____ Deserts are in southern Africa.

3. One of the world's largest lakes is _____.

4. The _____ was formed millions of years ago when the Earth's crust parted.

5. Mount Kenya and _____ are tall, isolated mountain peaks in eastern Africa.

6. One of Africa's largest language groups is _____.

7. _____ were trained speakers who told the history of the village through amusing tales.

8. Cultural exchange took place for centuries between Africa and

_____.

Main Idea Activities 8.2

The Kingdoms of Kush and Aksum

VOCABULARY Some expressions to understand:

- **corridor of trade (187):** trade route
- **maintain cultural ties (187):** share languages and customs
- **external trade (190):** trade outside a region

Some terms to understand:

- **roots (187):** beginnings
- **conversion (190):** change from one belief or religion to another
- **erosion (190):** loss of soil due to flooding or wind

ORGANIZING INFORMATION Decide whether each description is true about Kush, Aksum, or both kingdoms. Then write each item in the correct place on the Venn diagram.

- lay in rugged Ethiopian highlands
- introduced Christianity into the region
- ruled a unified Egypt in about 710 B.C.
- Meroë may have been a center of ironwork.
- controlled important trade routes between the Red Sea and Egypt
- located to the west of the Red Sea

The Kingdoms of Kush and Aksum

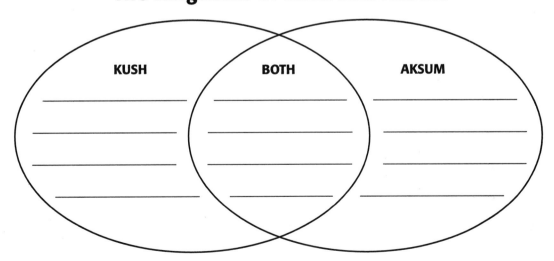

Chapter 8, Main Idea Activities 8.2, continued

UNDERSTANDING MAIN IDEAS For each of the following, write the letter of the best choice in the space provided.

_____ **1.** Why did the kingdom of Kush thrive?
   a. It was located on an important corridor of trade.
   b. It had deposits of silver, gold, and other minerals.
   c. It was a great source of ivory.
   d. It was located in Egypt.

_____ **2.** The wealth of Aksum increased as
   a. it became a military power.
   b. the kingdom of Kush declined.
   c. it gained more control of trade in eastern Africa.
   d. all of the above.

_____ **3.** Christianity appealed to the people of Aksum because
   a. they were ready for a new religion.
   b. it incorporated many of their traditions.
   c. 'Ēzānā forced people to convert.
   d. Constantine was a Christian ruler.

_____ **4.** Which of these is NOT a reason for the decline of Aksum?
   a. Erosion made the land less productive.
   b. Persians took over the Red Sea trade.
   c. Islamic Arabs won control of the Red Sea.
   d. Christianity lost its appeal among the people.

REVIEWING FACTS Choose the correct items from the following list to complete the statements below.

Ethiopian Church   the Red Sea   Napata   Meroë   Nubia

1. The kingdom of Kush arose in the area known as _____.

2. The capital of Kush was _____, a city along the Nile and Karmah.

3. At the height of their civilization, the people of _____ built pyramids.

4. Aksum controlled trade between inland Africa and _____.

5. King 'Ēzānā's conversion laid the foundations of the _____.

Name _____ Class _____ Date _____

VOCABULARY Some terms to understand:

- **emerged (191):** rose up or came out
- **demand (192):** to call for as necessary
- **dwindling (192):** becoming less
- **eyewitness (193):** one who gives a report of what he or she has seen
- **supporter (194):** one who promotes an interest, such as education and the arts
- **pilgrimage (194):** a trip made to visit a holy place
- **province (195):** a region of a country that has its own local government

ORGANIZING INFORMATION The following items describe the contributions of each African leader: Mohammed I Askia, Sonni ʿAlī , Mansa Mūsā, Tunka Manin. Use the items to fill in the chart.

- made a pilgrimage to Mecca
- great ruler of Ghana
- supported a revival of Islamic scholarship in Timbuktu
- divided Songhai into several provinces
- built a fleet of warships to patrol the Niger River
- built Songhai into a strong kingdom
- commanded army of 200,000 warriors

Great African Rulers	
Mohammed I Askia • supported a revival of Islamic scholarship in Timbuktu	**Sonni ʿAlī**
Mansa Mūsā	**Tunka Manin** • under his rule, Timbuktu became a commercial center

Chapter 8, Main Idea Activities 8.3, continued

CLASSIFYING INFORMATION Mark each item *W* for West Africa or *E* for East Africa.

_____ **1.** Swahili

_____ **2.** Madagascar

_____ **3.** Atlantic Ocean

_____ **4.** Ghana

_____ **5.** Mali

_____ **6.** Gao

_____ **7.** Kumbi

_____ **8.** Lake Chad

_____ **9.** Great Zimbabwe

_____ **10.** Mogadishu

_____ **11.** Niger River

_____ **12.** Timbuktu

_____ **13.** Indian Ocean

_____ **14.** Kilwa

UNDERSTANDING MAIN IDEAS For each of the following, write the letter of the best choice in the space provided.

_____ **1.** What religion heavily influenced the trade based in coastal East Africa?
  a. Islam
  b. Christianity
  c. Bantu
  d. Indian

_____ **2.** What did the wealth of kingdoms in West Africa depend upon?
  a. control of gold and salt trade routes across the Sahara
  b. control of trade routes to the south
  c. control of gold and salt trade routes across the Mediterranean Sea
  d. control of trade routes along the Nile

_____ **3.** Why did Sonni 'Alī patrol the Niger River with ships?
  a. The city of Gao was located on the Niger.
  b. It was a major shipping route.
  c. It ran through much of his kingdom.
  d. all of the above

_____ **4.** In general, the cities of West Africa were
  a. centers of wealth and culture.
  b. poor farming villages.
  c. wealthy centers of farming.
  d. isolated centers of wealth.

Main Idea Activities 9.1

The Earliest Americans

VOCABULARY Some terms to understand:

- **terrain (200):** physical features of land
- **underworld (201):** the place of departed souls
- **creator (201):** one who makes or creates
- **migrations (202):** annual movements of animals from place to place
- **glaciers (202):** a large mass of ice or snow that moves very slowly across land
- **subsistence (202):** the minimum amount necessary to support life

ORGANIZING INFORMATION Fill in the chart by writing the events in the correct sequence. Use your text to check the order of events.

- The earliest known farming communities began in Mexico.
- Early peoples from Asia migrated to the Americas.
- Villages and towns began to grow.
- The climate changed and large animals became extinct.
- The early migrants had to rely on plants as a food source.

The Development of American Agriculture

1. _____

2. _____

3. _____

4. _____

5. _____

UNDERSTANDING MAIN IDEAS For each of the following, write the letter of the best choice in the space provided.

_____ **1.** Where did the earliest Americans come from?
a. Asia
b. Europe
c. Canada
d. Mexico

_____ **2.** During the Ice Age, the bottom of the Bering Strait became a
a. river system.
b. thin piece of ice.
c. narrow strip of water.
d. land bridge.

_____ **3.** Creation myths are important to historians because they provide
a. information about a supreme being.
b. stories about people emerging from the underworld.
c. evidence of a people's customs and values.
d. explanations of how the world was formed.

_____ **4.** When glaciers melted, the main food source for hunter-gatherers was
a. plant life.
b. game animals.
c. the ocean.
d. icebergs.

_____ **5.** Early Americans turned from hunting to gathering because
a. Native American farmers invented the plow.
b. they had to use large animals for farming.
c. large prehistoric animals became extinct.
d. all their villages were surrounded by farmlands.

EVALUATING INFORMATION Mark each statement *T* if it is true or *F* if it is false.

_____ **1.** Many historians think that early Americans may have followed animal herds across the land bridge.

_____ **2.** Among the animals that early Americans hunted were modern elephants.

_____ **3.** Farming evolved as hunter-gatherers gradually relied on plants as a food source.

_____ **4.** Farming enabled people to build lasting settlements.

Cultures of North America

VOCABULARY Some terms to understand:

- **diversity (203):** the condition of being different; variety
- **present-day (203):** current; now
- **permanent (205):** continuing without change; lasting
- **droughts (205):** periods in which there is not enough water
- **mounds (207):** small hills
- **far-flung (207):** spread over a wide area

ORGANIZING INFORMATION Place each item where it belongs in the graphic organizer.

- people lived in teepees
- created totem poles
- relied on fishing
- Cahokia was a center of ceremony and trade.
- people hunted buffalo
- included the Hohokam people
- one group called the Hopewell
- built irrigation systems in dry regions

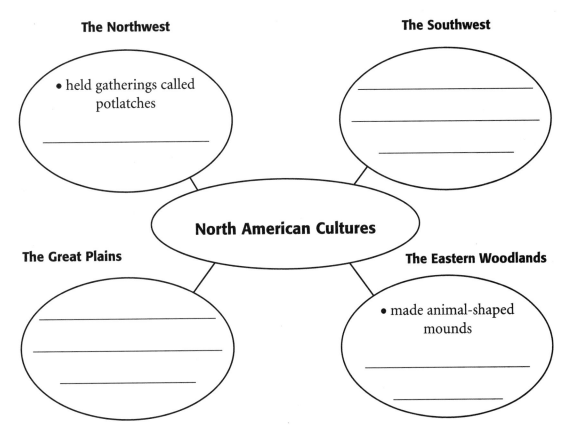

The Northwest

- held gatherings called potlatches
_____

The Southwest

_____
_____
_____

North American Cultures

The Great Plains

_____
_____

The Eastern Woodlands

- made animal-shaped mounds
_____
_____

Chapter 9, Main Idea Activities 9.2, continued

EVALUATING INFORMATION Mark each statement *T* if it is true or *F* if it is false.

_____ **1.** In large areas of the North American western desert, water was hard to find.

_____ **2.** The people who lived along the northwest coast of North America are remembered for their totem poles.

_____ **3.** The Plains people always hunted on horseback.

_____ **4.** The buffalo became sacred in the religion of the Plains people.

_____ **5.** Jewelry, tools, and weapons found in burial mounds reveal that the Hopewell were skilled artists.

_____ **6.** Cahokians carried on a far-flung trade for jewelry and tools.

UNDERSTANDING MAIN IDEAS For each of the following, write the letter of the best choice in the space provided.

_____ **1.** What crops did the Hohokam people raise?
 a. rice, corn, beans, and squash
 b. corn, beans, and cotton
 c. flax and cotton
 d. wheat, beans, and cotton

_____ **2.** What tale did the Zuni Pueblo tell about corn?
 a. It got its pleasant taste when the witches tasted it.
 b. It got its pleasant taste when crow, coyote, and owl tasted it.
 c. Crow, coyote, and owl learned to stay out of the fields.
 d. The taste of corn has grown hot like chili peppers.

_____ **3.** What did scientists find in Hopewell burial mounds that showed that trade connected diverse people across America?
 a. the teeth of grizzly bears and sharks
 b. jewelry, tools, weapons
 c. animals
 d. buffalo teeth

_____ **4.** What activity enabled Native Americans of the Eastern Woodlands to develop complex and extensive cultures?
 a. long-distance trade
 b. hunting animals
 c. mound building
 d. ceremonies

CHAPTER 9

Main Idea Activities 9.3

Mesoamerica and Andean South America

VOCABULARY Some terms to understand:

• **elite (209):** special group of people; the socially superior part of society

• **pictographic (209):** illustrated by pictures

• **accurate (209):** correct; without errors

• **catastrophes (210):** violent, usually destructive natural events

• **prestige (210):** fame or respect that comes from success or having wealth

• **pack animals (211):** animals trained to carry things

UNDERSTANDING MAIN IDEAS For each of the following, write the letter of the best choice in the space provided.

_____ 1. What was this building used for?
    a. to store grain
    b. to watch the stars and planets
    c. as a temple to Quetzalcoatl
    d. to honor the sun god, Tonatiuh

[Art Spec No.:
PN03MAC09ART003A-C]
[spot art 003A: Mayan
observatory as shown on
page 209 of PE]

_____ 2. What does the picture show?
    a. a chinampa
    b. a Mayan observatory
    c. the Mayan Calendar Stone
    d. the Aztec Calendar Stone

[spot art 003B: the Aztec
calendar stone as shown on
page 210 of PE]

_____ 3. What does this statue represent?
    a. Aztec artisans
    b. a prehistoric animal
    c. the god Quetzalcoatl
    d. the power of warriors

[spot art 003C: statue
of Quetzalcoatl as shown on
page 210 PE]

Chapter 9, Main Idea Activities 9.3, continued

CLASSIFYING INFORMATION Each of the following descriptions refers to a group of people in Mesoamerica and Andean South America. Use the space provided to indicate whether each description below refers to the Olmec (O), Chavin (C), Maya (M), Toltec (T), Aztec (A), or Inca (I)

_____ **1.** perhaps the most advanced people in the Americas

_____ **2.** worshipped a god that was part jaguar and part human

_____ **3.** spread the worship of their god, Quetzalcoatl

_____ **4.** decorated ceramic religious vessels with images of cats

_____ **5.** farmed on chinampas, or raised fields

_____ **6.** developed the only complete writing system in early America

_____ **7.** in the Andes Mountains of South America

_____ **8.** developed a counting system that included the number zero

_____ **9.** spoke Quechua, a language still spoken by millions of people in South America

_____ **10.** could perform operations on the brain

_____ **11.** built the city Tenochtitlán

_____ **12.** occupied most of the Yucatan peninsula to present-day El Salvador

_____ **13.** ruled a vast empire with hundreds of language groups

_____ **14.** could predict eclipses and good times for harvest

_____ **15.** had a name that meant "children of the sun"

_____ **16.** fed the sun god human sacrifices

_____ **17.** kept records by means of quipu

_____ **18.** left behind giant stone heads carved from basalt

_____ **19.** their capital city was Tula

_____ **20.** used llamas to carry their goods through mountainous terrain

CHAPTER 10   Main Idea Activities 10.1

Modern Chapter 1   **The Byzantine Empire**

VOCABULARY Some terms to understand:

- **revive (222):** to bring back
- **preservation (222):** the act of keeping safe from harm or decay
- **benefit (222):** help or useful aid
- **strategically (224):** in a manner that is important in planning for war or maintaining power
- **revenues (224):** earnings; money
- **patriarch (224):** head; leader
- **friction (226):** discord between two persons or parties
- **adoration (227):** devoted love or worship

ORGANIZING INFORMATION Use the following items to complete the graphic organizer.

- mosaic
- Cyrillic
- Hagia Sophia
- Justinian Code
- Greek fire
- icon

CONTRIBUTIONS OF THE BYZANTINE EMPIRE TO CIVILIZATION	
• collection of Roman laws	_____
• liquid that bursts into flame	_____
• holy picture that inspires devotion	_____
• alphabet created for Slavs	_____
• picture made from small pieces of enamel, glass, or stone	_____
• a round dome over a rectangular building	_____

EVALUATING INFORMATION Mark each statement *T* if it is true or *F* if it is false.

_____ **1.** The Byzantine Empire made the most contributions to civilization during the reign of Justinian.

_____ **2.** Justinian ordered scholars to collect Roman laws and make them useful.

_____ **3.** Justinian neglected the status of women.

_____ **4.** Officials of the empire were clever and efficient, but uninterested in getting paid.

_____ **5.** The Christian church in the Byzantine Empire was the same as that of the West.

_____ **6.** For iconoclasts, pictures of the saints should not be honored.

_____ **7.** In the West, icons helped Christians who could not read understand their religion.

_____ **8.** The Eastern Orthodox Church in Constantinople was the same as the Catholic Church in Rome.

_____ **9.** The dome of the Hagia Sophia was copied from the Romans.

_____ **10.** The Byzantine Empire lasted for 200 years until its conquest by Ottoman Turks.

REVIEWING FACTS Choose the correct items from the following list to complete the statements below.

Father   Seljuq Turks   dowry   heresy   Institutes

1. The third part of the Justinian Code, which serves as a guide for students, is called

the _____.

2. In Roman law, the money or goods a wife brought to a husband in marriage is called

a _____.

3. A _____ is an opinion that conflicts with official church beliefs.

4. In a Byzantine Church, the image of the _____ was found at the dome.

5. The worst threat to the Byzantine Empire in A.D. 1000 came from the

_____ from Asia.

 **CHAPTER 10**

Modern Chapter **1**

Main Idea Activities 10.2

The Rise of Russia

VOCABULARY Some terms to understand:

- **crisscross (229):** to go or pass back and forth
- **successors (230):** people who come after someone
- **prospered (230):** got rich
- **principality (230):** a small state usually ruled by a prince
- **frescoes (231):** paintings with water colors on damp plaster
- **agricultural (232):** having to do with farms

ORGANIZING INFORMATION Complete the pyramid about the social classes in Kievan Russia by using the following items. Write the most powerful class at the top down to the least powerful class at the bottom.

- boyars
- town artisans and merchants
- local princes and their families
- peasants

SOCIAL CLASSES IN KIEVAN RUSSIA

Chapter 10, Main Idea Activities 10.2, continued

EVALUATING INFORMATION Mark each statement *T* if it is true or *F* if it is false.

_____ **1.** Eurasia is a mountain range forming the boundary between Europe and Asia.

_____ **2.** Transportation and trade routes were possible because of the many rivers in the Eurasian plains.

_____ **3.** The Avars, Huns, and Magyars were natives of Eurasia.

_____ **4.** Attracted by the trade, the Vikings from Scandinavia sailed to the southern part of eastern Europe.

_____ **5.** A people called Rus, led by Rurik, came to rule the Slavs in A.D. 862.

_____ **6.** Kiev was one of the cities that grew along the plain.

_____ **7.** Agriculture was the source of Kiev's wealth and power.

_____ **8.** The princes of Kievan Russia were independent.

MATCHING Match the letters of the items in the second column with the correct items in the first column.

_____ **1.** Pravda Russkia

_____ **2.** hymns and sermons

_____ **3.** veche

_____ **4.** boyars

_____ **5.** Vladimir I

_____ **6.** Slavs

_____ **7.** taiga

_____ **8.** steppe

a. a grassy and mostly treeless plain

b. the source of the word "slave"

c. nobles who made up councils that advised Kievan princes

d. Russia's first law code introduced by Yaroslav the Wise

e. converted to Christianity and ordered all Kievans to do the same

f. an area of great forests that gets a lot of rain

g. town meeting in Kievan Russia

h. dominant forms of writing during the Kievan period of wealth

Main Idea Activities 10.3

Modern Chapter **1**

Russia and the Mongols

VOCABULARY Some terms to understand:

- **merciless (233):** cruel; showing no pity
- **outlying (233):** outside of a central area
- **sacked (233):** destroyed
- **assert (234):** insist on; claim
- **acquiring (234):** getting; taking
- **faithful (234):** members of the church
- **chandeliers (235):** lights that usually hang from the ceiling

ORGANIZING INFORMATION Complete the graphic organizer by putting the date next to each event.

- 1169 and 1203
- 1055
- 1547
- 1113 to 1125
- 1480
- 1240
- 1589

THE RISE OF RUSSIA	
• Ivan the Great led Russia to independence from Mongols.	_____
• Vladimir Monomakh regained Kiev and ruled it.	_____
• Mongols conquered and destroyed cities in Kievan Russia.	_____
• Moscow became the center of the Russian Orthodox Church.	_____
• Polovtsy gained control of the area south of Kiev.	_____
• Ivan the Terrible became czar with absolute power.	_____
• Groups of princes sacked Kiev.	_____

Chapter 10, Main Idea Activities 10.3, continued

EVALUATING INFORMATION Mark each statement *T* if it is true or *F* if it is false.

_____ **1.** Kiev began to lose power because the rulers' sons started fighting among themselves.

_____ **2.** The Mongols were the first invaders of Kiev.

_____ **3.** The Mongols taxed the Slavs heavily, probably in goods and services.

_____ **4.** The Slavs, Poles, and Mongols all shared the same religion.

_____ **5.** Ivan III united Russia and recognized the Mongol khan as ruler.

_____ **6.** Ivan IV modernized the laws of Russia.

_____ **7.** Siberia became a Russian territory under Ivan the Terrible.

_____ **8.** When the Turks took Constantinople, it had little effect on the Russian church.

UNDERSTANDING MAIN IDEAS For each of the following, write the letter of the best choice in the space provided.

_____ **1.** The Polovtsy were a Turkish people who
  a. interfered with Kiev's trade.
  b. were close allies with Kievan Russia.
  c. controlled the area to the north of Kiev.
  d. came from the Asian steppe east of the Ural Mountains.

_____ **2.** The long Mongol rule over Russia
  a. had little effect on the Russian people.
  b. destroyed the possibility of an independent Russia.
  c. influenced Slavic society in language and customs.
  d. did not end until the late 1800s.

_____ **3.** When Russians said that Moscow was the "third Rome," they meant that it
  a. was the third great capital of the Roman Empire.
  b. had become the new center of the Orthodox church.
  c. could no longer be seen as an important center of the Christian church.
  d. had fallen because of heresy.

_____ **4.** Russian churches of the period were
  a. generally quite small and dark inside.
  b. built to inspire awe and religious wonder.
  c. large flat buildings that had no domes on top.
  d. built in order to honor Constantinople as the center of the church.

Name _____ Class _____ Date _____

VOCABULARY Some terms to understand:

- **gulf (240):** a large area of ocean that reaches inland
- **revelation (240):** something that is made known, such as a truth or instruction from God
- **harass (241):** to bother
- **submission (242):** the act of surrendering or giving up power
- **clergy (242):** ministers, priests, rabbis, etc.
- **congregational (242):** something done in a gathering of people

ORGANIZING INFORMATION Write each name from the list in the correct spot on the map.

- Arabian Desert
- Arabian Sea
- Yemen
- Red Sea
- Syrian Desert
- Medina
- Persian Gulf
- Mecca
- Jidda

ARABIAN PENINSULA

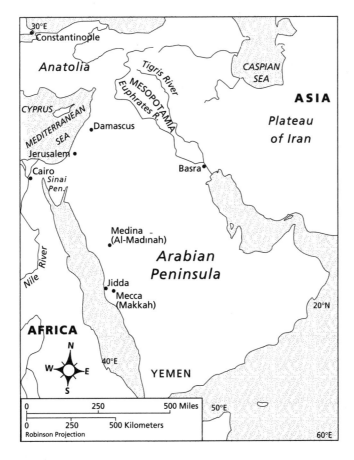

Chapter 11, Main Idea Activities 11.1, continued

EVALUATING INFORMATION Mark each statement *T* if it is true or *F* if it is false.

_____ **1.** Most of the Arabian Peninsula is desert.

_____ **2.** Because desert dwellers could not grow crops, many herded sheep and camels.

_____ **3.** In areas along the coasts, townspeople became fishermen.

_____ **4.** Like many Arabs in Mecca, Muhammad made a living as a shepherd.

_____ **5.** The angel Jibreel supposedly told Muhammad that he was a prophet.

_____ **6.** The merchant rulers of Mecca readily accepted Muhammad's teachings.

_____ **7.** Every year Arab pilgrims came to Mecca to worship their idols at the Kaaba.

_____ **8.** Muhammad converted many of the bedouin tribes to his religion.

_____ **9.** Muslim belief is based on Islam or obeying God's will.

_____ **10.** Muslims lead their lives according to the Qur'an, their holy book.

REVIEWING FACTS Choose the correct items from the following list to complete the statements below.

jihad	Kaaba	Five Pillars of Islam
mosques	sheikh	hijrah

1. The leader of a bedouin tribe is called a _____.

2. Muhammad's journey from Mecca to Yathrib is known as the

_____.

3. Muhammad rededicated the stone in _____ to the worship of Allah.

4. Muslims recognize the _____, or the struggle to defend the faith.

5. In Islam, there are five basic acts of worship, called the _____.

6. Muslims worship in _____.

Name _____ Class _____ Date _____

VOCABULARY Some terms to understand:

• **successor (243):** heir; next in line

• **tolerant (243):** willing to let others have their own beliefs

• **split (245):** separation or division

• **worth (245):** value

• **symbolic (247):** having the function of standing for something else

UNDERSTANDING MAIN IDEAS For each of the following, write the letter of the best answer in the space provided.

_____ **1.** What does this calligraphy symbolize or mean?
  a. one of the greatest Sufi mystics
  b. Rābi'ah al-'Adawīyah
  c. "In the name of Allah Most Gracious, Most Merciful"
  d. all of the above

_____ **2.** What kind of place does this picture show?
  a. mosque, or place of worship
  b. trading post where goods are exchanged
  c. church of the Eastern Orthodox religion
  d. center for learning in ancient arts

_____ **3.** The image in this picture is Abū Bakr. He is important to Muslims because
  a. he was a follower of Muhammad.
  b. he was the Muslim general who invaded Europe.
  c. he was the greatest sultan of the Turks.
  d. he succeeded Muhammad as leader of Islam.

EVALUATING INFORMATION Mark each statement *T* if it is true or *F* if it is false.

_____ **1.** Muslim conquerors demanded that all people convert to their faith.

_____ **2.** Disagreements about the choice of caliph split the Muslim community.

_____ **3.** Sunni Muslims believe that religious matters should be agreed upon by all Muslim people.

_____ **4.** Most of the world's Muslims are Shi'ah Muslims.

_____ **5.** The Turks took over the Arabs as the ruling force in Islam.

_____ **6.** Initially, the Turkish sultan had no power over the Muslim caliph in Baghdad.

REVIEWING FACTS Choose the correct items from the following list to complete the statements below.

Sufi	'Umar	Shi'ah	imams
Moors	Sunni	caliph	Jews

1. _____ means "successor to the Prophet."

2. Under the leadership of _____, Muslims took control of Iraq.

3. Muslims called Christians and _____ "People of the Book."

4. _____ Muslims believed that agreement among the Muslim people should settle religious matters.

5. The Shi'ah Muslims believed that _____ should decide religious and worldly matters.

6. The Muslim mystics, known as _____, tried to live simple lives for God.

7. The Muslims who followed 'Alī became known as _____.

8. The Muslims who made Spain their home were called the

_____.

Main Idea Activities 11.3

Modern Chapter **2**

Islamic Civilization

VOCABULARY Some terms to understand:

- **divorced (249):** lawfully dissolved a marriage
- **secluded (249):** hidden from public view
- **pharmaceutical (250):** having to do with drugs and medicines
- **distillation (250):** to draw out the part that is pure
- **dissection (250):** cutting apart carefully to observe the parts
- **diagnose (250):** to examine a patient and name his or her disease
- **hygiene (250):** a system for keeping people clean and free from germs
- **treat (250):** to give medicines or services to cure a disease

ORGANIZING INFORMATION The Muslim world traded ideas and goods with many cultures. Fill in the chart by placing each item under the culture from which the idea, raw materials, or goods originated.

- textiles from silk
- fine leather goods
- ideas of the philosophers
- Arabic numerals
- steel swords from Toledo
- papermaking technique
- the astrolabe
- an ancient system of mathematics

An Exchange of Cultures	
China	**Spain**
_____ _____	_____ _____
Greece	**India**
_____ _____	_____ _____

EVALUATING INFORMATION Mark each statement *T* if it is true or *F* if it is false.

_____ **1.** The Muslim Empire was the center of trade between Europe, Asia, and Africa.

_____ **2.** Many Europeans thought the Muslim world was a source of advanced knowledge.

_____ **3.** The Muslims were told to keep their slaves.

_____ **4.** If a marriage was arranged, a Muslim woman could not refuse it.

_____ **5.** Some of the most important Muslim contributions were to medicinal science.

_____ **6.** Muslim art shows human and animals forms.

UNDERSTANDING MAIN IDEAS For each of the following, write the letter of the best choice in the space provided.

_____ **1.** In Islamic families, every member had
  a. control of the family property.
  b. specific roles and duties.
  c. the right to contribute to the family's needs.
  d. his or her own slave.

_____ **2.** Medicine based on Arab Muslim medical advances
  a. was taught in universities throughout Europe.
  b. preserved old medical knowledge.
  c. helped great Islamic thinkers to become doctors.
  d. enabled physicians to understand Muslims.

_____ **3.** Islamic architecture focused on showing
  a. the glory of Islam.
  b. images of God.
  c. Muslim achievements.
  d. the wealth of Muslims.

_____ **4.** Why did Islamic art emphasize geometric and floral patterns?
  a. These were more interesting than battle scenes.
  b. The design of mosques had become too elaborate.
  c. Religious art cannot show human or animal form.
  d. The rulers preferred these patterns.

CHAPTER 12   Main Idea Activities 12.1

Modern Chapter **3**

China Under the Sui, Tang, and Sung Dynasties

VOCABULARY Some terms to understand:

• **disruption (266):** destroying or breaking apart order

• **reuniting (266):** bringing together again

• **ethics (269):** standards of right and wrong

• **tribute (269):** payment paid for protection or peace by one ruler or nation to another

• **caravans (270):** group of merchants traveling together

• **sponsorship (270):** the process of formally supporting or endorsing another person

• **landlords (270):** people who own land or buildings that are rented to others

• **orphanages (271):** homes for children who have no parents

ORGANIZING INFORMATION Complete the chart about important events and accomplishments of the Sui, Tang, and Sung Dynasties in China by writing the letter of each item in the correct box.

A. Buddhism reached its peak

B. more people lived in cities than ever before

C. prevented cheating on civil service tests

D. high point in Chinese literature

E. defeated by invading Turks in 615

F. brought back Confucianism

G. new type of rice helped farmers grow more crops

H. built the Grand Canal

I. unable to conquer southern Manchuria and northern Korea

Sui, Tang, and Sung Dynasties		
Sui	**Tang**	**Sung**

Chapter 12, Main Idea Activities 12.1, continued

EVALUATING INFORMATION Mark each statement *T* if it is true or *F* if it is false.

_____ **1.** The Sui dynasty came to power after a long period without order in China.

_____ **2.** The Grand Canal was one of the great building feats of the ancient world.

_____ **3.** The early Tang rulers expanded China's frontiers and its influence.

_____ **4.** There were few people writing poetry during the Tang dynasty.

_____ **5.** Missionaries from China spread Buddhism to India.

_____ **6.** In the last century of the Tang dynasty, the rulers did not like Buddhism.

_____ **7.** Sung emperors had to make a large payment each year to avoid war with the Mongols.

_____ **8.** Sung artisans made beautiful porcelain pottery.

_____ **9.** The two important changes in life for peasants under the Sung dynasty were improved farming methods and the absence of taxes.

_____ **10.** The custom of footbinding, the tying of women's feet, began during the Sung dynasty.

REVIEWING FACTS Choose the correct items from the following list to complete the statements below.

| porcelain | Empress Wu | Tang |
| gunpowder | ruling | |

1. Li Bo and Du Fu were poets during the _____ dynasty.

2. _____ strongly supported Buddhism.

3. Neo-Confucianism was the main religion of China's _____ classes until the early 1900s.

4. One of China's most valuable exports under the Sung emperors was

_____.

5. During the Han dynasty _____ was invented and was first used in warfare in A.D. 900.

Main Idea Activities 12.2

Modern Chapter 3

The Mongol Empire

VOCABULARY Some terms to understand:

- **cavalry (272):** soldiers who fight on horseback
- **maneuvers (272):** planned attacks or movements of an army
- **catapult (272):** ancient weapon for shooting stones
- **fostered (274):** helped to grow
- **courier (274):** messenger
- **principal (275):** main
- **kinsmen (275):** relatives

ORGANIZING INFORMATION Complete the graphic organizer about the events during the Mongol Empire by writing the following events in correct order.

- Kublai Khan got the title of Great Kahn.
- Genghis Khan and Mongols captured Beijing and renamed it Khanbalik.
- The Yuan dynasty was overthrown.
- Kublai Khan began the Yuan dynasty.
- Batu invades Europe around 1240.
- Yuan forces defeated the Sung dynasty.

IMPORTANT EVENTS DURING THE MONGOL EMPIRE

1.

2.

3.

4.

5.

6.

Chapter 12, Main Idea Activities 12.2, continued

EVALUATING INFORMATION Mark each statement *T* if it is true or *F* if it is false.

_____ **1.** The Mongols lived in the rugged steppe region in the south of China.

_____ **2.** Mongol soldiers rode horses and were very skilled fighters.

_____ **3.** The Mongols captured Japan in the early 1200s.

_____ **4.** The Yuan dynasty was started by Kublai Kahn.

_____ **5.** Mongol rule had little effect on life in China.

_____ **6.** The Mongol leaders used horses to improve communications in China.

_____ **7.** There was a lot of tension between the Mongol rulers and the Chinese people.

_____ **8.** One change made by the Mongols in China was to increase contact with Europe.

REVIEWING FACTS Choose the correct item from the following list to complete the statements below.

| cavalry | Batu | Kublai Kahn |
| Golden Horde | Marco Polo | Genghis Kahn |

1. The _____ was the name given to the Mongol invaders by Europeans.

2. To supply food from southern farmlands, _____ made the Grand Canal hundreds of miles longer.

3. The Italian traveler who wrote about the Mongol court was

_____ .

4. The Mongols used _____ to defeat their enemies in battle.

5. _____ , a grandson of Genghis Khan, invaded Russia, Poland, and Hungary.

6. The fiercest Mongol leader of all was _____ .

 Main Idea Activities 12.3

Modern Chapter 3   **Japan, Korea, and Southeast Asia**

VOCABULARY Some terms to understand:

- **typhoons (276):** hurricanes; huge storms that sweep in from the ocean
- **fiercely (278):** extremely; very
- **disobedience (278):** not following orders
- **scriptures (280):** religious writings
- **embodied (280):** found
- **peninsula (280):** a landmass that is almost surrounded by water
- **colony (281):** area that is governed by another country
- **embraced (283):** accept; take on

ORGANIZING INFORMATION Complete the chart about ways that China and India influenced Japan, Korea, and Southeast Asia using the following items. Many items will be true for more than one country. Write the letter for each item in the appropriate box or boxes.

A. Chinese Buddhism

B. Confucian traditions and ideas

C. Chinese writing

D. Hindu and Indian beliefs

E. metalworking techniques

F. Chinese model of government

G. Sanskrit language

Influences of China on Japan, Korea, and Southeast Asia			
Japan	**Korea**	**Vietnam**	**Non-Vietnam Southeast Asia**

Chapter 12, Main Idea Activities 12.3, continued

EVALUATING INFORMATION Mark each statement *T* if it is true or *F* if it is false.

_____ **1.** The world's first novel, *The Tale of Genji,* was written by a woman and told about her travels to China and India.

_____ **2.** The first family to gain control over the feudal Japanese government was the Fujiwara.

_____ **3.** The Minamoto clan was the first to have a general called a shogun.

_____ **4.** The Japanese believed in a daimyo, a nature spirit.

_____ **5.** Zen Buddhism taught salvation through enlightenment.

_____ **6.** In ancient times, people from mainland Asia passed through Korea to go to the neighboring islands.

UNDERSTANDING MAIN IDEAS For each of the following, write the letter of the best choice in the space provided.

_____ **1.** Japan does not have a lot of farmland, and its farmers
    a. are unable to produce much food.
    b. never tried to produce food other than what they could eat.
    c. have been able to produce a great deal of food.
    d. mostly gave up farming to become fishermen.

_____ **2.** Shinto religious worship involves
    a. prayers and rituals to please the nature spirits.
    b. reading religious writings every day.
    c. living a life without owning anything.
    d. following the strict laws of Shinto leaders.

_____ **3.** Korean leaders selected government workers by
    a. using a testing process to see who would be best.
    b. choosing only people they knew.
    c. picking people who were related to government officials.
    d. choosing the first people who wanted the job.

_____ **4.** An important difference between ancient Korea and China was
    a. China formed a middle class between the nobles and the peasants.
    b. Korea had a strong nobility who influenced the government.
    c. Korea had a much stronger government.
    d. Korea had a well-developed and educated middle class.

Main Idea Activities 13.1

Modern Chapter **4**

The Rise of the Franks

VOCABULARY Some terms to understand:

- **merged (288):** joined together
- **coronation (289):** the crowning of a king or queen
- **monarchs (289):** kings or queens; rulers
- **conscious (290):** aware
- **fidelity (290):** loyalty
- **splintered (291):** broken apart
- **undermined (292):** weakened

ORGANIZING INFORMATION Fill in the graphic organizer by arranging the following items in sequence.

- Pépin III was crowned; Carolingian rule began.
- Pépin II and his successors united the Frankish kingdoms.
- Clovis became ruler of Frankish tribes.
- The Papal States were created.
- Charles Martel defeated the Spanish Moors

THE RISE OF THE FRANKS

7. With papal support, Charlemagne inherited Frankish throne.

6.

5.

4.

3.

2. Franks seized and ruled southwestern Gaul (now France).

1.

EVALUATING INFORMATION Mark each statement *T* if it is true or *F* if it is false.

_____ **1.** The Middle Ages in Europe ended the classical age and started the modern world.

_____ **2.** The Franks were a loosely organized Germanic peoples.

_____ **3.** Clovis advanced in his conquests because he had the support of the Christian church.

_____ **4.** The Merovingian kings who ruled after Clovis were generally strong.

_____ **5.** European Christians believed that the pope's blessing came directly from God.

_____ **6.** Charlemagne spent much of his time consulting with the pope.

_____ **7.** Charlemagne's title as "Emperor of the Romans" was not important to western Europeans.

_____ **8.** A count ruled each region of Charlemagne's empire independently.

_____ **9.** Education had little value during Charlemagne's reign.

_____ **10.** The division of the empire among Charlemagne's sons and the invasion of the Vikings led to the empire's decline.

REVIEWING FACTS Choose the correct item from the following list to complete the statements below.

missi dominici   Carolingians   France
Middle Ages   Papal States

1. The medieval period of European development is also known as the

_____.

2. Pépin III's coronation established the _____, a new line of Frankish rulers.

3. A gift of land to the pope called the Donation of Pépin created the

_____.

4. Charlemagne's "new Rome" centered on what is now _____ and Germany.

5. Charlemagne appointed the _____, or "lord's messengers" to help him govern the empire.

Main Idea Activities 13.2

Modern Chapter **4**   **Feudalism and the Manorial System**

VOCABULARY Some terms to understand:

- **transaction (294):** deal; act of doing business
- **immensely (295):** very
- **decrees (295):** laws; official orders
- **authority (297):** right to control; power
- **purchased (297):** bought
- **dowries (298):** property or money that a woman brings to the man she marries
- **graphic (299):** using pictures
- **gallantly (299):** nobly; politely

ORGANIZING INFORMATION Complete the chart about lords and peasants in the feudal system. Write each item on the line in the correct section.

- knight   • squire
- vassal   • serf
- lord   • page

Who's Who in Feudalism	
Person	**Description**
	one who grants land to others
	warrior and protector of the castle
	teenager who serves as knight's attendant
	peasant who works the land
	one who receives a fief or land grant
	young boy who serves as knight's helper

EVALUATING INFORMATION Mark each statement *T* if it is true or *F* if it is false.

_____ **1.** In the feudal system, the lesser noble who received a land grant could not own the land.

_____ **2.** A grant of land by a lord was called a fief.

_____ **3.** In feudal times, trials were decided by a jury.

_____ **4.** The manorial system shaped the economy of Europe during the Middle Ages.

_____ **5.** Peasants in medieval times worked hard but were allowed leave for relaxation.

_____ **6.** Chivalry did not improve the rough manners of early feudal lords.

REVIEWING FACTS Choose the correct item from the following list to complete the statements below.

domain	coat of arms	compurgation	fief
primogeniture	feudalism	chain mail	moat
serf	keep		

1. The system of government by local independent lords or nobles during the 900s in Europe is called _____.

2. The person who granted land in the manorial system was a lord and the grant of land was called a _____.

3. The system of inheritance from father to oldest son is called

_____.

4. A knight's armor made of interlocking metal links is a _____.

5. One way a person is tried in medieval times was by oath taking or

_____.

6. A third of the land that the lord of the manor kept for himself was his

_____.

7. The term _____ is another word for peasant.

8. The ditch surrounding the lord's castle was a _____.

9. The main part of a castle was the _____.

10. A graphic symbol on the dress of a knight that identified him was a

_____.

CHAPTER **13**

Main Idea Activities 13.3

Modern Chapter **4**

The Church

VOCABULARY Some terms to understand:

- **clergy (300):** people such as priests, ministers, or rabbis who are officials in an organized religion and do religious work

- **hierarchy (300):** an order of things

- **parish (300):** district or area that has its own church

- **matrimony (300):** marriage

- **fasting (301):** not eating

- **institution (302):** organization set up for a social or public purpose

- **labored (303):** worked

- **criticism (303):** disapproving comments

ORGANIZING INFORMATION List on the pyramid the different parts of the early European church using the following items. List the parts in order of importance with the most important at the top.

- cardinals
- bishops
- parish priests
- archbishops
- pope

THE CHURCH HIERARCHY

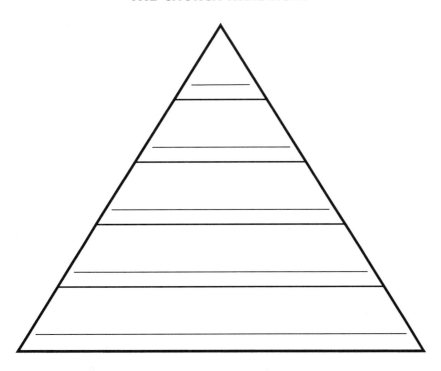

Chapter 13, Main Idea Activities 13.3, continued

EVALUATING INFORMATION Mark each statement *T* if it is true or *F* if it is false.

_____ **1.** The medieval church served as a government in many parts of Europe.

_____ **2.** During medieval times, parish priests could give all seven sacraments.

_____ **3.** In many cases, kings and nobles were able to control who became a bishop.

_____ **4.** Monks and nuns are called regulars because they lived by very strict rules.

_____ **5.** Monasteries and convents remained poor because they took care of the needy.

_____ **6.** The church had little or no effect on political life during the Middle Ages.

_____ **7.** The church did not allow anyone to question the principles of the Christian religion.

_____ **8.** During the Inquisition, the Dominicans were asked to unite the Christian world.

MATCHING Match the descriptions in the first column with the terms or names in the second column.

_____ **1.** a Christian ritual to gain God's direct favor

_____ **2.** a bishop's official church

_____ **3.** group of counselors who advise the pope

_____ **4.** "princes of the church"

_____ **5.** way of life in convents and monasteries

_____ **6.** he created the rules for monastic life

_____ **7.** the church's own code of law

_____ **8.** he brought Christianity to Ireland

_____ **9.** all churches in a region can be closed with this ruling

_____ **10.** practise of buying high positions in the church hierarchy

a. cardinals

b. canon law

c. simony

d. sacraments

e. curia

f. monasticism

g. cathedral

h. interdict

i. St. Benedict

j. St. Patrick

Main Idea Activities 13.4

Modern Chapter **4**   **The Struggle for Power in England and France**

VOCABULARY An expression to understand:

• **took the throne (305):** became king

Some terms to understand:

• **heir (305):** person who inherits something, often a son or daughter

• **monarchy (305):** government by a king or queen

• **middle class (307):** class of people between the very rich and unskilled laborers

• **statutes (307):** set laws

• **jurisdiction (308):** area of power or control

• **shrewd (309):** clever

• **convened (309):** called together

ORGANIZING INFORMATION Complete the chart about government in England between 886 and 1307. Put the following items where they belong in the sequence chart.

• King John was forced to accept the Magna Carta.

• Simon de Montfort built middle class support for nobles.

• Henry I sent traveling judges throughout the country.

• Alfred the Great made peace with the Danes.

EVENTS IN ENGLISH GOVERNMENT 886–1307

1.
2. William the Conqueror shaped England's feudal system.
3.
4.
5.
6. Edward I divided the court into three branches

Chapter 13, Main Idea Activities 13.4, continued

CLASSIFYING INFORMATION Mark each of the following with an *E* if it took place under English rule or an *F* if it took place under French rule.

_____ **1.** Norman laws, customs, and languages were introduced to the kingdom.

_____ **2.** Feudal lords ruled the rest of the kingdom from their own domains.

_____ **3.** The king scattered fiefs and lords throughout the kingdom.

_____ **4.** The king set up an accurate tax system and gathered records of people's properties in a Doomsday Book.

_____ **5.** The king took control of the lands of noble families who had died out.

_____ **6.** The kings made Parliament the highest of royal courts.

_____ **7.** The Estates General became part of the government.

_____ **8.** The Magna Carta outlined the rights of ordinary people.

UNDERSTANDING MAIN IDEAS For each of the following, write the letter of the best choice in the space provided.

_____ **1.** Which of these statements is true about William the Conqueror?
  a. He had an heir who would become king.
  b. All English lords were not vassals of William.
  c. The Anglo-Saxons rejected his Norman customs and language.
  d. He crossed the English Channel but was defeated by Harold of Wessex.

_____ **2.** Which event immediately followed the murder of Thomas Becket?
  a. Harold of Wessex became king of England.
  b. William stopped the lords from uniting against him.
  c. Canterbury became a popular destination for pilgrims.
  d. Henry I sent traveling judges throughout the country to try cases.

_____ **3.** Which of these statements does NOT apply to England's common law?
  a. It was applied equally to all subjects.
  b. It kept track of the king's financial accounts.
  c. It was created to meet constantly changing conditions.
  d. It was based on decisions made by the new royal courts.

_____ **4.** By involving the Estates General in his government, Philip IV was able to
  a. increase his royal holdings.
  b. influence the selection of the next pope, Clement V.
  c. arrest Pope Boniface VII because he opposed the Capetians.
  d. secure widespread support in his struggle against the church.

Main Idea Activities 13.5

Modern Chapter **4**

The Clash over Germany and Italy

VOCABULARY Some terms to understand:

- **seize (310):** take with force
- **figurehead (310):** leader who has no real power
- **papacy (311):** government by a pope
- **temporal (311):** not religious, worldly
- **firmament (312):** arch of the sky or heavens
- **pontifical (312):** of the pope
- **quarreled (313):** fought
- **fragmented (313):** divided into separate sections

ORGANIZING INFORMATION Complete the chart about the struggles between the popes and the European rulers using the following statements.

- Thought that kings should be able to choose bishops.
- Had the great power of excommunication.
- Believed that people's souls were more important than their bodies.
- Placed England under interdiction.
- Chose four popes during the 1000s.
- Thought of the church as a branch of the imperial government.

| Struggles Between Popes and European Rulers ||
Popes	European Rulers

Chapter 13, Main Idea Activities 13.5, continued

EVALUATING INFORMATION Mark each statement *T* if it is true or *F* if it is false.

_____ **1.** Descendants of Charlemagne, called Holy Roman Emperors, ruled Italy.

_____ **2.** The Holy Roman Empire was very powerful until the mid-1900s.

_____ **3.** Henry III thought the church should support the Holy Roman Empire.

_____ **4.** Pope Gregory VII believed that rulers and ordinary people were subject to the will of the church.

_____ **5.** Frederick Barbarossa was able to control all the Lombardi city-states.

_____ **6.** Pope Innocent III used his power to force kings to do what he wanted.

_____ **7.** Papal power weakened after the death of Innocent III.

_____ **8.** During the 1200s, Germany and Italy were finally united.

REVIEWING ACTS Choose the correct item from the following list to complete the statements below.

Concordat of Worms	lay investiture	King Henry III
Lombardy	Italy	Otto I

1. Because he helped Pope John XII in his struggle with the Roman nobles, the German

king _____ was named Emperor of the Romans.

2. The disagreement between Pope Gregory VII and Henry IV was about

_____.

3. Like Charlemagne, _____ considered the church a branch of the imperial government.

4. According to the _____, only the pope could choose a bishop.

5. The trading centers of Bologna, Padua, Verona, and Milan were in the region of

_____.

6. By the end of the 1200s, _____ remained divided into three regions.

CHAPTER 14

Main Idea Activities 14.1

Modern Chapter **5**

The Crusades

VOCABULARY Some words to understand:

- **pilgrims (318):** travelers to a foreign land or a holy place
- **expedition (318):** a trip undertaken for a specific purpose like a war
- **forge (319):** to move forward steadily but gradually
- **massacre (319):** violent, random killing of a number of people
- **disgrace (320):** the condition of being out of favor or a cause of shame
- **looted (321):** robbed or stolen on a large scale and by violence
- **mob (321):** a large, disorderly crowd often tending to violent action

ORGANIZING INFORMATION Use the following items to complete the chart below.

- French knights
- Frederick Barbarossa, Philip II, and Richard III
- French and Italian lords
- Louis VII and Conrad III
- crusaders return in disgrace
- Richard forges pact with Muslims
- crusaders attack Constantinople
- crusaders capture the Holy Land

The Major Crusades		
Years	**Leaders**	**Outcome**
• The First Crusade (1096–1099)	•	•
• The Second Crusade (1147–1149)	•	•
• The Third Crusade (1189–1192)	•	•
• The Fourth Crusade (1202–1204)	•	•

EVALUATING INFORMATION Mark each statement *T* if it is true or *F* if it is false.

_____ **1.** The Crusades were fought to regain the Holy Land from the Arabs who conquered Palestine in the late 1000s.

_____ **2.** Pope Urban II called a meeting of church leaders and feudal lords to organize the Crusades in Rome.

_____ **3.** A cross of cloth on their clothes identified the crusaders as Christians.

_____ **4.** Some crusaders joined to gain land and wealth in Palestine.

_____ **5.** All the Crusades failed, including the first.

_____ **6.** The armies wearing wool and leather garments suffered in their long march to Palestine in the heat.

_____ **7.** With the Crusades, the European kings became more powerful and the pope more important.

_____ **8.** The European army taught the Muslims how to use gunpowder.

_____ **9.** Italian cities became major trading centers during the Crusades.

_____ **10.** Ships returning from the Holy Land loaded with unusual goods established new trading patterns in Europe.

REVIEWING FACTS Choose the correct items from the following list to complete the statements below.

southwest Asia	feudalism	Holy Land	60
crossbow	Acre	catapult	Asia Minor
100	Byzantine emperor		

1. Palestine among Christians is called the _____.

2. It was the _____ who asked Pope Urban II for help to regain Palestine.

3. On their way to Palestine, the crusaders marched through

_____.

4. After the First Crusade, Europeans held on to the Holy Land for

_____ years.

5. Venetians controlled trade in Constantinople for _____ years.

6. When the Muslims captured the city of _____, the last Christian stronghold, the Crusades ended.

7. The crusaders used the _____, a new weapon that could penetrate a plate armor.

8. The crusaders learned from the Muslims how to throw rocks using a

_____.

9. Political changes during the Crusades put an end to _____.

10. Ships coming back from Palestine carried food from all of

_____.

CHAPTER **14**   Main Idea Activities 14.2

Modern Chapter **5**   **The Revival of Trade**

VOCABULARY Some words to understand:

- **manors (323):** usually large landed estates granted by a king to a feudal lord
- **go-betweens (323):** people who act as messengers or intermediaries between parties
- **site (323):** location
- **league (323):** an association or alliance of nations for a common purpose
- **changed hands (325):** passed from the possession of one person to that of another
- **outlook (325):** point of view

ORGANIZING INFORMATION Fill in the graphic organizer by writing the letter of the items where they belong.

A. Kiev and Flanders   **D.** Baltic goods like fish, fur, timber

B. Bremen, Hamburg, and Lübeck   **E.** Asian goods carried by ships from Palestine

C. Genoa, Pisa, and Venice   **F.** goods from Constantinople, fine wool

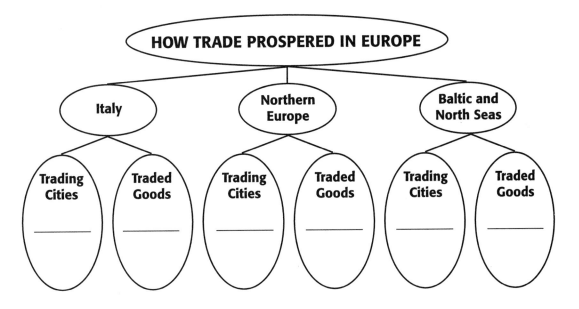

EVALUATING INFORMATION Mark each statement *T* if it is true or *F* if it is false.

_____ **1.** Italy was the earliest site of trade revival after the Crusades.

_____ **2.** Trade routes from Italy to central and northern Europe did not help cities along its path of progress.

_____ **3.** Because Germany's central government was weak, German trading cities formed the Hanseatic League, which grew to 100 members.

Chapter 14, Main Idea Activities 14.2, continued

_____ **4.** As trade expanded in the towns, merchants avoided the fairs held in church yards where Asian goods were sold.

_____ **5.** Business was conducted during those years without the use of money.

_____ **6.** The system of manufacturing, banking, and investing known to this day began during the revival of trade in Europe in the Middle Ages.

_____ **7.** Manufacturing took place in workers' homes and in shops and factories.

_____ **8.** The first bankers were money changers who exchanged currencies during the fairs.

_____ **9.** Lending money was an important service of the early bankers, and most law codes allowed the collection of interest on loans used for business.

_____ **10.** During this time, Europeans began investing capital and made the first steps toward the present-day market economy.

UNDERSTANDING MAIN IDEAS For each of the following, write the letter of the best choice in the space provided.

_____ **1.** How did European city-states help trade grow during the Crusades?
 a. They acted as go-betweens for traders between Asia and Europe.
 b. They manufactured their own goods.
 c. They held village fairs.
 d. They started investing more capital.

_____ **2.** Which of these goods were in demand in Europe during the Middle Ages?
 a. luxury goods, including dyes, medicines, silks, and spices
 b. manufactured goods like oil and soap
 c. traded goods such as leather and woolen cloth
 d. locally produced wine and glassware

_____ **3.** What other role did the fairs play besides serving as markets for imported goods?
 a. serving as a teaching place
 b. serving as a place to relax for traveling merchants
 c. serving as a performance location for children
 d. serving as a social event at which to share news and ideas

_____ **4.** What characteristic of a market economy today can be traced to the Middle Ages?
 a. Land, labor, and capital are controlled by individuals.
 b. Little money ever changes hands.
 c. Goods and services are exchanged for other goods and services.
 d. Manufacturing takes place in homes.

CHAPTER 14

Modern Chapter **5**

Main Idea Activities 14.3

The Growth of Towns

VOCABULARY Some words to understand:

- **resorted (327):** to have recourse to or to act
- **involved (327):** obliged to take part
- **stable (328):** firmly established
- **serfs (328):** a class of servants in the feudal system who worked the soil
- **plague (330):** an epidemic disease causing high rates of death
- **gutter (330):** low area at a roadside to carry off surface water
- **uprising (330):** a usually localized revolt

ORGANIZING INFORMATION Fill in the graphic organizer by arranging the items below showing the steps to becoming a master in a guild.

- A young man becomes a journeyman.
- Parents bring a boy to a master.
- He is taken in as an apprentice.
- Parents pay the master to house, feed, and clothe him.
- The young man opens his shop.
- The guild approves the young man's masterpiece.
- The young man receives wages.
- He trains for nine years.

STEPS TO BECOMING A MASTER IN A GUILD

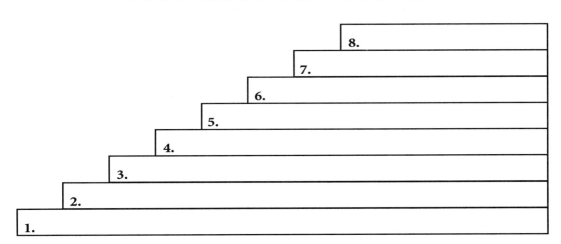

Chapter 14, Main Idea Activities 14.3, continued

EVALUATING INFORMATION Mark each statement *T* if it is true or *F* if it is false.

_____ **1.** As towns grew in the Middle Ages, people left farming and began to make and trade goods.

_____ **2.** Since some lords still controlled the towns, people never gained rights.

_____ **3.** One of the four basic rights freed people from work on the manor.

_____ **4.** Under the rules of a guild, merchants could trade without a fee in any town with an established guild.

_____ **5.** The guilds helped members who were in trouble but not their families.

_____ **6.** Craft guilds had masters to train boys and men who wanted to learn skills.

_____ **7.** The rise of the middle class started from among members of the merchants and craft guilds.

_____ **8.** Cities in the Middle Ages were built on large tracts of land and had plenty of space.

_____ **9.** The plague, called the Black Death, reached Europe through the trade routes that began and ended in Asia.

_____ **10.** After the plague, the few workers who survived demanded higher wages and staged uprisings when they weren't given.

UNDERSTANDING MAIN IDEAS For each of the following, write the letter of the best choice in the space provided.

_____ **1.** Towns started to grow during the Middle Ages because of an increase in
  a. trade activites.
  b. farming villages.
  c. serfs on manors.
  d. control of towns by lords.

_____ **2.** Merchants and craftsmen organized themselves into guilds and became what is known to this day as the
  a. middle class.
  b. king's advisers.
  c. serf owners.
  d. nobles.

_____ **3.** The towns that grew in the Middle Ages gave serfs
  a. jobs in the city.
  b. a chance to repay debt.
  c. new skills for the manor.
  d. time to learn new farming methods.

_____ **4.** Many cities during the Middle Ages stood on hilltops or lay along river bends because they
  a. were easier to defend.
  b. had more light and fresh air.
  c. were easier to build.
  d. attracted fewer people.

Modern Chapter **5** **Life and Culture in the Middle Ages**

VOCABULARY Some words to understand:

- **chivalry (332):** the system, spirit, ways, or customs of medieval knighthood
- **realm (332):** kingdom, sphere, domain
- **prestige (333):** fine reputation based on past performance or merit
- **forerunner (333):** one that goes ahead and tells or indicates the coming of another
- **theology (333):** the study and interpretation of religious faith and practice
- **winches (334):** machines that have rollers on which a rope is coiled for hauling or hoisting
- **vaults (334):** an arched structure of masonry or concrete usually forming a ceiling or roof

ORGANIZING INFORMATION Complete the graphic organizer using the following forms of vernacular literature:

- romance
- animal story or fable
- long poem or epic
- miracle or morality plays

LITERATURE IN THE MIDDLE AGES

1. _____
   Song of Roland

2. _____
   King Arthur and the Knights of the Round Table

3. _____
   Raynard the Fox

4. _____
   Noah's Flood

Chapter 14, Main Idea Activities 14.4, continued

EVALUATING INFORMATION Mark each statement *T* if it is true or *F* if it is false.

_____ **1.** During the Middle Ages, vernacular language, or everyday language, began to replace Latin, the written and spoken language of educated Europeans.

_____ **2.** French, Italian, Spanish, German, and English as known today did not come from vernacular languages.

_____ **3.** In the early Middle Ages, anyone could study with the nobles and clergy in the schools run by monasteries.

_____ **4.** Present-day universities began as guilds formed by teachers and students.

_____ **5.** Medieval philosophers attempted to fuse together faith and reason but failed.

_____ **6.** Scientists of the time dealt only with mathematics and optics or the study of light.

_____ **7.** Everyday life became easier because of better designs for winches and pulleys, iron plows, and oxen yokes.

_____ **8.** Church architecture was the main art form during the Middle Ages.

_____ **9.** Gothic churches became the center not only of spiritual but also economic and social life.

_____ **10.** The Gothic cathedrals, known as monuments to God, expressed the highest artistic skills of the medieval world.

REVIEWING FACTS Choose the correct names from the following list to complete the statements below.

Geoffrey Chaucer   Dante Alighieri   Thomas Aquinas   Peter Abelard

1. _____ wrote *The Divine Comedy* and is thought of by many historians as the father of the Italian language.

2. _____ wrote his famous *Canterbury Tales* in Middle English.

3. _____, an important philosopher of scholasticism, wrote a book called *Sic et Non*.

4. _____ summarized medieval Christian thought and is probably the greatest medieval philosopher.

CHAPTER 14

Modern Chapter **5**

Main Idea Activities 14.5

Wars and the Growth of Nations

VOCABULARY Some words to understand:

- **vassal (336):** one in a subservient or subordinate position, as in "servant vassal"

- **dynasty (336):** a powerful group or family that maintains position for a considerable time

- **badge (337):** something worn to show that a person belongs to a certain group

- **scheming (338):** to form plans; to engage in intrigue

- **fervent (338):** marked by a great warmth of feeling; ardent

- **stronghold (338):** a fortified place; a fortress

ORGANIZING INFORMATION Fill in the chart by using the items below

- Ferdinand and Isabella wanted an all-Catholic Spain
- English royalty, using the rose as badge, fought over throne
- Edward III claimed French throne
- French House of Burgundy took English side
- New weapons of war used; parliament gained power over king
- Henry Tudor began strong English monarchy
- Charles the VII of Orleans won, crowned king, and drove English out
- Muslims' last stronghold captured; Spain united

Wars in the Middle Ages		
War	**Cause**	**Effect**
• The Hundred Years' War (1337–1453)	•	•
• The War of the Roses (1455–1485)	•	•
• War in the House of Burgundy and Orleans (1337–1429)	•	•
• War Against the Moors (1429–1515)	•	•

Chapter 14, Main Idea Activities 14.5, continued

EVALUATING INFORMATION Mark each statement *T* if it is true or *F* if it is false.

_____ **1.** Edward III of England did not have rights to the French throne.

_____ **2.** At the end of the Hundred Years' War in 1453, England kept its French lands except Calais.

_____ **3.** New weapons like the longbow and cannon proved that castles were not strong enough to protect the lords.

_____ **4.** As the war dragged on, the English king's power grew stronger.

_____ **5.** Joan of Arc helped the House of Orleans win back France.

_____ **6.** French peasants gained their freedom under the strong king, Louis XI.

_____ **7.** Many leaders of industry and trade left Spain because they did not want to be baptized Catholics.

_____ **8.** Only the Holy Roman Empire remained weak in Europe after the wars ended.

_____ **9.** Maximillian I of the Habsburg family married into the more powerful royal houses, strengthening his rule and uniting the Holy Roman Empire.

_____ **10.** Independent princes in Italy held on to their kingdoms but recognized the pope.

UNDERSTANDING MAIN IDEAS Choose the correct items from the following list to complete the statements below.

     nations   Holy Roman Empire   freedom   monarchy

1. The Hundred Years' War not only weakened knightly warfare but also the

_____ as well.

2. Unlike in England, a strong French monarchy united the country but gave the

peasants very little _____.

3. Most of the independent kingdoms of Europe united and became the

_____ of England, France, and Spain after the wars.

4. The Habsburg family became the most powerful family in Europe but it could not

unite the _____.

CHAPTER 14
Modern Chapter 5

Main Idea Activities 14.6

Challenges to Church Power

VOCABULARY Some words to understand:

• **clergy (341):** body of religious officials (priests, ministers, and rabbis)

• **heresy (341):** religious opinion contrary to church doctrine

• **envoys (341):** representatives sent by one government to another; ambassadors

• **undermine (343):** to weaken or wear away secretly or gradually

• **excommunicated (343):** to take away officially the rights of church membership

• **profound (343):** deeply felt

• **alter(343):** to change partly but not completely

ORGANIZING INFORMATION Complete the graphic organizer by arranging the items below in the correct sequence.

• Popes were kept in Avignon during the Babylonian Captivity.

• The Council of Constance ended the Great Schism.

• Boniface decreed that popes had power over wordly affairs.

• The Great Schism: church was divided into opposing groups.

• John Wycliffe attacked the wealth of the church.

• Jan Hus angered the clergy and was burned at the stake.

Events that Led to the Decline of Church Power

1. _____	3. _____	5. _____
_____	_____	_____
_____	_____	_____

2. _____	4. _____	6. _____
_____	_____	_____
_____	_____	_____

Chapter 14, Main Idea Activities 14.6, continued

EVALUATING INFORMATION Mark each statement *T* if it is true and *F* if its false.

_____ **1.** The worldly power of the church weakened under strong governments.

_____ **2.** Townspeople supported the government and found fault with the great wealth of the church.

_____ **3.** The people thought church laws had nothing to do with trade and industry.

_____ **4.** In the conflict between King Philip and Pope Boniface, the king won by imposing taxes on the church.

_____ **5.** The Babylonian Captivity showed the power of the French monarchy over the church.

_____ **6.** During the Great Schism, only one pope had the support of rulers.

_____ **7.** The Council of Constance ended the Great Schism and supported the French and Italian popes.

_____ **8.** Writers of the *Defender of the Faith* believed that the pope had nothing to do with worldly matters.

_____ **9.** John Wycliffe believed that people should be allowed to read and interpret the Bible by themselves.

_____ **10.** Jan Hus was burned at the stake for his teachings about the Bible.

UNDERSTANDING MAIN IDEAS Choose the correct items from the following list to complete the statements below.

    Defender of the Faith   Avignon   reforms   Innocent III   practices

1. The last of the powerful popes was _____.

2. After Innocent III, people began to question church _____.

3. The pope's residence was in _____ from 1309 to 1377.

4. The views in _____ were opposite those of Pope Boniface's *Unam Sanctum.*

5. The attacks on the power of the pope by John Wycliffe began

_____ that would change the church.

CHAPTER **15**

Modern Chapter **6**

Main Idea Activities 15.1

The Italian Renaissance

VOCABULARY Some terms to understand:

- **literature (354):** written works of high quality
- **achievements (354):** successful results gained by effort
- **rhetoric (355):** the art of speaking effectively
- **authentic (355):** original, real, actual
- **scholarship (355):** learning through study, research, and intelligent thought
- **frescoes (358):** paintings done on freshly spread moist lime plaster with water-based pigments

ORGANIZING INFORMATION Use the following items to complete the chart below.

- Niccolò Machiavelli
- Leonardo da Vinci
- admiration for human achievement
- humanities
- Francesco Petrarch
- perspective

Art	Literature	Thought
• Michelangelo	•	•
•	•	•
•	• Castiglione's *The Book of the Courtier*	• new emphasis on education

EVALUATING INFORMATION Mark each statement *T* if it is true or *F* if it is false.

_____ **1.** Medieval scholars tried to break away from Christian teachings.

_____ **2.** During the Renaissance many people excelled as both poets and scientists.

_____ **3.** Isabella d'Este worked to oppress artistic expression in Italy.

_____ **4.** In *The Book of the Courtier,* Castiglione showed how gentlemen and women should act in society.

_____ **5.** The humanities include the study of grammar, history, poetry, and rhetoric.

_____ **6.** Jews were free to live and practice their religion the way they wanted during the Renaissance.

_____ **7.** Machiavelli's *The Prince* argued that rulers should be more compassionate.

_____ **8.** Painters developed a more realistic style during the Renaissance.

_____ **9.** Leonardo da Vinci used science and math to improve his paintings.

_____ **10.** Perspective, in the artistic sense, means seeing more than one meaning in a work.

REVIEWING FACTS Choose the correct items from the following list to complete the statements below.

Roman glory	perspective	realistic
classical	ancient world	power
meaningful life	Hebrew	arts

1. Italian Renaissance scholars studied the _____ to explore its great achievements.

2. Ruins of the Roman Empire reminded Italians of _____.

3. Christian scholars during the Renaissance learned _____ so as to study the Bible in its original language.

4. Humanists maintained that every person should lead a _____.

5. Knowledge of _____, Greek, and Latin became a mark of an educated person.

6. Machiavelli argued that a ruler should be concerned only with

_____ and political success.

7. Renaissance artists created _____ scenes and images.

8. By using a technique called _____, Renaissance artists created an illusion of depth on a flat canvas.

Modern Chapter **6**

Main Idea Activities 15.2

The Northern Renaissance

VOCABULARY Some terms to understand:

- **printing press (359):** machine capable of reproducing pictures and text by stamping them onto paper
- **monastery (360):** place where monks and other Christians lived and prayed
- **imagery (361):** language that helps a reader to imagine something
- **ridicule (360):** to criticize harshly; to mock

ORGANIZING INFORMATION Put each of the following names where they belong in the chart below.

- Desiderius Erasmus
- Jan and Hubert van Eyck
- Pieter Brueghel
- Thomas More

Northern Renaissance Outlook		
Ideas	**Writers**	**Painters**
• believed that scholars had made Christian faith less spiritual		
• imagined a society where everyone worked to support one another		
• paid great attention to detail, such as facial expressions		
• used art to criticize intolerance and cruelty		

EVALUATING INFORMATION Mark each statement *T* if it is true or *F* if it is false.

_____ **1.** The Chinese were the first to develop a method of printing.

_____ **2.** The northern Renaissance involved a study of early Christian thought.

_____ **3.** Marlowe and Shakespeare wrote plays about human situations.

_____ **4.** The Flemish school is a scholarly university in northern Europe.

_____ **5.** Pieter Brueghel used his art to comment on the injustices he saw around him.

_____ **6.** Only Italian artists used the technique of perspective in their paintings.

_____ **7.** Erasmus criticized the church for its lack of spirituality and love for ceremony.

_____ **8.** Thomas More wrote *Utopia*, a text which advocated communal living.

_____ **9.** Johannes Gutenberg invented the first European printing press.

_____ **10.** Scribes stood to benefit from the invention of the printing press.

UNDERSTANDING MAIN IDEAS For each of the following, write the letter of the best choice in the space provided.

_____ **1.** The Renaissance brought with it new
    a. ships from South Asia.
    b. goods to be traded.
    c. emphasis on the individual.
    d. rulers and governments.

_____ **2.** The Italian Renaissance spread to the north through trade and the use of
    a. soldiers.
    b. men on horseback.
    c. the printing press.
    d. singing troubadours.

_____ **3.** The Renaissance can be described as a period of increased
    a. travel to the colonies.
    b. trade with other coutries.
    c. scholarly thought.
    d. study of events.

_____ **4.** Because of the interest in many branches of knowledge, the Renaissance led to an increase in the number of
    a. palaces.
    b. universities.
    c. laboratories.
    d. churches.

CHAPTER 15

Main Idea Activities 15.3

Modern Chapter **6**

The Protestant Reformation

VOCABULARY Some terms to understand:

• **reformation (363):** a period of change for an existing institution

• **vice (363):** habitual behavior considered to be bad

• **pardon (363):** forgiveness for an offense

• **pious (364):** showing a love of or a commitment to a religion

• **salvation (364):** deliverance from the power and effects of sin

• **revelation (364):** deep insight believed to be true

• **sect (365):** informal religious group

• **vicar (366):** overseer of a parish

MATCHING Place the letters of the descriptions next to the appropriate names and terms.

_____ **1.** Edict of Nantes

_____ **2.** theocracy

_____ **3.** Martin Luther

_____ **4.** Charles V

_____ **5.** "the elect"

_____ **6.** Huguenots

_____ **7.** Johann Tetzel

_____ **8.** Henry VIII

_____ **9.** Calvinism

_____ **10.** 95 theses

_____ **11.** Indulgence

_____ **12.** Peace of Augsburg

a. emperor who attempted to stop the spread of Protestantism

b. divine forgiveness of sins by the Church

c. French nobles who adopted Calvinism

d. government run by a religious group

e. monk who traveled through Germany selling indulgences and angered many Christians

f. Protestant movement started by Vicar Huldrych Zwingli, who died early in its development

g. king of England who broke from the Catholic church because he wanted a divorce

h. list of grievances against the Catholic church which were posted on a church door

i. Catholic monk who broke with the church because he disagreed with its practices

j. treaty ending a war between Catholics and Protestants that gave Protestants some religious freedom

k. those whom the Calvinists believed God had chosen to save

l. ended the Catholic persecution of the French Huguenots

EVALUATING INFORMATION Mark each statement *T* if it is true or *F* if it is false.

_____ **1.** Calvinists believed in the rights of the individual.

_____ **2.** The Catholics of France welcomed the French who became Huguenots.

_____ **3.** Before Henry VIII wanted to divorce his wife, he was a strong supporter of the Catholic faith.

_____ **4.** After Martin Luther broke with the Catholic Church, many other reformers began to do the same.

_____ **5.** Martin Luther believed that the Catholic Church had forgotten religion and cared only for profit.

_____ **6.** Frederick the Wise attempted to capture Martin Luther.

_____ **7.** Most Protestants and Catholics are not affected by their religious disagreements.

_____ **8.** Calvinism made dancing, cards, and profanity illegal.

_____ **9.** The Edict of Nantes came about after the French Catholics had tried for years to destroy the Huguenots.

_____ **10.** Martin Luther translated the Bible into German so the peasants could read it for themselves.

INTERPRETING VISUAL IMAGES Examine the woodcut below about pro-Catholic forces attacking Huguenots in France in 1572. Then answer the following questions.

[PN03MACC015ART003A ART—BLACK AND WHITE VERSION OF GERMAN WOODCUT ON PAGE 367 OF WH03 THE HUMAN JOURNEY PE]

1. What are the pro-Catholic soldiers doing? _____

_____

2. What do you think happened next? _____

_____

CHAPTER **15**   Main Idea Activities 15.4

Modern Chapter **6**   **The Catholic Reformation**

VOCABULARY Some terms to understand:

- **doctrine (368):** formal beliefs of a religious group
- **devout (368):** having strong religious faith; unquestioning
- **Inquisition (368):** practice of seeking out and punishing those who disagreed with the Catholic Church
- **heresy (368):** any thought or idea which disagrees with Catholic doctrine
- **free will (369):** the belief in the individual's ability to make choices, free from any influence

ORGANIZING INFORMATION Use the following items to complete the web below.

- defined official church position on matters of doctrine
- most effective agents in spreading Catholicism
- produced educated supporters of the church
- emphasized the need for ceremonies

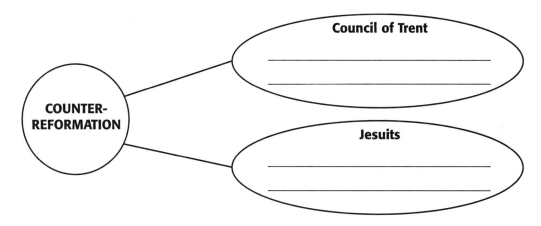

EVALUATING INFORMATION Mark each statement *T* if it is true or *F* if it is false.

_____ **1.** Pope Paul IV established the *Index of Important Books.*

_____ **2.** Pope Paul III used the Inquisition to strengthen the Catholic position in Italy.

_____ **3.** The Protestants and Catholics, for the most part, got along peacefully.

_____ **4.** One result of the Reformation and the Counter-Reformation was an increased interest in education.

_____ **5.** One of the roots of the Protestant Reformation was the writings of the humanist Erasmus.

_____ **6.** The Jesuits were a Protestant group who went about arguing against Catholicism.

_____ **7.** At the Council of Trent in 1545, much of Catholic doctrine was organized and made official.

_____ **8.** The Counter-Reformation was an attempt by Pope Paul III to stop the Protestant movement and strengthen belief in the Catholic Church.

_____ **9.** Before the printing press, the Catholic Church did not forbid books, it burned them.

_____ **10.** During the hundred years or so of the Reformation and the Counter-Reformation, wars and violence were very common as people coped with changes to their spiritual world.

REVIEWING FACTS Choose the correct items from the following list to complete the statements below.

heresy	salvation	Erasmus	Loyola
Jesuits	chastity	Pope	Protestantism

1. One of the results of the Counter-Revolution was the weakening of the power of the

_____.

2. The _____ were a Catholic order that believed in obeying the pope and doing good deeds to earn salvation.

3. The movement to do good deeds, live pious Catholic lives, and be obedient to the

pope was started by a man named _____.

4. Catholics believed that _____ could only be attained through the church.

5. The Jesuits took vows of poverty, _____ and loyalty to the pope.

6. An early critic of the Catholic Church who inspired others was

_____.

7. The primary motivation of the Counter-Reformation was to stop the threat to

Catholic power from _____.

8. Pope Paul III forbade books and tortured individuals in an attempt to combat

_____.

CHAPTER **15**

Modern Chapter **6**

Main Idea Activities 15.5

Culture and Daily Life

VOCABULARY Some terms to understand:

- **superstitions (372):** unfounded beliefs in magic, mysticism, or otherworldly powers, to explain events in daily life
- **famine (372):** an extreme shortage of food affecting a large population
- **baptism (372):** the Christian ceremony, conducted shortly after birth, which allows the individual to officially enter the religion
- **preachers (375):** traveling speakers who spoke for a particular idea or belief
- **peddlers (375):** traveling salespeople
- **serfdom (376):** the practice, whereby peasants live on the land of a lord, and pay the lord with labor, crops, and money.

ORGANIZING INFORMATION Use the following items to complete the chart below.

- Raising food used up all the daylight hours
- Farming was time-consuming
- Villagers lived in close-knit communities.
- Villagers played games and celebrated holidays.

Changes to Daily Life	
Cause	**Effect**
	Anyone who upset village traditions was treated harshly.
People need time to relax.	

EVALUATING INFORMATION Mark each statement *T* if it is true or *F* if it is false.

_____ **1.** People have used forks and spoons since the Middle Ages.

_____ **2.** Peasants made up 85 percent to 90 percent of the European population.

_____ **3.** A plague known as the Black Death killed one-third of the European population in the 1300s.

Chapter 15, Main Idea Activities 15.5, continued

_____ **4.** Catholics and Protestants educated the people because they believed in the virtues of education.

_____ **5.** As a result of the printing press, most peasants learned to read.

_____ **6.** Villagers were quick to punish anyone who acted oddly or broke tradition.

_____ **7.** Villagers were too ignorant to understand their class inequality.

_____ **8.** People accused weak members of the community of being witches because it gave them a sense of control over their own lives.

_____ **9.** Moving to large urban areas helped reduce the reliance on superstition.

_____ **10.** Most villagers believed that misfortune was God's will.

REVIEWING FACTS Choose the correct items from the following list to complete the statements below.

exorcise	almanac	inflation	preachers
Black Death	peddlers	priest	wise person

1. Religious thought was spread through the peasant population primarily through the

work of _____.

2. Because the population began to increase, prices for goods also went up, which is

called _____.

3. Many peasants turned to a _____ to explain the events in the world around them.

4. A book of predictions about the weather and farming which became popular in the

1500s is the _____.

5. A priest would have to _____ the evil spirit out of a person who was believed to be a witch.

6. _____ traveled through villages selling books, food, and other things.

7. The plague which killed one in every three people in the 1300s was called the

_____.

8. Peasants relied on the _____ to baptize their children and pray for crops.

 **CHAPTER 16**

Modern Chapter **7**

Main Idea Activities 16.1

The Scientific Revolution

VOCABULARY Some terms to understand:

• **barometer (382):** instrument used to measure pressure in the atmosphere

• **thermometer (382):** instrument used to measure heat

• **gravity (385):** force which pulls smaller objects toward far larger ones

• **circulation (385):** movement of blood through the body

ORGANIZING INFORMATION Write the name of each scientist in the correct circle.

• Copernicus   • Kepler   • Galileo   • Newton

• Vesalius   • Harvey   • Boyle   • Lavoisier

        • Priestley

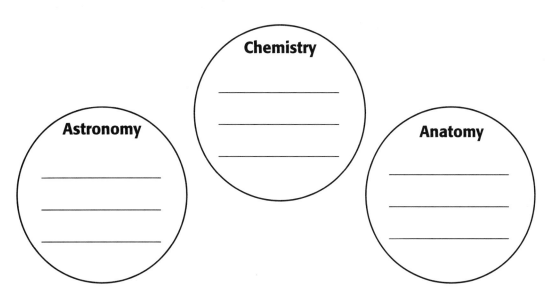

EVALUATING INFORMATION Mark each statement *T* if it is true or *F* if it is false.

_____ **1.** The scientific method of experimentation and verification led to a major change in life for all people.

_____ **2.** Lavoisier proved that while matter can change form, it cannot be destroyed or created.

_____ **3.** Robert Boyle proved that gas changes size when heated or cooled.

_____ **4.** René Descartes believed that he could not prove his own existence by thought.

_____ **5.** Francis Bacon believed that scientific theories could be developed through observation.

_____ **6.** While Copernicus, Kepler, and Galileo helped prove the heliocentric theory, Isaac Newton explained why.

_____ **7.** The Catholic Church helped to fund many of the new sciences because of its belief in the power of knowledge.

_____ **8.** For over a thousand years, from the beginning of A.D. until the Renaissance, almost no new knowledge was developed by European nations about the world.

_____ **9.** Research and experimentation have always been obvious methods of forming conclusions.

_____ **10.** The changing ideas that came out of the Renaissance helped bring about the Scientific Revolution.

REVIEWING FACTS Choose the correct items from the following list to complete the statements below.

alchemists	Galileo	circulation	natural philosophers
geocentric	anatomy	motion	Kepler

1. William Harvey studied _____ and described the workings of veins and arteries.

2. _____ attempted to change ordinary metals into precious metals using a mixture of science and magic.

3. Vesalius made major advances in _____ by studying the human body.

4. By using his own device, the telescope, _____ argued that every heavenly body revolves around the Earth.

5. Those people who based their conclusions on ancient Greek and Roman scholars, primarily Aristotle, were called _____.

6. Isaac Newton studied and wrote laws on _____.

7. The _____ theory of the universe had existed for thousands of years and argued that the Earth was the center of the universe.

8. _____ was the first to argue that the Earth was not the center of the universe.

CHAPTER 16   Main Idea Activities 16.2

Modern Chapter 7   The Foundations of European Exploration

VOCABULARY Some terms to understand:

- **exploration (389):** the search for new land, riches, routes, etc.

- **navigation (389):** the system of establishing location and direction so as not to become lost

- **technology (389):** man-made tools of ever-increasing complexity, which aid human existence

- **geographers (389):** scholars who study the physical features of the Earth in order to understand the relative location of different points

- **magnetize (389):** to induce properties of electric attraction to a piece of metal so that it always points to the north.

ORGANIZING INFORMATION Complete the chart below using the information provided.

- banks began printing uniform money

- banks could lend large sums of money to explorers and governments

- allowed explorers to know their location better and explore more accurately

- desire for religious freedom and greater curiosity about the world

- governments began to pursue riches from the territories it claimed

Factors	Specific Causes	Influence on Exploration and Colonization
Technological Advances	invention of the compass	
Economic Conditions		
Mercantilism	government efforts to obtain more wealth than rival nations	
Social Changes		many more people were willing to leave Europe

Chapter 16, Main Idea Activities 16.2, continued

EVALUATING INFORMATION Mark each statement *T* if it is true or *F* if it is false.

_____ **1.** Most scholars knew before Columbus's famous voyage that the Earth was round.

_____ **2.** Europeans colonized other lands for non-financial reasons.

_____ **3.** A joint-stock company was an early example of selling shares in a company.

_____ **4.** Mercantilism was the theory that money was a destructive influence.

_____ **5.** Governments used tariffs to make the products produced in their own country appear cheaper.

_____ **6.** Governments gave money called subsidies to new businesses.

_____ **7.** A primary role of the colonies was to provide a captive market to the mother nation.

_____ **8.** The Renaissance and the Scientific Revolution helped convince people to travel overseas by making them more curious about the world.

_____ **9.** Until improvements in shipbuilding in the 1500s, ships had to use oars to travel upwind.

_____ **10.** Money and riches were not the primary motivators during the Age of Exploration.

REVIEWING FACTS Choose the correct items from the following list to complete the statements below.

compass   galleys   discovery   ducat   precious metals

1. Before the 1300s, the value of coins changed according to the amount of

_____ they contained.

2. Until the 1400s, European sailors used long boats known as

_____.

3. Two of the most dependable Italian coins in the 1200s were the gold florin of

Florence and the _____ of Venice.

4. The _____ was one of the most important instruments developed during the Age of Exploration.

5. Spain, France, and Portugal built overseas empires through conquest and

_____.

CHAPTER 16

Modern Chapter **7**

Main Idea Activities 16.3

Voyages of Portugal and Spain

VOCABULARY Some terms to understand:

- **voyage (392):** a long trip or journey over water
- **route (392):** a chosen path to be traveled
- **inhabitants (393):** people who live in a certain area
- **edict (394):** a command or rule, passed down by a ruler
- **annex (399):** to make a neighboring nation or state part of another, usually larger nation or state

ORGANIZING INFORMATION Use the following items to complete the graphic organizer below.

- Brazil
- Central and South America
- eastern and western coasts of Africa
- Asia and the East Indies
- New World
- Philippines

Portugal

_____

_____

_____

Spain

_____

_____

_____

EVALUATING INFORMATION Mark each statement *T* if it is true or *F* if it is false.

_____ **1.** Slave traders were cautious with their slaves because they did not want to lose any while traveling.

_____ **2.** African kingdoms fought against the European slave trade.

_____ **3.** Spain conquered Portugal because it had over-extended its resources and could not defend itself.

_____ **4.** Columbus never knew that he had discovered a new western continent.

_____ **5.** Vikings had been to the Americas long before Columbus arrived.

Chapter 16, Main Idea Activities 16.3, continued

_____ **6.** One of the items which Europeans introduced to the Americas was smallpox, which killed many Native Americans.

_____ **7.** Development and progress in Africa was severely damaged because the European slave traders took so many healthy young Africans.

_____ **8.** Overseas trade with Asia was desirable because overland caravans were taxed by the nations they passed through and took a long time to arrive.

_____ **9.** Christopher Columbus studied the writings of Marco Polo and Ptolemy to form his conclusions about the westward trip to India.

_____ **10.** Spain and Portugal went to war because they both claimed the same colonial territories.

MATCHING Place the letters of the descriptions next to the appropriate names and terms.

_____ **1.** spices

_____ **2.** Ferdinand Magellan

_____ **3.** horses

_____ **4.** the Columbian Exchange

_____ **5.** Amerigo Vespucci

_____ **6.** Asia

_____ **7.** *Nina*

_____ **8.** Portugal

_____ **9.** Brazil

_____ **10.** Prince Henry

_____ **11.** middle passage

_____ **12.** Queen Isabella

a. one section of the triangular trade which involved carrying slaves out of Africa

b. a major trade item desired by Europeans

c. explorer who first realized that the New World was not part of Asia

d. nation that conquered many areas of India

e. monarch who encouraged and financed many early Portugese explorers

f. explorer who died while traveling around the world

g. nation that began as a conquered colony

h. person who financed Columbus' voyage in 1492

i. one valuable item which Europeans introduced to the Americas

j. Vasco da Gama found an overwater route to this area

k. one of the ships in Columbus' expedition

l. the introduction of goods from America to Europe and vice versa

CHAPTER 16

Modern Chapter **7**

Main Idea Activities 16.4

The Spanish and Dutch Empires

VOCABULARY An expression to understand:

• **guerilla warfare (403):** irregular warfare consisting, in part, of harassment, sabotage, and surprise.

Some terms to understand:

• **conquest (400):** the effort to violently take over and control another group of people
• **viceroy (401):** a governor of a state or province who represents a king
• **armada (402):** a fleet of warships
• **efficient (403):** being productive without waste
• **dike (403):** a bank of earth or wall constructed to control or confine water

ORGANIZING INFORMATION Complete the chart below. List the causes of the decline of the Spanish Empire listed below in the appropriate boxes.

• Spain was a consumer nation because it lacked a functioning middle class
• large profits from the colonies drove inflation up
• fought continuous holy wars for Spain and the Holy Roman Empire
• lost possession of the Netherlands

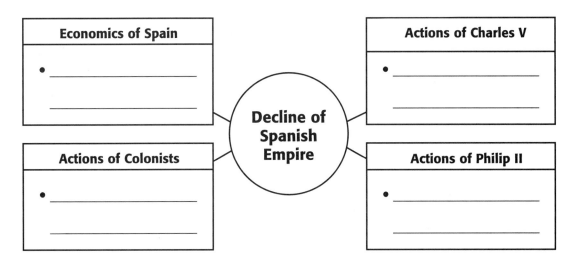

EVALUATING INFORMATION Mark each statement *T* if it is true or *F* if it is false.

_____ **1.** Ponce de León discovered Mexico.

_____ **2.** The Spanish built Mexico City on top of the Aztec city of Tenochtitlán.

_____ **3.** The possession of guns and horses, and the spread of diseases allowed the Spanish to conquer both the Aztec and Incan civilizations.

_____ **4.** The primary objective for conquering Native American populations was to obtain slaves.

_____ **5.** Spain attempted to stop all other European nations from reaching the Americas.

_____ **6.** Before Philip II's reign, the Netherlands was part of the Spanish Empire.

_____ **7.** The Dutch formed their own trading empire in South America and Mexico.

_____ **8.** The Dutch tried to convert conquered people to Christianity and impose their own laws on the native people.

_____ **9.** The primary cause of Spain's decline was the depletion of the country's resources by King Philip II's religious wars and persecution.

_____ **10.** The Dutch were the only people allowed to have a trading base in Japan because they did not try to convert the Japanese to Christianity.

UNDERSTANDING MAIN IDEAS For each of the following, write the letter of the best choice in the space provided.

_____ **1.** The main assets of Spain's colonies were
   a. a rich culture.
   b. a wealth of traded goods.
   c. products unknown in Europe.
   d. mineral resources.

_____ **2.** Spain's rivals tried to get some of its wealth by
   a. organizing into an army to invade Spain.
   b. conquering Spanish colonies.
   c. trading in Spanish-American ports.
   d. engaging in religious wars.

_____ **3.** The Dutch colony at the Cape of Good Hope allowed the Dutch to
   a. build very efficient ships.
   b. become expert sailors.
   c. convert native people to Christianity.
   d. protect their trade routes in Asia.

_____ **4.** Which of the following was not a reason for Spain's decline?
   a. Spanish nobles preferred military service.
   b. The population decreased as people moved to the colonies.
   c. There was less demand for Spanish-made products.
   d. People became discontented with high taxes and inflation.

CHAPTER 17

Modern Chapter 8

Main Idea Activities 17.1

The Ming and Qing Dynasties

VOCABULARY Some terms to understand:

- **fleet (412):** group of ships
- **seafaring (413):** traveling by sea
- **philosophy (413):** beliefs, concepts, and attitudes of a person or group
- **self-sufficient (413):** able to function without help from others
- **minority (414):** the smaller in number of two groups as a whole
- **emigration (414):** movement of people from their country to another
- **nutritional (415):** relating to diet or food
- **scholarship (415):** learning or study
- **bribes (416):** money or favors given to convince someone to do something

ORGANIZING INFORMATION Complete the chart about the four classes of people under Confucianism. Match each of the following items with one of the classes in the chart.

- made beautiful and useful objects
- produced food and paid taxes that supported the empire
- sold objects that peasants and artisans made or produced
- read books and served as staff of the royal government

The Four Classes of People Under Confucianism	
Scholar-gentry	• _____
Farmers	• _____
Artisans	• _____
Merchants	• _____

Chapter 17, Main Idea Activities 17.1, continued

CLASSIFYING INFORMATION Mark these statements as either *M* (for something that was true during the Ming dynasty) or *Q* (for something that was true during the Qing dynasty).

_____ **1.** During the early period, trade was mostly done by sea.

_____ **2.** The leaders were Manchu people.

_____ **3.** Some regions became centers for weaving cotton cloth.

_____ **4.** The leaders made the Great Wall of China stronger.

_____ **5.** The White Lotus Rebellion weakened the dynasty.

_____ **6.** The emperors defeated the Mongols in 1368.

REVIEWING FACTS Choose the correct item from the following list to complete the statements below.

family	White Lotus Rebellion	sweet potato
junks	queue	philology

_____ **1.** Chinese ships called _____ sailed to India in 1405.

_____ **2.** By forcing Chinese men to wear their hair in a _____, or braided tail, the Qing rulers showed their power over the Chinese.

_____ **3.** During the Ming and Qing dynasties, the _____ was a very important part of life.

_____ **4.** The _____ became known as "the poor man's food" in southern China.

_____ **5.** Chinese scholars studied _____, the history of literature and language.

_____ **6.** Members of a Buddhist cult led the _____, a peasant uprising.

Modern Chapter **8**

VOCABULARY Some terms to understand:

• **inner circle (417):** people who are nearest the center, especially of influence to a leader

• **monopoly (418):** exclusive ownership or control

• **addiction (418):** uncontrollable need for a habit-forming drug

• **embassy (419):** an office for one country's ambassador and staff within another country

• **concessions (421):** grants of property or rights by a government

• **sovereignty (421):** freedom from external control

• **sham (421):** not true; fake

ORGANIZING INFORMATION Complete the chart about foreign nations and China by writing the following events in chronological order.

• Taiping Rebellion weakens Qing dynasty. Foreign nations demand more treaty ports.

• Chinese ask Britain to stop bringing opium into China.

• Opium War ends. China gives Hong Kong to the British in the Treaty of Nanjing.

• Chinese and British fight the Opium War.

• British begin shipping opium to China.

• Jesuit missionaries become advisors to the Qing emperor.

Foreign Nations and China

1. _____
   _____

2. _____
   _____

3. _____
   _____

4. _____
   _____

5. _____
   _____

EVALUATING INFORMATION Mark each statement *T* if it is true or *F* if it is false.

_____ **1.** Portugal was the first European country to trade with China.

_____ **2.** Jesuit missionaries never had much power in China.

_____ **3.** The British traded with China in order to get tea for England.

_____ **4.** Supporters of free trade agreed to the British monopoly on tea trade.

_____ **5.** When the Chinese demanded that opium sales should stop, the British responded quickly.

_____ **6.** After the Opium War, Qing officials had to negotiate on British terms.

_____ **7.** Great Britain was the only country that wanted to trade with China.

_____ **8.** The British viewed Chinese interests as more important than British needs.

MATCHING Match the letters of the items in the second column with the correct items in the first column.

_____ **1.** used astronomy to get approval of the Chinese emperor

_____ **2.** were afraid that Christianity would make them less powerful

_____ **3.** came to China to buy silk and tea

_____ **4.** the idea that government should not restrict trade

_____ **5.** addictive product the British used to exchange for tea

_____ **6.** opened five new ports to British trade

_____ **7.** foreign people in a country follow the laws of their home country

_____ **8.** signed by the Chinese because they were afraid of new wars with Europeans

a. Qing rulers

b. free trade

c. "unequal treaties"

d. Jesuit missionaries

e. Treaty of Nanjing

f. opium

g. the British

h. extraterritoriality

Name _____ Class _____ Date _____

VOCABULARY Some terms to understand:

• **bitter (422):** hard to bear

• **alliances (423):** agreements between people to help each other

• **decentralized (424):** spread out among different areas

• **courtiers (424):** people who live at a royal court

• **muskets (424):** guns; rifles

• **prohibited (425):** did not allow

• **handicrafts (426):** articles made by hand, such as pottery

• **reluctantly (427):** without wanting to

ORGANIZING INFORMATION List on the pyramid the different parts of the Japanese government and social classes. List the parts in order of importance from the greatest to the least.

• merchants   • daimyo   • samurai

• artisans   • shogun   • peasants

Government and Social Classes in Tokugawa Japan

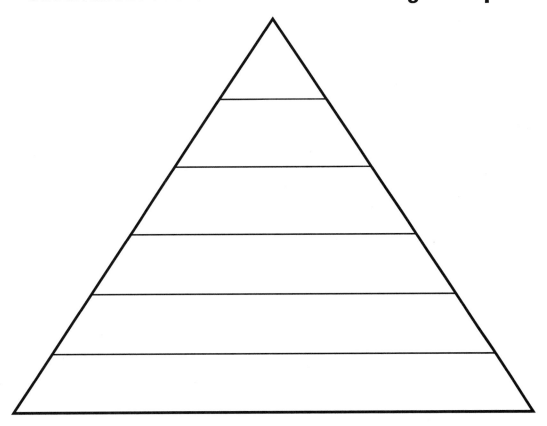

Chapter 17, Main Idea Activities 17.3, continued

EVALUATING INFORMATION Mark each statement *T* if it is true or *F* if it is false.

_____ **1.** After a long time of war, three powerful daimyo set up a strong feudal system in Japan.

_____ **2.** Each Japanese daimyo had great power within his own area.

_____ **3.** The Tokugawa ruled the entire country directly.

_____ **4.** Tokugawa shoguns decided that Christianity was good for Japan.

_____ **5.** Under Tokugawa rule, Japan had very little contact with other countries.

_____ **6.** A person's social class in Tokugawa Japan was determined by his or her skills.

_____ **7.** As cities grew in size, people in Tokugawa Japan became poorer.

_____ **8.** Anti-Tokugawa forces restored the power of the emperor.

UNDERSTANDING MAIN IDEAS For each of the following, write the letter of the best choice in the space provided.

_____ **1.** The Tokugawa shoguns made the daimyo live at the capital every other year
    a. to punish them when they were not loyal.
    b. in order to keep them from becoming too strong.
    c. to help them get to know each other and make them stronger.
    d. because they did not believe in holding anyone against their will.

_____ **2.** The Tokugawa shoguns did not allow trade with other countries because
    a. they wanted to control China and other Asian nations.
    b. they were worried that the Japanese people would all leave the country.
    c. they wanted to keep Japan isolated from other countries.
    d. there were too many languages to learn in a very short time.

_____ **3.** Increased wealth during Tokugawa Japan led to the rise of
    a. foreign trade.
    b. central power.
    c. the common people.
    d. a popular culture.

_____ **4.** Matthew Perry came to Japan two times in order to
    a. open Japanese ports to trade with the United States.
    b. help foreign nations open consulates.
    c. take the Japanese emperor to the United States.
    d. remove all American people from Japan.

CHAPTER 18 — Main Idea Activities 18.1

Modern Chapter **9**   **The Ottoman Empire**

VOCABULARY Some expressions to understand:

- **career of conquest (432):** spending much of one's life conquering other lands or people
- **to its height (433):** greatest degree of success
- **marked the start (434):** showed the beginning

Other terms to understand:

- **capital (432):** city where the government of a country or state is located
- **deference (434):** respect
- **bypassed (435):** found a way around
- **bureaucracy (435):** officials running different parts of a government

ORGANIZING INFORMATION Complete the time line by matching the following events with the dates on the time line. Write the letter for each event on the line next to the correct date.

A. Süleyman the Magnificent conquers Hungary

B. birth of Timur

C. beginning of the rule of Süleyman the Magnificent

D. Murad's army defeats European crusaders at the Battle of Varna

E. Mehmed II conquers Constantinople

F. first Ottoman sultan is appointed

The Rise of the Ottoman Empire

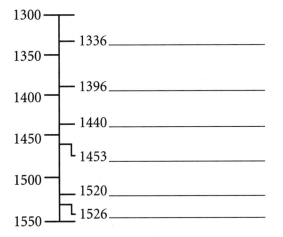

1300
1336 _____
1350
1396 _____
1400
1440 _____
1450
1453 _____
1500
1520 _____
1550
1526 _____

EVALUATING INFORMATION Mark each statement *T* if it is true or *F* if it is false.

_____ **1.** The first Ottomans were Turkish soldiers who had come to Asia Minor to escape the Mongols.

_____ **2.** The Janissaries never gained importance in the Ottoman Empire because they were war captives and slaves.

_____ **3.** The Ottomans defeated Timur at the Battle of Ankara.

_____ **4.** Mehmed II conquered Constantinople and renamed the city Istanbul.

_____ **5.** During the rule of Süleyman, the Ottomans ruled most of eastern Europe, western Asia, and northern Africa.

_____ **6.** The supreme ruler of Ottoman society was the grand vizier.

_____ **7.** The ordinary Ottoman subjects were called *reaya,* which means "protected flock."

_____ **8.** The leaders of Ottoman society were born to their positions.

_____ **9.** Millets were separate religious communities that governed themselves.

_____ **10.** After the death of Süleyman the Magnificent, the Ottoman Empire became stronger.

REVIEWING FACTS Choose the correct item from the following list to complete the statements below.

Murad II   Osmar   Turkey   Genghis Kahn   the Lawgiver

1. The ghazi leader whose tribe members became known as Ottomans was named

_____.

2. Timur, the Turko-Mongol leader, claimed he was descended from the great Mongol

_____.

3. After the Ottoman civil war in the 1400s, _____ took power and began expanding the empire.

4. The greatest Ottoman leader was called _____ by his own people.

5. When the Republic of _____ was created, the Ottoman Empire finally ended.

CHAPTER 18   Main Idea Activities 18.2

Modern Chapter **9**   **The Safavid Empire**

VOCABULARY Some terms to understand:

- **persecuted (436):** caused to suffer again and again
- **proclaimed (436):** said; stated
- **convert (436):** cause a change in religion
- **identity (437):** self
- **rectangular (438):** a shape that has two pairs of equal sides and one pair is longer than the other
- **arcade (438):** walkway with an arched roof
- **inns (438):** hotels
- **inept (438):** not skilled

ORGANIZING INFORMATION Complete the chart about the causes of events in the Safavid Empire. For each item listed in the right column write one of the following causes in the left column.

- 'Abbās wanted to defeat the Ottomans and Uzbeks.
- Persians killed or imprisoned many Safavids.
- Shi'ah became the religion of the Safavid Empire.
- Rulers after 'Abbās were inept.

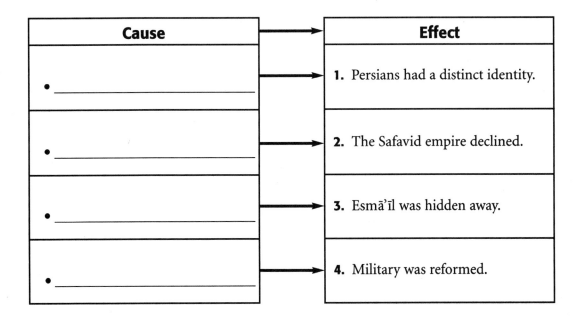

Cause		Effect
• _____	→	**1.** Persians had a distinct identity.
• _____	→	**2.** The Safavid empire declined.
• _____	→	**3.** Esmā'īl was hidden away.
• _____	→	**4.** Military was reformed.

Causes of Events in the Safavid Empire

Chapter 18, Main Idea Activities 18.2, continued

EVALUATING INFORMATION Mark each statement *T* if it is true or *F* if it is false.

_____ **1.** Much of what was the Safavid Empire is now Iran.

_____ **2.** Esmā'īl upset the Ottomans and Uzbeks because he converted Safavids to Shi'ah Muslims.

_____ **3.** Shi'ah gave Persians an identity distinct from Turks and Arabs.

_____ **4.** 'Abbās was not able to beat the Turks and Uzbeks.

_____ **5.** The reign of 'Abbās was a time of economic development.

_____ **6.** Carpet weaving became a major industry during the Safavid Empire.

_____ **7.** After 'Abbās died, the Safavid rulers became very strong.

_____ **8.** In time, Persia split into a number of small states.

MATCHING Match the letters of the items in the second column with the correct items in the first column.

_____ **1.** head of the family after which the Safavids were named

_____ **2.** the Safavid army who wore red hats

_____ **3.** first Safavid ruler who took the ancient title of shah

_____ **4.** battle in which the Safavids were beaten

_____ **5.** son of Esmā'īl who lost territory to the Ottomans and Uzbeks

_____ **6.** reformed the army, encouraged manufacturing and trade

a. Safī od-Dīn
b. 'Abbās
c. kizilbash
d. Tahmāsp
e. Çaldiran
f. Esmā'īl

CHAPTER **18**

Modern Chapter **9**

Main Idea Activities 18.3

The Mughal Empire in India

VOCABULARY Some terms to understand:

- **descendant (439):** person born into the same family or group as another person
- **miniature (440):** very small copy of a real object
- **impressive quantities (440):** large amounts
- **abuses (443):** wrong or bad acts
- **vigorous (443):** having a lot of energy
- **observance (443):** following or keeping

ORGANIZING INFORMATION Complete the chart about three Mughal rulers by using the following items. List each item under the correct ruler.

- increased taxes to support wars in Persia
- demanded strict following of Islamic laws
- tolerant of all religions
- built the Taj Mahal
- revolts and economic problems weakened his empire
- known as the greatest Mughal emperor

Three Mughal Rulers		
Akbar	**Shah Jahān**	**Aurangzeb**

EVALUATING INFORMATION Mark each statement *T* if it is true or *F* if it is false.

_____ **1.** During the 1300s Turkish Muslims controlled India.

_____ **2.** Bābur lost in Delhi because he was greatly outnumbered.

_____ **3.** Bābur's grandson, Akbar, became emperor at the age of 35.

_____ **4.** The economy declined during Akbar's reign.

_____ **5.** The Taj Mahal was built as a tomb for Shah Jahān's wife.

_____ **6.** The Sikh religion is a blend of Hindu, Muslim, and Christian religions.

_____ **7.** Aurangzeb was a very popular Mughal emperor.

_____ **8.** There were many revolts because of Aurangzeb's actions.

UNDERSTANDING MAIN IDEAS For each of the following, write the letter of the best choice in the space provided.

_____ **1.** What role did Bābur play in the Mughal Empire?
   a. supporter of the arts
   b. reformer
   c. founder
   d. divine ruler

_____ **2.** Under whose rule did literature in the Hindi and Urdu languages develop?
   a. Akbar
   b. Bābur
   c. Shah Jahān
   d. Aurangzeb

_____ **3.** Why did Shah Jahān increase taxes?
   a. The empire included both northern and southern India.
   b. His subjects wanted to pay him only half of their crops.
   c. Military campaigns against Persia were expensive.
   d. He wanted workers from Central Asia to build the Taj Mahal.

_____ **4.** The Sikh faith, which called for devotion to one god, conflicted with
   a. Nanak's teachings.
   b. Mughal culture.
   c. Shah Jahān's plans.
   d. Hindu beliefs.

_____ **5.** The strict policies of Aurangzeb caused
   a. the building of thousands of Hindu temples.
   b. religious riots throughout the empire.
   c. great celebrations that included wine and music.
   d. elephants to crush protestors.

Main Idea Activities 19.1

Modern Chapter **10**   **France in the Age of Absolutism**

VOCABULARY An expression to understand:

- **concentrated it in the hands of (455):** gave most of it to

Other terms:

- **industry (455):** business and manufacturing
- **absolute (455):** total; complete
- **grandeur (455):** splendor or magnificence; being very grand
- **eliminating (456):** getting rid of
- **dominating (457):** controlling
- **profitable (458):** money making

ORGANIZING INFORMATION Complete the chart about three French leaders by using the following items. List each item under the correct leader.

- caused Protestants to flee France by doing away with the Edict of Nantes
- led military attacks on towns held by Huguenots
- converted to Catholicism to help bring peace and unity to France
- wanted to protect the rights of Protestants
- controlled the nobles by having them live at his palace
- made the intendants, or king's officials, more powerful

Ideas About Ruling France

1. Henry IV	• _____ • _____
2. Cardinal Richelieu	• _____ • _____
3. Louis XIV	• _____ • _____

EVALUATING INFORMATION Mark each statement *T* if it is true or *F* if it is false.

_____ **1.** The French tax system in the 1500s was very fair to the middle and lower classes.

_____ **2.** To make the king's power supreme, Cardinal Richelieu strengthened the nobles.

_____ **3.** The Thirty Years' War began as a Protestant rebellion against the Holy Roman Empire.

_____ **4.** Cardinal Richelieu kept France fighting in the front lines during the Thirty Years' War.

_____ **5.** Cardinal Richelieu believed the Edict of Nantes was good for the monarchy.

_____ **6.** During the reign of Louis XIV, 200,000 Huguenots left France.

_____ **7.** To fight his four wars, Louis XIV had the most powerful army in Europe.

_____ **8.** Other countries in Europe did not mind France's increasing power.

REVIEWING FACTS Choose the correct items from the following list to complete the statements below.

intendants	balance of power	Treaty of Westphalia
Jean-Baptiste Colbert	Versailles	Treaty of Utrecht

1. The Thirty Years' War ended with the _____, granting independence to the Netherlands and Switzerland.

2. Louis XIV's beautiful palace, _____, represented the grandeur and the power of the monarchy.

3. _____ were King Louis XIV's representatives in the French provinces.

4. _____ took steps to eliminate corruption and waste in the French tax systems.

5. Louis XIV's wars to extend his territory brought other Europeans together to achieve a

_____ against France.

6. France and Spain could never be united in accordance with the

_____ .

CHAPTER  19

Modern Chapter **10**

Main Idea Activities 19.2

Russia in the Age of Absolutism

VOCABULARY Some terms to understand:

- **origins (459):** beginnings
- **disguised (460):** change dress or looks to keep from being recognized
- **worsened (462):** made more unfavorable
- **innumerable (462):** very many
- **oration (462):** speech
- **vast (464):** very large; huge

ORGANIZING INFORMATION Complete the chart about Peter the Great and Catherine the Great by using the following items.

- extended Russian borders into central Europe
- opened access to Siberia
- built a new capital in St. Petersburg
- modernized and Westernized Russia
- created a new class of nobles based on "service nobility"
- gained control of most of the northern shore of the Black Sea

Peter and Catherine of Russia	
Peter the Great	**Catherine the Great**
• _____	• _____
• _____	• _____
• _____	• _____

(Chapter 19, Main Idea Activities 19.2, continued)

EVALUATING INFORMATION Mark each statement *T* if it is true or *F* if it is false.

_____ **1.** Russia was separated from western Europe by a large ocean.

_____ **2.** Because Russia was ruled by Mongols for 200 years, it was very similar to western Europe.

_____ **3.** The Romanovs added to the power of the czars in Russia.

_____ **4.** Peter the Great wanted to keep Russia from being like western Europe.

_____ **5.** Peter the Great had complete control of the government.

_____ **6.** The Russian Orthodox Church strongly supported Peter the Great.

_____ **7.** Most Russians in the 1700s were very poor.

_____ **8.** Catherine the Great wanted more land and sea ports for Russia.

UNDERSTANDING MAIN IDEAS For each of the following, write the letter of the best choice in the space provided.

_____ **1.** Under Peter the Great and Catherine the Great, Russia became
   a. separated from the rest of Europe.
   b. the center of European power.
   c. both Catholic and Protestant.
   d. a Westernized and powerful nation.

_____ **2.** Both Peter the Great and Catherine the Great wanted to
   a. keep Russia the same as it had been for centuries.
   b. open up ports on the sea for trade.
   c. force Russians to speak and read only Russian.
   d. live peaceful lives and not bother any other countries.

_____ **3.** Some of the social changes that took place in Russia under Peter the Great were
   a. women took greater part in the community and men shaved their beards.
   b. women stopped being active in the community and men stopped shaving.
   c. the army became weaker and there was more trade.
   d. the army became stronger and there was less trade.

_____ **4.** Both Peter the Great and Catherine the Great
   a. did not improve the lives of the serfs, who stayed poor.
   b. made every effort to improve the lives of poor people.
   c. spent large amounts of money on aid to foreign countries.
   d. told the nobles that they could no longer control the serfs.

CHAPTER 19   Main Idea Activities 19.3

Modern Chapter **10**   **Central Europe in the Age of Absolutism**

VOCABULARY Some terms to understand:

• **ambitious (466):** full of desire to get a high position or place in the world

• **lavish (466):** extreme; excessive

• **efficient (466):** able to do the most with the least waste

• **thoroughly (466):** completely

• **ceded (467):** given up to

• **tolerance (469):** letting other people do as they wish

• **prosperity (469):** good fortune

ORGANIZING INFORMATION Complete the chart by matching the changing alliances of Austria and Prussia. List each item below next to the correct war.

• Great Britain

• France and Russia

• Bavaria, Spain, France

• Great Britain, Russia, the Netherlands

• Russia

• Great Britain withdraws from conflict

Shift of European Alliances in the mid-1700s		
The Wars	**Alliances**	
	Austria	**Prussia**
1. War of Austrian Succession		
2. Diplomatic Revolution		
3. Seven Years' War		

Chapter 19, Main Idea Activities 19.3, continued

EVALUATING INFORMATION Mark each statement *T* if it is true or *F* if it is false.

_____ **1.** The Habsburg empire under Maria Theresa was easy to rule.

_____ **2.** Austria's chief rival was the Hohenzollern family in Russia.

_____ **3.** Frederick William, also called the Great Elector, unified his army but failed to rebuild his state.

_____ **4.** Frederick William I imitated Louis XIV's ruling style and gained the title as king of Prussia.

_____ **5.** In the Diplomatic Revolution, the European countries kept the same allies.

_____ **6.** The Seven Years' War began in North America as the French and Indian War.

_____ **7.** After the Seven Years' War, European nations wanted to keep fighting.

_____ **8.** Frederick the Great helped rebuild Prussia after years of fighting wars.

UNDERSTANDING MAIN IDEAS For each of the following, write the letter of the best choice in the space provided.

_____ **1.** The rivalry between Austria and Prussia began when the Hohenzollerns, Prussia's ruling family,
    a. made friends with France and Great Britain.
    b. took land that belonged to the Catholic Church.
    c. improved diplomatic relations with Bavaria.
    d. expanded the territory to the north and south.

_____ **2.** The War of Austrian Succession began after
    a. the Prussians invaded Austria.
    b. the Habsburgs invaded Prussia.
    c. the Silesians invaded Prussia.
    d. the Prussians invaded Silesia.

_____ **3.** At the end of the Seven Years' War
    a. Prussia had clearly won the war.
    b. there was no clear winner.
    c. Austria and Britain were the winners.
    d. France had lost the war, while the other countries had won.

_____ **4.** The fighting and losses in the Seven Years' War
    a. made many countries want to find new lands to conquer.
    b. had little effect on the people of Europe.
    c. led to a period of peace in Europe.
    d. left many European countries with extra wealth.

CHAPTER 19   Main Idea Activities 19.4

Modern Chapter **10**   **The English Monarchy**

VOCABULARY An expression to understand:

• **harsh lines of her destiny (471):** the serious responsibilities of being queen of England

Some terms to understand:

• **ruthless (470):** showing no mercy; cruel
• **provoked (470):** brought about; stirred up
• **radiant (471):** shining; bright
• **invincible (471):** unbeatable
• **disunity (471):** lack of unity; not unified
• **customs (473):** taxes paid to a government on items brought from other countries
• **negotiations (473):** talks to arrange terms or work out an agreement

ORGANIZING INFORMATION Complete the graphic organizer about English rulers by writing the following items in the correct bubble.

• approved a new translation of the Bible
• had more tolerant religious policies
• managed Parliament successfully
• was determined to restore Catholicism in England
• persecuted Protestants and caused rebellion
• believed in the divine right of kings

English Rulers

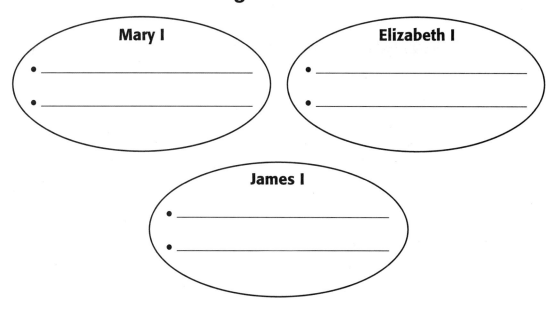

Chapter 19, Main Idea Activities 19.4, continued

EVALUATING INFORMATION Mark each statement *T* if it is true or *F* if it is false.

_____ **1.** The first Tudor king, Henry VII, made England stable and prosperous.

_____ **2.** Henry VIII established the Anglican Church in England because the pope allied with his enemies.

_____ **3.** The first reigning queen of England was Elizabeth I.

_____ **4.** Mary I married Philip II because she wanted to become a Catholic.

_____ **5.** The invincible Armada attacked England because Elizabeth I helped Protestants prosper in Spanish lands.

_____ **6.** The Tudor monarchs wanted all English subjects to be Anglicans.

_____ **7.** Puritans favored the religious policies of Elizabeth I.

_____ **8.** James I was king of both England and Scotland.

UNDERSTANDING MAIN IDEAS For each of the following, write the letter of the best choice in the space provided.

_____ **1.** How did Mary I earn her reputation as "Bloody Mary"?
    a. She wore a red gown to her coronation.
    b. She told Parliament to put red carpeting in buildings.
    c. She had more than 300 Protestants burned at the stake.
    d. She began a rebellion in which many people died.

_____ **2.** Which of these religious policies angered the Puritans?
    a. Tudor monarchs wanted all English subjects to be Anglicans.
    b. The Anglican Church kept some Catholic practices.
    c. Non-Anglican Protestants were allowed to become Catholics.
    d. No further changes to the church were allowed.

_____ **3.** Among the accomplishments of Elizabeth I was the
    a. challenge to royal power.
    b. anger of Puritans.
    c. victory over Spain.
    d. tolerance of other religions.

_____ **4.** Monarchs in England tried to rule with absolute power but met serious opposition from
    a. European leaders.
    b. Anglicans and Catholics.
    c. Parliament.
    d. nobles.

Main Idea Activities 20.1

CHAPTER 20

Modern Chapter **11**   **Civil War and Revolution**

VOCABULARY Some terms to understand:

• **isolated (478):** set apart

• **dismissed (478):** sent away

• **civil liberties (478):** rights and freedoms of people

• **dispossessed (479):** kicked out

• **severing (480):** cutting

• **suppress (481):** stop; put down

• **dissent (481):** statements that disagree with someone or a stated policy

• **quarreled (482):** fought; argued

ORGANIZING INFORMATION Complete the chart about events in England between 1638 and 1660 by writing the following items in chronological order.

• Cromwell had Charles I killed.

• Cromwell ruled as lord protector.

• Long Parliament began.

• Parliament passed Petition of Right.

• Civil War broke out.

• Cromwell failed to set up a constitution.

Events in England 1638–1660
1. _____
2. Charles I refused to call Parliament to session. _____
3. _____
4. _____
5. _____
6. _____
7. _____
8. Parliament invited Charles II to be King of England. _____

Chapter 20, Main Idea Activities 20.1, continued

EVALUATING INFORMATION Mark each statement *T* if it is true or *F* if it is false.

_____ **1.** Charles I thought that kings should share power with Parliament.

_____ **2.** Parliament passed the Petition of Right because Charles I was treating people unjustly.

_____ **3.** Charles I wanted to raise money to fight against the Scots and Irish.

_____ **4.** Because Parliament refused to let Charles raise a bigger army, he tried to use his army to force Parliament.

_____ **5.** In the English civil war that followed the king's actions, Oliver Cromwell fought for Charles I.

_____ **6.** After Charles I was defeated, Cromwell had him imprisoned for life.

_____ **7.** Cromwell based his rule on the support of the army.

_____ **8.** After Cromwell died, his son increased his own power.

MATCHING Match the letters of the items in the second column with the correct items in the first column.

_____ **1.** stated that the king could not tax people without agreement of Parliament

_____ **2.** passed a law that Parliament must meet at least once every three years

_____ **3.** people on the side of the king in the English civil war

_____ **4.** people on the side of Parliament in the English civil war

_____ **5.** defeated Charles I in the English civil war

_____ **6.** got rid of the king and the House of Lords

_____ **7.** a system of government in which there is no king and people have some rights; a democratic republic

_____ **8.** stated that all goods shipped to England had to be carried by English ships or by ships of the country that made the goods

a. Rump Parliament

b. Navigation Act of 1651

c. Long Parliament

d. New Model Army

e. commonwealth

f. Roundheads

g. Petition of Right

h. Cavaliers

CHAPTER **20**   Main Idea Activities 20.2

Modern Chapter **11**   **Constitutional Monarchy in England**

VOCABULARY Some terms to understand:

- **restrictions (483):** rules or guidelines for
- **cynical (483):** someone who tends to believe that other people are not honest or sincere
- **abandon (483):** give up
- **rebellious (484):** to go against authority
- **antagonized (484):** created dislike in
- **spurred (484):** encouraged; made
- **bloodless (484):** without violence
- **chaos (485):** great confusion or disorder
- **supreme (487):** more powerful

ORGANIZING INFORMATION Complete the chart about the ideas of Thomas Hobbes and John Locke by using the following items. Write each item under the correct person's name.

- People need a government.
- People make a social contract with leaders.
- Individual rights are more important than laws.
- People act only from self-interest.
- Only the strong survive in the natural world.
- A tyrant can be justly overthrown.

The Ideas of Thomas Hobbes and John Locke	
Thomas Hobbes	**John Locke**
• _____	• _____
• _____	• _____
• _____	• _____

Chapter 20, Main Idea Activities 20.2, continued

EVALUATING INFORMATION Mark each statement *T* if it is true or *F* if it is false.

_____ **1.** Charles II began the period in England called the Restoration.

_____ **2.** The people of England were hoping to have a Catholic king again.

_____ **3.** The Glorious Revolution took place without anyone being killed.

_____ **4.** During the time of William and Mary, Parliament passed the English Bill of Rights, which said that Parliament had control over English rulers.

_____ **5.** By 1700, Parliament had given up most of its power.

_____ **6.** In 1707, England and Scotland were joined to become Great Britain.

_____ **7.** During the 1700s, the prime minister ran the government in Britain.

_____ **8.** The British system of limited constitutional monarchy did not last long.

REVIEWING FACTS Choose the correct items from the following list to complete the statements below.

Toleration Act	Restoration	Whigs	Habeas Corpus Act
cabinet	prime minister	English Bill of Rights	Tories

1. The _____ was a political party that usually supported the Anglican Church.

2. The _____ stated that no ruler could tax the people without asking Parliament.

3. The _____ granted religious freedom to some people.

4. When Charles II became king, the _____ period began and the period without a king or queen ended.

5. The _____ was a political party that wanted a strong Parliament instead of a Catholic ruler.

6. The _____ was made up of leaders from Parliament who advised the prime minister.

7. Parliament passed the _____ in order to protect the rights of people who had been arrested.

8. As Parliament became more powerful, the _____ ran the government instead of the king or queen.

Name _____ Class _____ Date _____

CHAPTER 20

Modern Chapter **11**

Main Idea Activities 20.3

English Colonial Expansion

VOCABULARY Some expressions to understand:

- **emerged supreme (491):** came out the winner
- **respectable occupation (493):** a job that other people respect or accept

Some terms to understand:

- **plundering (491):** attacking ships and taking their cargoes
- **voluntarily (492):** because a person wants to
- **manufacturing (493):** making by hand or machine
- **forbade (493):** refused to allow
- **smuggling (493):** to import or export goods secretly or illegally

ORGANIZING INFORMATION Complete the chart about English explorers by using the following items. Write each item under the correct person's name.

- helped to defeat the Spanish Armada
- searched for the Northwest Passage in northern North America
- explored the bay in northern Canada that now has his name
- plundered foreign ships, particularly those of Spain
- Venetian sea captain who explored the coasts of Newfoundland and Nova Scotia
- gave England its first claim in North America

English Explorers		
John Cabot	**Sir Francis Drake**	**Henry Hudson**
• _____ _____ • _____ _____	• _____ _____ • _____ _____	• _____ _____ • _____ _____

EVALUATING INFORMATION Mark each statement *T* if it is true or *F* if it is false.

_____ **1.** During the 1600s, England had too many problems at home to explore the rest of the world.

_____ **2.** The sea dogs were sea captains and pirates who helped England.

_____ **3.** Repeated raids from Africa greatly angered King Philip II of Spain.

_____ **4.** The British were not able to set up trading posts in India.

_____ **5.** The first British settlements in North America were in Canada.

_____ **6.** The British thought that England existed for the benefit of its colonies.

_____ **7.** Britain passed laws that restricted trade by colonists.

_____ **8.** North American colonists were very happy with British rule.

REVIEWING FACTS Choose the correct items from the following list to complete the statements below.

Henry Hudson	British East India Company	Sir Francis Drake
John Cabot	sea dogs	mercantilism

1. Trading posts in Malaya and the East Indies were set up by the

_____.

2. Queen Elizabeth told Philip II of Spain that she was not able to keep the

_____ from attacking his ships.

3. King Henry VII of England hired _____ to explore North America.

4. A year after sailing for the Dutch, _____ explored far northern Canada for the English.

5. Under the idea of _____ colonies were to serve their home country.

6. One of the sea dogs, _____, sailed all the way around the world.

CHAPTER **20**   Main Idea Activities 20.4

Modern Chapter **11**   **The Enlightenment**

VOCABULARY Some terms to understand:

- **privileged (494):** people who have special favor or rights
- **minority (494):** small group; less than half of a group
- **solely (494):** singly; exclusively
- **predictable (494):** can be told ahead of time
- **governed (494):** controlled; ran
- **harmony (494):** peace; without bothering others
- **exemplified (495):** be an example of
- **satires (495):** writings that attack or make fun of something
- **suppress (495):** put down

ORGANIZING INFORMATION Complete the diagram below by writing the following names above the ideas or principles they believed.

- Montesquieu
- Voltaire
- Rousseau
- Wollstonecraft

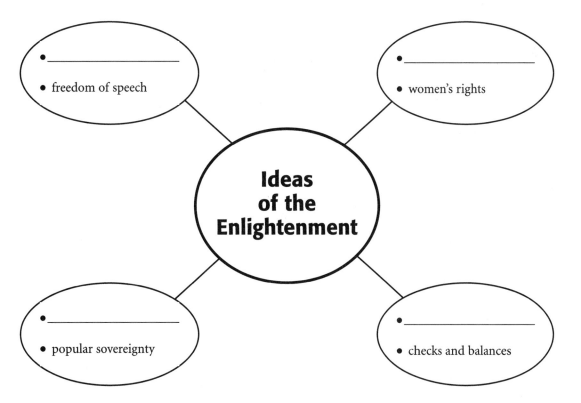

- _____
  - freedom of speech

- _____
  - women's rights

Ideas of the Enlightenment

- _____
  - popular sovereignty

- _____
  - checks and balances

Chapter 20, Main Idea Activities 20.4, continued

EVALUATING INFORMATION Mark each statement *T* if it is true or *F* if it is false.

_____ **1.** The 1700s in Europe were called the Age of Enlightenment.

_____ **2.** Enlightenment thinkers believed that natural law was not important.

_____ **3.** Denis Diderot published a huge handbook called *The Dictionary*.

_____ **4.** Many thinkers in France thought that England had the best political system.

_____ **5.** Voltaire was put in prison twice for writing against French nobility.

_____ **6.** During the Enlightenment, many philosophers thought that governments should be controlled by the people.

_____ **7.** In England, Mary Wollstonecraft argued that the ideals of the Enlightenment should be true for women as well as men.

_____ **8.** In enlightened despotism, the government is ruled by a monarch who would ignore the principles of the Enlightenment.

UNDERSTANDING MAIN IDEAS For each of the following, write the letter of the best choice in the space provided.

_____ **1.** In *The Encyclopedia* many people wrote their ideas about
   a. exploring North America.
   b. how the common people had enough rights and power.
   c. the Enlightenment, the church, the government, and more.
   d. how philosophers were interesting people but did not have useful ideas.

_____ **2.** The French authorities
   a. put Denis Diderot and other philosophers in prison for their ideas.
   b. were pleased that people were willing to criticize the government.
   c. burned all the copies of *The Encyclopedia*.
   d. helped Diderot and others publish *The Encyclopedia*.

_____ **3.** Philosophers such as Baron de Montesquieu
   a. criticized the power and privilege of kings, clergy, and nobles.
   b. suggested that the king and nobles join forces against the clergy.
   c. were not interested in the workings of government.
   d. thought that all governments should have two parts.

_____ **4.** In the *Social Contract*, Jean-Jacques Rousseau wrote that
   a. environment had little effect on a person's life.
   b. people were born neither good nor bad.
   c. people were naturally good but were changed by their environment.
   d. no person should be allowed to choose his or her own government.

CHAPTER 20 · Main Idea Activities 20.5

Modern Chapter **11** · **The American Revolution**

VOCABULARY Some terms to understand:

- **inherent (497):** belonging to someone as a permanent quality
- **debt (497):** something owed to another person or thing
- **mortgages (498):** documents that state the legal right to a piece of property, which are given as security to a bank that has loaned money to buy the property
- **obedience (498):** doing what one is told to do
- **milestone (499):** an important event
- **unanimity (501):** when all people agree about something
- **fray (501):** fight
- **daunting (502):** very challenging; difficult

ORGANIZING INFORMATION Complete the chart below by listing the following items as principles of either the Articles of Confederation or the Constitution of the United States.

- one-house Congress in which each state had one vote
- Congress could not vote for taxes or coin money
- government divided into legislative, executive, and judicial branches
- individual states had all the power; very weak central government
- federal government could declare war, raise armies, and make treaties
- set up executive branch headed by the president and enforced laws

Articles of Confederation:

- _____
- _____
- _____

Constitution:

- _____
- _____
- _____

Chapter 20, Main Idea Activities 20.5, continued

EVALUATING INFORMATION Mark each statement *T* if it is true or *F* if it is false.

_____ **1.** After the French and Indian War, the British controlled much of North America.

_____ **2.** The British expected the American colonies to help them pay for the French and Indian War.

_____ **3.** Almost all American colonists wanted to remain part of Great Britain.

_____ **4.** The Declaration of Independence set up the United States government.

_____ **5.** It was not hard for the colonists to build a strong army.

_____ **6.** After winning the war, the colonists had to create a new government.

_____ **7.** The American Constitution has not worked very well over the years.

_____ **8.** The American Revolution put into practice ideas of the Enlightenment.

MATCHING Match the letters of the items in the second column with the correct items in the first column.

_____ **1.** prime minister under King George III who carried out harsh policies against the American colonies

_____ **2.** colonists who supported the king in the American Revolution

_____ **3.** colonists who wanted to break from Britain in the American Revolution

_____ **4.** the person who wrote most of the Declaration of Independence

_____ **5.** colonial leader who negotiated treaty with Britain after the Revolutionary War

_____ **6.** interprets the laws under the Constitution

_____ **7.** makes the laws under the Constitution

_____ **8.** first ten amendments to the Constitution that guarantee freedom of religion, speech, the press, assembly, and petition

a. judicial branch of government

b. Patriots

c. Lord North

d. Benjamin Franklin

e. legislative branch of government

f. Loyalists

g. Bill of Rights

h. Thomas Jefferson

Main Idea Activities 21.1

Modern Chapter **12**

The Roots of Revolution

VOCABULARY Some terms to understand:

- **conspicuously (508):** obviously; remarkably
- **materialistic (508):** only interested in money, possessions, or things
- **irresponsible (508):** not doing their jobs well or with care
- **urban (509):** about cities
- **laborers (509):** workers
- **took to the streets (509):** went out into the streets
- **prospered (509):** made money; lived very well
- **stoked the fires of (510):** added to
- **deluge (510):** flood; in this case serious problems and reaction from the French people

ORGANIZING INFORMATION Complete the chart about the three estates in France before the French Revolution by using the following items. Write the letter of each item in the correct part of the chart.

A. Roman Catholic clergy who held vast lands and collected rents, taxes, and fees

B. 97 percent of the people, with no voice in government

C. city workers, artisans, and rural peasants

D. less than two percent of the population, whose sons inherited their titles and lands

E. less than one percent of the population

F. nobles who paid few taxes and held the highest positions in government

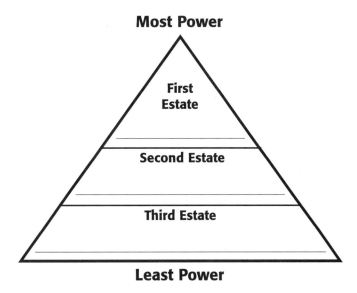

The Three Estates in France

Most Power

First Estate

Second Estate

Third Estate

Least Power

EVALUATING INFORMATION Mark each statement *T* if it is true or *F* if it is false.

_____ **1.** By 1780 France had been ruled for more than 100 years by an absolute monarch.

_____ **2.** Before the French Revolution, France was made up of three classes.

_____ **3.** The Third Estate had the most power in France.

_____ **4.** During the mid-1700s, most people in France were happy with the king.

_____ **5.** The peasants, workers, and bourgeoisie all had the same problems.

_____ **6.** The French kings tried very hard to solve the problems of the poor.

_____ **7.** When the Estates General met in 1789, the Third Estate would not do what the king wanted.

_____ **8.** The Third Estate declared itself the National Assembly.

UNDERSTANDING MAIN IDEAS For each of the following, write the letter of the best choice in the space provided.

_____ **1.** The First Estate was wealthy and powerful because
   a. the church owned about 15 percent of the land in France.
   b. the nobles gave the peasants half their lands.
   c. the clergy became discontented with the old system.
   d. the kings gave them all the wealth they could.

_____ **2.** The discontent in France during the mid-1700s came from
   a. only one factor: that the king had left the country.
   b. several factors, including population growth and higher rents.
   c. rural landowners lowering the rents on land.
   d. the price of goods going down and an increase in wages to laborers.

_____ **3.** Because the bourgeoisie became more wealthy in the 1700s, they
   a. wanted political power to go with their economic strength.
   b. wished to share their wealth with the First Estate.
   c. were not interested in gaining political power, which they left to the king.
   d. wanted the government to continue controlling business.

_____ **4.** After the Third Estate created the National Assembly, they
   a. voted to make sure that Louis XVI kept absolute power.
   b. decided that they would play tennis until the king stepped down.
   c. decided that the National Assembly should meet once each year.
   d. said they would not stop meeting until they had written a constitution.

Modern Chapter **12**

The French Revolution

VOCABULARY Some terms to understand:

- **took action (512):** responded
- **looted (512):** robbed; stole
- **stormed (513):** rushed; violently attacked
- **abuses (513):** wrong or cruel treatment
- **paying down (514):** reducing the amount of
- **proceeds (514):** money from the sales of property
- **inexperienced (515):** having no experience or skill
- **deadlocked (515):** unable to reach an agreement

ORGANIZING INFORMATION Complete the chart about the events of the French Revolution by writing the following items in chronological order.

- Legislative Assembly meets for the first time.
- National Assembly creates the Declaration of the Rights of Man.
- France declares war on Austria in 1792.
- Constitution of 1791 is written.
- The people of Paris loot and destroy the Bastille prison.
- The office of king is suspended, and Louis XVI is put in prison.

Events of the French Revolution

1.

2.

3.

4.

5.

6.

Chapter 21, Main Idea Activities 21.2, continued

EVALUATING INFORMATION Mark each statement *T* if it is true or *F* if it is false.

_____ **1.** King Louis XVI ordered the people of Paris to destroy the Bastille.

_____ **2.** After the Bastille was destroyed, people were afraid the nobles would stop the Revolution so they attacked local manor houses throughout France.

_____ **3.** The National Assembly tried to stop violence by passing reforms.

_____ **4.** The Declaration of the Rights of Man and of the Citizen dealt with basic human rights and political powers.

_____ **5.** The nobles who left France stopped caring about what happened there.

_____ **6.** The leaders of the Revolution believed that the church did not need to be reformed.

_____ **7.** Louis XVI plotted with foreign powers to overthrow the constitution.

_____ **8.** The leaders of some European countries wanted to stop the Revolution in France.

REVIEWING FACTS Choose the correct items from the following list to complete the statements below.

conservatives	Civil Constitution of the Clergy	radicals
Great Fear	moderates	émigrés
departments	Olympe de Gouges	

1. The _____ swept across France as peasants attacked nobles and clergy.

2. _____ believed that women should have the same rights as men.

3. The _____ were nobles who left France during the Revolution.

4. The National Assembly divided France into 83 _____, or districts.

5. In the _____, the National Assembly said that people should elect their local church members.

6. The group known as _____ wanted to get rid of the king.

7. In the Legislative Assembly the _____ had no extreme views.

8. The _____ wanted a king with limited powers.

VOCABULARY Some terms to understand:

- **perish (519):** die
- **emigrated (519):** moved to another country
- **suppression (519):** stopping by force
- **luxurious (519):** the finest quality
- **universal (520):** for everyone
- **quell (520):** stop; put down
- **genius (521):** very great power, ability, or skill
- **morale (521):** enthusiasm, confidence, or loyalty of an individual or group

ORGANIZING INFORMATION Complete the chart below by using the following items.

- set up the Committee of Public Safety
- had five leaders who ran the government
- said that the crown of France was lying on the ground waiting to be picked up
- abolished slavery in France's colonies
- neither the radicals nor the conservatives liked this government
- seized power in a *coup d'état*

French Government		
National Convention	**The Directory**	**Napoléon**
• _____ _____ _____ • _____ _____ _____	• _____ _____ _____ • _____ _____ _____	• _____ _____ _____ • _____ _____ _____

Name _____ Class _____ Date _____

EVALUATING INFORMATION Mark each statement *T* if it is true or *F* if it is false.

_____ **1.** Under the National Convention every man in France could vote.

_____ **2.** When Louis XVI was executed, people in other countries did not care.

_____ **3.** During the Reign of Terror, the leaders of the Revolution killed anyone they thought did not support them.

_____ **4.** The National Convention was not able to make democratic reforms.

_____ **5.** The leaders of other European countries feared that the French would try to overthrow royalty outside France.

_____ **6.** Under the Directory, the wealthy once again controlled the government.

_____ **7.** Napoléon Bonaparte first became well known as a general in the army.

_____ **8.** Napoléon took power in a *coup d'état*, which meant that the people chose him in an election.

MATCHING Match the letter of each item in the second column with the number of the correct item in the first column.

_____ **1.** means that all men can vote in an election

_____ **2.** a powerful Jacobin who was executed by Robespierre

_____ **3.** the Reign of Terror ended when he died

_____ **4.** a doctor and Jacobin leader who was assassinated by Charlotte Corday

_____ **5.** a period during which many people were killed to suppress opposition to the Revolution

_____ **6.** unmarried men between 18 and 25 had to be in the military

_____ **7.** being against the Revolution

_____ **8.** a leader of French society who became Napoléon's wife

a. conscription
b. Maximilien Robespierre
c. Joséphine de Beauharnais
d. counterrevolutionary
e. George-Jacques Danton
f. Jean-Paul Marat
g. universal manhood suffrage
h. Reign of Terror

Main Idea Activities 21.4

Modern Chapter **12**

The Napoléonic Era

VOCABULARY Some terms to understand:

- **procedure (523):** way of doing something
- **established (524):** set up
- **deserted (524):** left
- **blockade (524):** blocking a place with force, often with ships; controlling what goes into or comes out of a place
- **coalition (525):** group that works together
- **annulled (526):** canceled
- **pension (527):** money to live on
- **resistance (527):** opposition; power against
- **disputes (527):** fights; arguments

ORGANIZING INFORMATION Complete the timeline by matching the following events with the dates on the timeline. Write the letter for each event on the line next to the correct date.

    A. Napoléon loses the Battle of Waterloo

    B. the Consulate is formed with Napoléon as First Consul

    C. Napoléon is beaten and the Bourbon monarchy is restored

    D. beginning of the Peninsular War

    E. Napoléon dies in exile on the island of St. Helena

    F. Napoléon's son, Napoléon II, is born

    G. Napoléon crowns himself emperor of the French Empire

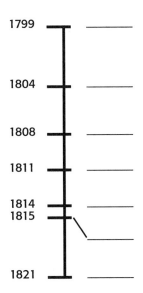

EVALUATING INFORMATION Mark each statement *T* if it is true or *F* if it is false.

_____ **1.** The people of France accepted Napoléon as dictator.

_____ **2.** Under the Consulate, the legislature could only approve or reject Napoléon's decisions.

_____ **3.** One of Napoléon's most lasting acts was to organize the laws of France.

_____ **4.** Napoléon was not interested in military actions outside of France.

_____ **5.** Napoléon's actions led to nationalism in many parts of Europe.

_____ **6.** The invasion of Russia by Napoléon was a complete success.

_____ **7.** After he was defeated, Napoléon accepted the rule of Louis XVIII.

_____ **8.** At the end of Napoléon's life he was Emperor of Elba.

UNDERSTANDING MAIN IDEAS For each of the following, write the letter of the best choice in the space provided.

_____ **1.** The Napoléonic Code
    a. organized French law into a system.
    b. explained how to win a battle.
    c. was Napoléon's writing about his life.
    d. was a handbook for how to act in the court of the emperor.

_____ **2.** In the Concordat, Napoléon was able to
    a. settle his differences with Britain.
    b. restore the monarchy to France but only with limited powers.
    c. agree with Russia that neither country would invade the other.
    d. end the conflict between France and the Roman Catholic Church.

_____ **3.** When Napoléon tried to defeat the British navy and invade Britain,
    a. he was able to create a lasting peace in Europe.
    b. he really was hoping to defeat Spain and Russia.
    c. the British fleet under Admiral Nelson defeated the French and Spanish.
    d. he was able to easily beat the navy but was not able to invade Britain.

_____ **4.** Napoléon's scorched-earth policy in Russia meant that the French
    a. burned or destroyed anything that the Russian army might use.
    b. were afraid that huge fires might break out during battles.
    c. allowed the Russians to retreat without bothering them.
    d. were able to capture Moscow and take over control of Russia.

Main Idea Activities 21.5

Modern Chapter 12

A Return to Peace

VOCABULARY Some terms to understand:

- **rebellions (529):** armed fight against a government or leader
- **principles (529):** basic beliefs
- **reshuffled (529):** moved around
- **boundaries (530):** borders
- **periodic (530):** from time to time
- **domestic (533):** within one's own country; not foreign
- **thwart (533):** stop; oppose
- **intervene (533):** become involved in

ORGANIZING INFORMATION Complete the chart by listing the following items as principles of reactionaries or liberals.

- ideas that came out during the American and French revolutions
- Holy Alliance
- individual rights were very important
- believed in absolutism
- supported freedom of speech and press
- said that former ruling families should be restored to their power

Reactionaries	Liberals
• _____	• _____
• _____	• _____
• _____	• _____

EVALUATING INFORMATION Mark each statement *T* if it is true or *F* if it is false.

_____ **1.** The Congress of Vienna met to restore order to Europe.

_____ **2.** Countries who suffered from Napoléon were paid back for their losses.

_____ **3.** After the Napoléonic Era, very few leaders wanted to return to the way things had been before the French Revolution.

_____ **4.** Conservative leaders in Europe liked the idea of nationalism.

_____ **5.** Most European rulers signed the Holy Alliance, which stated that they would rule as Christians.

_____ **6.** Prince Metternich was a strong supporter of liberal ideals.

_____ **7.** Metternich spied on revolutionary organizations and people.

_____ **8.** Great Britain was sympathetic to liberal movements because it had a representative form of government.

MATCHING Match the letters of the items in the second column with the correct items in the first column.

_____ **1.** meeting of hundreds of delegates to settle territorial questions

_____ **2.** all former rulers would be restored to their thrones

_____ **3.** French representative at Congress of Vienna who supported legitimacy

_____ **4.** payment by France for damages it had caused under Napoléon

_____ **5.** the four allies who had defeated Napoléon plus France

_____ **6.** form of international governance to maintain balance of power in Europe

_____ **7.** Austrian leader who was very conservative

_____ **8.** Greece won independence from Turkey in 1829

a. Charles-Maurice de Talleyrand-Périgord

b. indemnity

c. legitimacy

d. Prince Metternich

e. Concert of Europe

f. Congress of Vienna

g. Treaty of Adrianople

h. Quintuple Alliance

Main Idea Activities 22.1

Modern Chapter 13   **Origins of the Industrial Revolution**

VOCABULARY Some terms to understand:

• **tenant farmers (544):** farmers who live on and work land that someone else owns and to whom they pay a portion of their crops as rent

• **replaceable (544):** one that can be removed and another put in its place

• **manual (546):** done by hand

• **unintended (546):** not planned for

• **portable (547):** capable of being carried from place to place

• **forges (547):** special fireplaces used for heating metal to hammer into shapes

• **tariffs (550):** taxes on imports or exports

• **reaper (550):** machine that cuts grain or gathers crops

ORGANIZING INFORMATION Use the following items to complete the chart below.

• the *Clermont*
• steam engine
• water-powered loom

• replaceable plow blades
• steam locomotive
• cotton gin

• seed drill
• iron
• canals with locks

Agriculture	Manufacturing	Transportation

EVALUATING INFORMATION Mark each statement *T* if it is true or *F* if it is false.

_____ **1.** The enclosure movement meant that lands were fenced off into small plots.

_____ **2.** When farmers rotated crops they left fields unplowed so that the soil could rebuild its nutrients.

_____ **3.** Land, money, equipment, and labor are the main factors of production.

_____ **4.** No inventor could improve on the hand-powered loom.

Chapter 22, Main Idea Activities 22.1, continued

_____ **5.** Steel was important because inventors could use it to make machines that could withstand high steam pressure.

_____ **6.** The steam engine improved land transportation but had no effect on water transportation.

_____ **7.** The Bessemer process was a cheap way of producing gas for streetlights.

_____ **8.** The telegraph never became a practical communication device.

_____ **9.** Charles Goodyear's vulcanization process is the basis of today's rubber industry.

_____ **10.** Great Britain was the last of the major European countries to become industrialized.

REVIEWING FACTS Choose the correct items from the following list to complete the statements below.

tariffs	factory system	steam engine	
"Turnip" Townshend	farm workers	battery	
dots and dashes	water power	Great Britain	cotton gin

1. _____ introduced the system of crop rotation into England.

2. By the 1800s, many _____ had been forced off the land and moved to the cities where they became a large source of labor.

3. Richard Arkwright's spinning mill of the 1780s was the start of the modern

_____ .

4. Because of Eli Whitney's _____, the southern United States became the major cotton producing center of the world.

5. Drawbacks to using _____ were that it was not reliable and could not be moved from place to place.

6. Locomotives and steamboats were both powered by _____ .

7. Morse code was a system of _____ used to transmit the alphabet.

8. The Italian scientist Alessandro Volta made the first _____, which provided a steady source of electric power.

9. The country that led the Industrial Revolution was _____ .

10. France imposed _____ on foreign goods to protect its own industries.

Main Idea Activities 22.2

Modern Chapter **13**

The Factory System

VOCABULARY Some terms to understand:

• **drudgery (551):** hard, tiresome, or disagreeable work

• **apprentice (551):** person legally bound to an expert who teaches the person a trade

• **domestic (551):** home based

• **capital (551):** money, tools, machinery, equipment, and supplies

• **sanitary facilities (552):** washrooms and restrooms

• **shabby (552):** poor, run-down, neglected

• **fictitious (553):** made-up; not real

• **management (553):** the people who direct or control a business

• **economists (553):** experts in the science that studies how goods are made, sold, and used

ORGANIZING INFORMATION Use the following items to complete the chart below.

• employed women and children
• workers worked on complete products
• workers did only part of a job
• workers fined for being late
• workers decided when to work
• employed skilled workers

Factory System	Domestic System
	• workers were paid for items completed
• workers were paid for hours worked	

EVALUATING INFORMATION Mark each statement *T* if it is true or *F* if it is false.

_____ **1.** The factory system had no effect on how people worked or lived their lives.

_____ **2.** Early textile factories preferred to hire children and young women because they worked for lower wages than men.

_____ **3.** Factory owners wanted to produce goods as cheaply as possible.

_____ **4.** In the early days, textile factories lured women to work by offering higher wages than they would earn in more traditional jobs.

_____ **5.** Women were often paid the same wages as men, even when the woman was the only wage earner in the family.

_____ **6.** Child-labor laws were strictly enforced from the earliest days of industrialization.

_____ **7.** Workers' living conditions, especially in the tenements, were generally far safer and more healthful than working conditions in factories.

_____ **8.** The Industrial Revolution shifted the balance of power from manufacturing to agriculture.

_____ **9.** The middle class that arose as a result of the Industrial Revolution was based on wealth rather than on birth.

_____ **10.** Most workers felt that neither they nor their children could ever belong to the middle class.

UNDERSTANDING MAIN IDEAS For each of the following, write the letter of the best choice in the space provided.

_____ **1.** Older skilled workers often found themselves unemployed because
a. they needed different skills and training than they had.
b. machines often broke down.
c. unskilled workers worked for lower wages.
d. households did not need their wages.

_____ **2.** Unlike workers in the domestic system, factory workers
a. took pride in the quality of the products they made.
b. were often highly paid and well trained.
c. could set their own hours.
d. worked under close supervision.

_____ **3.** The working conditions in early factories can best be described as
a. safe.
b. primitive and dangerous.
c. similar to domestic working conditions.
d. shabby.

_____ **4.** Middle-class men and women
a. gained their social position by luck.
b. worked in factories in conditions of great hardship.
c. were not allowed to own property.
d. lived and dressed like the upper classes.

CHAPTER 22 — Main Idea Activities 22.3

Modern Chapter 13 **New Methods and Business Organizations**

VOCABULARY Some terms to understand:

- **industrialist (555):** person who owns or manages a large business or industry
- **conveyor belt (556):** mechanical device that carries items from one place to another
- **proprietorship (557):** ownership
- **stock (557):** ownership of a business divided into portions or shares
- **financier (557):** person skilled in managing large sums of money
- **concessions (557):** land or privileges given by a government to a business
- **decline (558):** loss of wealth or value
- **cascading (558):** flowing like a waterfall
- **economy (558):** system of managing how goods are produced, distributed, and consumed

ORGANIZING INFORMATION Use the following items to complete the chart below.

- assembly line
- United States Steel Company
- interchangeable parts for guns

Person	Accomplishment
Eli Whitney	
Henry Ford	
J. P. Morgan	

EVALUATING INFORMATION Mark each statement *T* if it is true or *F* if it is false.

_____ **1.** Under capitalism, the government owns the means of production.

_____ **2.** During the Industrial Revolution, manufacturers replaced merchants as leaders of business.

_____ **3.** Using machines had no effect at all on how much workers could produce.

_____ **4.** An advantage to using interchangeable parts in muskets was that the muskets could easily be repaired.

_____ **5.** Mass production means producing large numbers of identical items.

_____ **6.** A worker on an automobile assembly line was responsible for producing the entire car.

_____ **7.** Use of an assembly line was important in the growth of the Ford Motor Company.

_____ **8.** Corporations are generally larger than sole proprietorships and partnerships.

_____ **9.** A monopoly exists when many corporations equally share the production and sale of a particular good or service.

_____ **10.** More workers are needed when there is a high demand for goods, but fewer workers are needed when demand decreases.

UNDERSTANDING MAIN IDEAS For each of the following, write the letter of the best choice in the space provided.

_____ **1.** The division of labor in the manufacturing process meant that
  a. skilled workers remained more important than unskilled workers.
  b. profit was not important to success.
  c. each worker was given a single task to perform.
  d. the cost of making something increased.

_____ **2.** Mass production allowed manufacturers to
  a. charge the highest possible price for what they made.
  b. provide jobs for skilled workers.
  c. work inefficiently.
  d. lower costs and sell goods for less.

_____ **3.** A monopoly exists when
  a. a company's expenses go down.
  b. the stockholders in a corporation provide money to expand the business.
  c. one corporation has almost complete control of the production or sale of a single item.
  d. one corporation sells another corporation necessary services.

_____ **4.** The alternating periods of prosperity and decline that the Industrial Revolution caused is called
  a. the business cycle.
  b. a cartel.
  c. a depression.
  d. a partnership.

VOCABULARY Some terms to understand:

• **abode (559):** place to live

• **exerting himself (559):** making an effort; trying hard

• **advantageous (559):** favorable, beneficial

• **unrestricted (560):** not limited

• **obstacle (560):** something that stands in the way of or stops progress

• **inevitable (560):** certain to happen; unavoidable

• **determine (560):** be the deciding factor in or cause of something

• **dismal (560):** dark, gloomy

• **meddle (560):** interfere in other people's affairs

• **dues (563):** money paid by a member to a group

ORGANIZING INFORMATION Use the following items to complete the chart below.

• Adam Smith   • David Ricardo

• Thomas Malthus   • John Stuart Mill

Theory or Belief	Proponent
The iron law of wages	
A government should work for the good of all its citizens.	
The law of supply and demand and the law of competition	
The connection between poverty and population growth	

EVALUATING INFORMATION Mark each statement *T* if it is true or *F* if it is false.

_____ **1.** Adam Smith is considered the founder of modern economics.

_____ **2.** According to the law of supply and demand, people would pay more for an item if it was scarce.

_____ **3.** In the free-enterprise system, strict laws and regulations control what businesses may do and the profits they may make.

_____ **4.** Economics became known as the "dismal science" because early economists believed that workers would always be poor.

_____ **5.** According to the law of wages, wages go down when there are not enough workers for all the jobs.

_____ **6.** According to the laissez-faire system, government should not try to control what business does.

_____ **7.** Humanitarians believed that writers should not speak out against selfish business practices.

_____ **8.** Early reform laws attempted to control the practice of child labor.

_____ **9.** Early reform laws established a system of improved wages for all workers.

_____ **10.** Workers have always had the legally protected right to strike.

REVIEWING FACTS Choose the correct items from the following list to complete the statements below.

unions	John Stuart Mill	enforce
inevitable	leave things alone	supply and demand
laws	mercantilism	

1. The economic theory called _____ stated that the world had only a fixed amount of wealth.

2. According to the law of _____ people would be willing to pay a high price for a scarce item in great demand.

3. According to many early economists, low wages and poverty among workers was

_____ .

4. The term *laissez-faire* means "_____."

5. Reformers believed that _____ were needed to improve wages and working conditions.

6. An important reformer named _____ believed that government should work for the good of all its citizens.

7. Early reform laws were not effective because they lacked a way to

_____ them.

8. Workers' associations called _____ used money from dues to pay workers who went on strike.

CHAPTER 22 Main Idea Activities 22.5

Modern Chapter **13** **Socialism**

VOCABULARY Some terms to understand:

- **advocated (564):** publicly favored or supported
- **common good (565):** the good of all
- **environment (565):** surroundings, conditions
- **patrician and plebian (565):** aristocrat and member of the lower class
- **reconstitution (565):** a return to its original form
- **amass (566):** gather, acquire
- **authoritarian (566):** state- or government-controlled

ORGANIZING INFORMATION Use the following items to complete the diagram below.

- Government owns the means of production
- dictatorship of the proletariat
- redistribution of wealth
- The people own the means of production
- "From each according to his abilities; to each according to his needs."
- classless society
- private property allowed

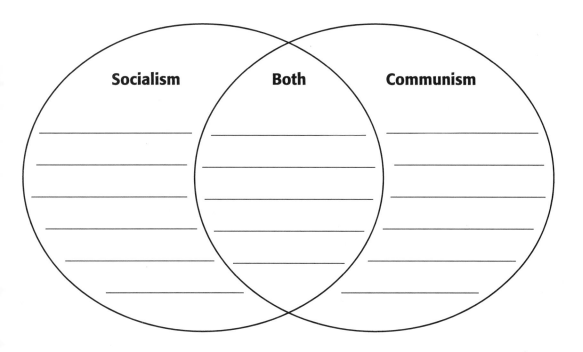

Chapter 22, Main Idea Activities 22.5, continued

EVALUATING INFORMATION Mark each statement *T* if it is true or *F* if it is false.

_____ **1.** Socialism arose because of what some saw as an unequal distribution of wealth in society.

_____ **2.** Utopian socialists believed that an armed struggle was needed to create a socialist society.

_____ **3.** The British reformer Robert Owen tried to establish socialist-style communities in the United States.

_____ **4.** Owen spent his personal money to build homes and schools for his workers and to improve their lives.

_____ **5.** Karl Marx believed that the entire capitalist system had to be destroyed.

_____ **6.** Marx believed that all wealth was created by workers, not by business owners.

_____ **7.** All socialists, even democratic socialists, believed that governments must be overthrown by revolution.

_____ **8.** Marx's Second International was torn apart by disagreements between radical and moderate elements within it.

UNDERSTANDING MAIN IDEAS For each of the following, write the letter of the best choice in the space provided.

_____ **1.** Socialists believed that laissez-faire capitalism was unfair because
　　a. it did not control populations.
　　b. it improved the lives of the wealthy.
　　c. the poor far outnumbered the rich.
　　d. businesses wanted to make profits.

_____ **2.** Utopian socialists believed that
　　a. everyone could work for the common good.
　　b. people had to be forced to help one another.
　　c. poverty could not be ended.
　　d. all governments had to be overthrown.

_____ **3.** Marx and Engels' form of socialism claimed that
　　a. socialism could not protect workers.
　　b. workers should become capitalists.
　　c. people and government should share power.
　　d. governments had to be overthrown by force.

CHAPTER **23**

Modern Chapter **14**

Main Idea Activities 23.1

Advances in Technology and Communication

VOCABULARY Some terms to understand:

- **curious (572):** strange, odd, unusual
- **electric current (573):** flow of electricity
- **illumination (573):** lighting
- **electrical circuit (573):** the complete path over which an electrical current flows
- **principles (575):** basic truths or beliefs

ORGANIZING INFORMATION Use the following items to complete the chart below.

- radio
- wireless telegraph
- telephone
- dams
- balloons
- lightbulb
- dynamo
- aerodynamics
- internal combustion engine

Electricity	Communications	Transportation

EVALUATING INFORMATION Mark each statement *T* if it is true or *F* if it is false.

_____ **1.** Scientific discoveries have little value or use in the business world.

_____ **2.** Electricity joined steam and water as an important source of power.

_____ **3.** A dynamo made it possible to generate electricity.

_____ **4.** The earliest lightbulbs glowed for months before they burned out.

_____ **5.** Using waterfalls was an unsuccessful way to generate electricity.

_____ **6.** Radio can send messages through the air without wires.

_____ **7.** Electromagnetic waves travel through space at the speed of sound.

Chapter 23, Main Idea Activities 23.1, continued

_____ **8.** Electromagnetic waves are invisible.

_____ **9.** Early electric motors were not practical for use in vehicles.

_____ **10.** Many inventors tried to make water-powered cars.

_____ **11.** The internal combustion engine uses gasoline as fuel.

_____ **12.** Heavier-than-air flight happened before lighter-than-air flight.

REVIEWING FACTS Choose the correct items from the following list to complete the statements below.

magnetism	hydroelectric	wires	fuel
ship-to-shore	Michael Faraday	Kitty Hawk	
electric current	outside	water power	

1. _____ discovered that electricity was not a fluid that passed through wires like pipes.

2. Scientists such as André Ampère studied the connection between electricity and

_____ .

3. A dynamo could be driven either by _____ or by magnetism.

4. A wire could be made to glow when an _____ was passed through it.

5. Electricity generated by water power is called _____ power.

6. Early telephones, unlike radio, needed _____ to send messages over.

7. Marconi's wireless was important because it permitted _____ and ship-to-ship communication.

8. In a steam engine, fuel is burned _____ the cylinder.

9. Internal combustion engines used oil or gasoline as _____ .

10. The first powered airplane flew at _____ .

Name _____ Class _____ Date _____

VOCABULARY Some terms to understand:

- **classical (576):** traditional; sound but not quite up-to-date

- **innovative (576):** bringing in new ways of doing things

- **organisms (576):** living bodies

- **adapted (577):** adjusted; made suitable

- **characteristics (577):** special qualities or features

- **controversial (577):** open to question; disputed; argued about

- **bacteria (578):** one-celled microscopic organisms

- **sanitary (579):** giving protection from dirt and filth

- **periodic table (580):** a chart that shows the chemical elements in related groups

- **diagnostic tool (581):** a tool used to identify a medical condition

ORGANIZING INFORMATION Use the following names to complete the chart below.

- Alexander Fleming
- Albert Einstein
- Wilhelm C. Röntgen
- Dmitry Mendeleyev
- Charles Darwin

- Rudolf Virchow
- Edward Jenner
- Schleiden and Swann
- Max Planck
- Robert Koch

- Gregor Mendel
- Pierre and Marie Curie
- Joseph Lister
- Louis Pasteur
- Jean-Baptiste Lamarck

Biology	Medicine	Physics and Chemistry

Chapter 23, Main Idea Activities 23.2, continued

EVALUATING INFORMATION Mark each statement *T* if it is true or *F* if it is false.

_____ **1.** Scientists have known for thousands of years that all living things are made up of tiny units of matter called cells.

_____ **2.** Organisms grow when cells divide and multiply.

_____ **3.** Lamarck's theory of inheritance has been proven true.

_____ **4.** Many people of the time believed that Darwin's theory of evolution was incorrect because it contradicted the Bible.

_____ **5.** Gregor Mendel proved that humans developed from animals.

_____ **6.** A vaccine made from cowpox protected people from smallpox.

_____ **7.** Antiseptics kept patients from dying from infections.

_____ **8.** The atom has been shown to be the smallest particle of matter.

UNDERSTANDING MAIN IDEAS For each of the following, write the letter of the best choice in the space provided.

_____ **1.** One of Pasteur's most important discoveries is that
  a. milk can ferment.
  b. plants pass down traits to their descendants.
  c. invisible bacteria cannot harm humans.
  d. germs cause sickness.

_____ **2.** Anesthetics such as ether
  a. make operations fatal.
  b. protect patients from germs.
  c. made longer operations possible.
  d. help maintain sanitary conditions in hospitals.

_____ **3.** Before Einstein, one of the most important discoveries in physics was that
  a. all matter is radioactive.
  b. even the nucleus of an atom is made up of smaller particles.
  c. x-rays have no scientific value.
  d. water never turns into a gas.

_____ **4.** One of Albert Einstein's important conclusions is that
  a. the three-dimensional universe has a fourth dimension—time.
  b. matter can never be transformed into energy.
  c. no one can accurately measure motion.
  d. matter can travel faster than light.

Name _____ Class _____ Date _____

 Main Idea Activities 23.3

Modern Chapter **14** **Social Sciences in the Industrial Age**

VOCABULARY Some terms to understand:

• **objective (583):** real, not just in one's mind

• **systematic (583):** orderly

• **excavation (584):** digging, unearthing

• **conditioned reflex (585):** behavior shaped by constant exposure to something

ORGANIZING INFORMATION Fill in the chart with the following items.

• study of human relationships

• study of past and present societies

• study of the mind and human behavior

• study of human culture through its artifacts

• cave paintings in France

• Pavlov, Freud

• Tylor, Frazer

• Spencer, Comte

ARCHAEOLOGY	ANTHROPOLOGY
• _____ • _____	• _____ • _____
SOCIOLOGY	PSYCHOLOGY
• _____ • _____	• _____ • _____

EVALUATING INFORMATION Mark each statement *T* if it is true or *F* if it is false.

_____ **1.** The social sciences study people as members of society.

_____ **2.** No one studied politics in a serious way until the 1900s.

_____ **3.** Social scientists refused to adopt the scientific manner of arranging and analyzing information.

_____ **4.** The study of history was changed by nationalism.

_____ **5.** Thanks to Voltaire, historians began to focus on the study of ordinary people.

_____ **6.** *Kultur* is the set of beliefs and behaviors that society shares.

_____ **7.** Anthropologists are not interested in comparing the customs of different cultures.

_____ **8.** Social Darwinism tries to explain why some societies succeed and others fail.

_____ **9.** Pavlov studied reflex actions.

_____ **10.** According to Freud, people are fully aware of their unconscious fears and desires.

UNDERSTANDING MAIN IDEAS For each of the following, write the letter of the best choice in the space provided.

_____ **1.** During the Industrial Age, the social sciences became more
  a. scientific.
  b. involved with the needs of the upper classes.
  c. subjective and opinion-based.
  d. separated from reality.

_____ **2.** Frazer's book *The Golden Bough* was important because it
  a. explained how governments work.
  b. advocated a cure for poverty.
  c. described the family tree of humanity.
  d. tried to show that different societies are similar.

_____ **3.** Social Darwinism lost its influence because it was seen as
  a. correct.
  b. not based on psychology.
  c. too simplistic.
  d. too nationalistic.

_____ **4.** Ivan Pavlov is best known for his study of
  a. unconscious fears and desires.
  b. conditioned reflexes.
  c. ancient Egypt.
  d. mental illness.

 **CHAPTER 23**   Main Idea Activities 23.4

Modern Chapter **14**   **Society and Culture in the Industrial Age**

VOCABULARY Some terms to understand:

- **rural (587):** in the countryside
- **residential (588):** area occupied by homes
- **outskirts (588):** outer parts or edges
- **vocational (589):** job related
- **regulate (590):** control
- **civic (590):** involving the general public

ORGANIZING INFORMATION Write the letter of each item where it belongs in the diagram below.

A. immigrants fleeing poverty   **D.** population shift from rural areas

B. decline in jobs on farms   **E.** immigrants fleeing oppression

C. factories located there   **F.** improvements in sanitation

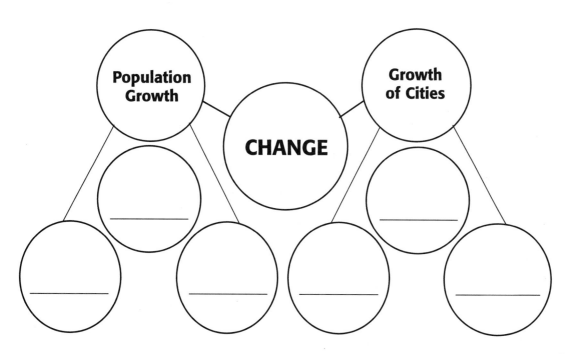

EVALUATING INFORMATION Mark each statement *T* if it is true or *F* if it is false.

_____ **1.** One of the greatest mass movements of people in history took place between 1870 and 1900.

_____ **2.** From 1870 to 1900, most immigrants moved from the United States to cities in Europe.

Chapter 23, Main Idea Activities 23.4, continued

_____ **3.** The increase in the number of factories had no effect on the demand for labor.

_____ **4.** Before the Industrial Revolution, most people in Europe and the United States lived in cities.

_____ **5.** Until 1900, most cities lacked sewers.

_____ **6.** Sir Robert Peel organized London's first permanent police force.

_____ **7.** The first people to move to the suburbs were the working class.

_____ **8.** One reason behind the growth of a free public school system was that industry needed workers who could read and write.

_____ **9.** Professional sports teams were organized when people had leisure time to attend games.

_____ **10.** The Louvre Museum in Paris was once a palace of the French kings.

REVIEWING FACTS Choose the correct items from the following list to complete the statements below.

life expectancy	public transportation	newspapers	public parks
lower class	sewers	refrigerated	Jane Addams

1. Until the late 1800s most cities did not have _____ or a system for waste disposal.

2. _____ founded a community service center for immigrants called Hull House.

3. _____ railroad cars made it possible to ship food safely.

4. The improvement of _____ helped people move faster from home in the suburbs to work.

5. Improvements in medicine and nutrition increased _____.

6. Generally, children from the _____ attended school only as long as the law required them to.

7. Writing became a full-time job because of the increase in the number of

_____.

8. By 1900, city governments had begun to set aside land inside the city for use as

_____.

CHAPTER 23

Modern Chapter **14**

Main Idea Activities 23.5

Literature, Music, and Art in the Industrial Age

VOCABULARY Some terms to understand:

• **instinct (592):** unlearned natural tendencies

• **inspirations (593):** ideas or feelings that brought about something

• **surge (593):** rise or swell up

• **lyric (593):** full of feelings or emotions

• **vitality (594):** strength, vigor, energy

• **impact (594):** forceful or dramatic effect

• **Victorian (596):** during the reign of Great Britain's Queen Victoria (1837–1901)

• **frankness (596):** open expression of ideas, with nothing held back

ORGANIZING INFORMATION Complete the diagram by writing the letter of the correct answer where it belongs.

A. *Legend of Sleepy Hollow* (Washington Irving)

B. Keats

C. *Faust*

D. Tchaikovsky, Verdi

E. Grimm Brothers's fairy tales

F. Beethoven, Schubert

G. Byron

H. *Ivanhoe*

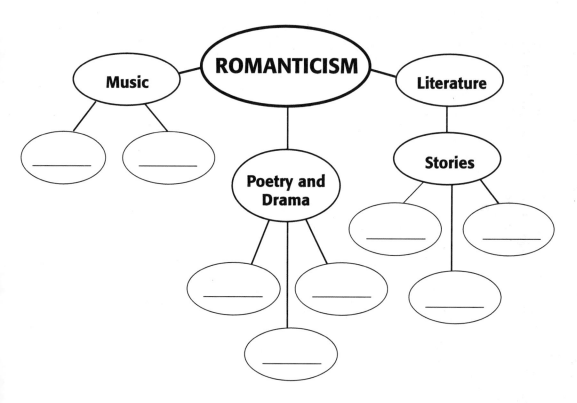

Chapter 23, Main Idea Activities 23.5, continued

EVALUATING INFORMATION Mark each statement *T* if it is true or *F* if it is false.

_____ **1.** The romantic writers and poets value emotion over reason.

_____ **2.** Writers such as Sir Walter Scott depicted the days of knighthood in all their gloomy misery.

_____ **3.** The music of the German composer Ludwig van Beethoven expressed many of the ideals of romanticism.

_____ **4.** The romantic movement produced many writers but almost no musicians.

_____ **5.** Two musicians whose music inspired feelings of nationalism are Giuseppe Verdi and Richard Wagner.

_____ **6.** The Gothic revival in architecture was an attempt to create a futuristic style.

_____ **7.** The daguerreotype is an early type of photograph introduced in 1839.

_____ **8.** The photographs of Jacob Riis attempted to romanticize the lives of the poor.

UNDERSTANDING MAIN IDEAS For each of the following, write the letter of the best choice in the space provided.

_____ **1.** Romantic writers and painters
    a. were dismissed by most critics as childish.
    b. wrote or painted about city life.
    c. appealed to reason rather than emotion.
    d. often chose topics from the past.

_____ **2.** Photography helped give rise to realism because
    a. photographs captured things as they really were.
    b. the photographers glorified war and poverty.
    c. photographers hated the outdoors.
    d. photography had no impact on modern society.

_____ **3.** An important difference between realism and romanticism is that
    a. realism was even more emotional than romanticism.
    b. realism dealt with the future, when all would be perfect.
    c. realism dealt with the lives of ordinary people.
    d. realism avoided depicting human misery.

_____ **4.** Naturalist writers such as Zola and Dickens
    a. preferred to write about distant places.
    b. wrote about social problems to bring about reform.
    c. used language that sugarcoated social problems.
    d. saw themselves as romantics rather than realists.

 **CHAPTER 24**   Main Idea Activities 24.1

Modern Chapter **15**   **Liberal Reforms in Great Britain and Its Empire**

VOCABULARY Some terms to understand:

- **intolerable (602):** unbearable, too much to endure
- **abolition (602):** formal elimination
- **intimidated (602):** made afraid, frightened
- **emancipation (602):** release from slavery or restraint
- **bribery (604):** giving or offering money to do something
- **fungus (604):** a disease-causing organism that makes plants wither and die
- **frustrated (605):** kept from accomplishing anything
- **disruptive (606):** rebellious, unruly
- **gridlock (607):** a state in which nothing moves

ORGANIZING INFORMATION Use the following items to complete the Venn diagram below.

- People with less property can vote.
- Only Anglicans hold office.
- Catholics, Jews, and non-Anglicans can vote.
- No secret ballot.
- Only property owners vote.
- Only males vote.

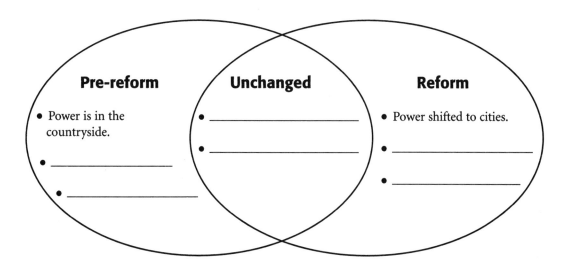

EVALUATING INFORMATION Mark each statement *T* if it is true or *F* if it is false.

_____ **1.** The philosophy of liberalism protected the rights of the large landowners.

_____ **2.** Only men of wealth and property could vote or hold office before voting reform occurred.

_____ **3.** Thanks to voting reform, the middle class had a real voice in Parliament.

_____ **4.** The Corn Laws allowed workers to buy food at artificially low prices.

_____ **5.** The Chartist movement got its name from a document called the People's Charter.

_____ **6.** None of the political reforms urged by the Chartist movement ever became law, and the movement fell apart.

_____ **7.** Under Disraeli as prime minister, the British Empire lost territory.

_____ **8.** Home rule was only one of the many issues that England and Ireland disagreed about while Gladstone was prime minister.

_____ **9.** The potato famine forced only a few Irish to emigrate to the United States.

_____ **10.** The Parliament Act of 1911 put full control over taxes and spending into the hands of the House of Commons.

REVIEWING FACTS Choose the correct items from the following list to complete the statements below.

aborigines	convicts	suffragettes
Emmeline Pankhurst	Canadian Pacific Railroad	self-government
New Zealand	secret ballot	

1. A _____ helps keep voters from being pressured or bribed.

2. _____ was an important advocate for women's voting rights.

3. Women who campaigned for the right to vote were called

_____ .

4. One factor that kept Canada in the British empire was Lord Durham's insistence on

_____ for Canada.

5. The _____ opened western Canada to immigration.

6. The first people whom Great Britain sent to live in Australia were

_____ .

7. The _____ of Australia suffered from racial discrimination and European diseases.

8. In 1893, _____ became the first country in the world to give women the right to vote.

Name _____ Class _____ Date _____

Modern Chapter **15**   **Expansion and Reform in the United States**

VOCABULARY Some terms to understand:

- **ordinance (609):** regulation, law
- **reservations (611):** land set aside by the government for the native peoples
- **emerged (611):** came forth
- **bitterness (611):** annoyance, resentment
- **ease (611):** make easier
- **restrictions (614):** limitations
- **conventions (614):** formal meetings for political purposes
- **ratification (614):** formal approval

ORGANIZING INFORMATION Use the following items to complete the time line below.

- Louisiana Purchase
- Florida Cession
- Gadsden Purchase
- Annexation of Hawaii
- Texas Annexation
- Northwest Territory
- Oregon Country
- Alaska Purchase

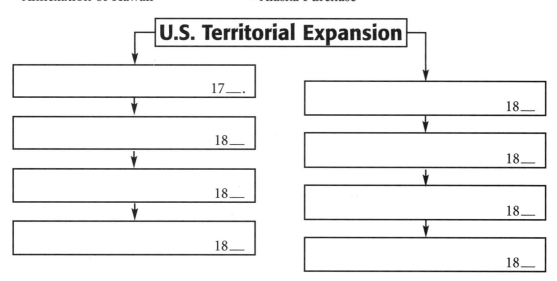

U.S. Territorial Expansion

| 17___. |
| 18___ |
| 18___ |
| 18___ |

| 18___ |
| 18___ |
| 18___ |
| 18___ |

EVALUATING INFORMATION Mark each statement *T* if it is true or *F* if it is false.

_____ **1.** By 1900, the United States had grown to almost four times its original size.

_____ **2.** Settlers in other parts of the United States did not enjoy the same rights as the people from the original thirteen colonies.

_____ **3.** A territory could become a state when its population reached 5,000 men, women, and children.

_____ **4.** The vast Louisiana Territory was once the property of Spain.

_____ **5.** The United States captured Texas from France.

_____ **6.** Arguments about abolishing slavery divided the northern and the southern states.

_____ **7.** President Abraham Lincoln vowed to stop the spread of slavery in territories that were not yet part of the United States.

_____ **8.** The Confederate States won the Civil War.

_____ **9.** Despite amendments to the Constitution, former slaves' rights were not always protected.

_____ **10.** The second wave of immigrants to the United States came from southern or eastern Europe.

UNDERSTANDING MAIN IDEAS For each of the following, write the letter of the best choice in the space provided.

_____ **1.** As the United States expanded westward in the 1800s,
  a. the country became more involved in the affairs of Europe.
  b. gold was found in every part of the United States.
  c. Native American people were pushed off their land.
  d. the United States conquered Canada in war.

_____ **2.** During the Civil War, the military leaders on both sides employed a strategy of
  a. total war.
  b. limited war.
  c. terrorism.
  d. sectionalism.

_____ **3.** Immigrants came to the United States to seek economic opportunities and to
  a. fight a war with Mexico.
  b. run away from their families.
  c. find work aboard ships.
  d. escape religious or political persecution.

_____ **4.** Elizabeth Cady Stanton and Lucretia Mott
  a. served as nurses during the Civil War.
  b. immigrated to the United States when they were very young.
  c. campaigned to win for women the right to vote.
  d. owned the railroads that carried immigrants west.

VOCABULARY Some terms to understand:

- **costly (615):** expensive in terms of lives, money, and resources
- **absolute (615):** having unrestricted power
- **instance (616):** example
- *coup d'état* **(617):** sudden change in government, often by force
- **censored (617):** kept from speaking openly and freely
- **mounting (618):** growing, increasing
- **goad (618):** prod, urge on
- **siege (618):** encircling a place with an army to capture it
- **decentralized (619):** spread out among local groups

ORGANIZING INFORMATION Use the following items to complete the chart below.

- Elected by the people
- Restricted free speech
- "Citizen King"
- Abdicated the throne
- Forced France to create a new constitution
- Replaced by the Second Republic
- Later elected and ruled as Emperor Napoléon III
- Staged a coup d'état

Louis Philippe	Louis-Napoléon

EVALUATING INFORMATION Mark each statement *T* if it is true or *F* if it is false.

_____ **1.** Louis XVIII was a constitutional monarch, but his successor, Charles X, was an absolute monarch.

_____ **2.** Under Louis Philippe, French workers and peasants held most of the power.

_____ **3.** The Revolution of 1848 forced Louis Philippe from power.

Chapter 24, Main Idea Activities 24.3, continued

_____ **4.** The constitution of the Second Republic allowed Louis-Napoléon to serve only one four-year term.

_____ **5.** Louis-Napoléon made use of his famous name and his promise to restore order to seize control of France.

_____ **6.** In the Crimean War, France fought Great Britain, Russia, and the Ottoman Empire.

_____ **7.** Napoléon III's attempt to control Mexico failed when the Mexicans overthrew and executed Archduke Maximilian in 1867.

_____ **8.** France was the victor in the Franco-Prussian war of 1870–1871.

_____ **9.** The Communards were attacked and defeated by their own government's soldiers in street-to-street fighting.

_____ **10.** After the Franco-Prussian War, France once again became a monarchy.

UNDERSTANDING MAIN IDEAS For each of the following, write the letter of the best choice in the space provided.

_____ **1.** One of Louis-Napoléon's goals was to
   a. restore the power of the National Assembly.
   b. improve life for workers and peasants.
   c. restore the empire and rule as Napoléon III.
   d. protect freedom of speech.

_____ **2.** Otto von Bismarck of Prussia used the Franco-Prussian War to
   a. win a place for Germany in the Crimea.
   b. help him unite the German states into a single country.
   c. create field hospitals for his troops.
   d. put Napoléon III on the throne of France.

_____ **3.** One of the results of the Franco-Prussian War was that
   a. Germany surrendered territory to France.
   b. the Communards surrendered to the Prussians.
   c. socialist reforms were allowed to occur.
   d. German troops occupied France.

_____ **4.** The Dreyfus scandal created tensions in France because
   a. the Panama Canal project failed.
   b. radical socialists threatened to revolt.
   c. an innocent military officer was wrongly imprisoned for treason.
   d. the French army was weak and lacked support.

CHAPTER (24)

Modern Chapter **15**

Main Idea Activities 24.4
Latin Americans Win Independence

VOCABULARY Some terms to understand:

- **conquistadors (621):** descendants of the Spanish conquerors
- **sea dogs (621):** veteran sailors
- **barriers (622):** obstacles to progress
- **exploit (622):** make unfair or selfish use of
- **Jesuits (622):** Roman Catholic order of priests
- **secluded (622):** kept apart
- **chaperoned (622):** watched over in public by an older person
- **outright (624):** open, without restraint
- **dispersed (624):** scattered
- **denounced (625):** publicly condemned
- **promote (626):** help to establish

ORGANIZING INFORMATION Match the name of the revolutionary leader with the country he is most closely associated with.

- Mexico   • Haiti   • Chile   • Peru   • Gran Colombia

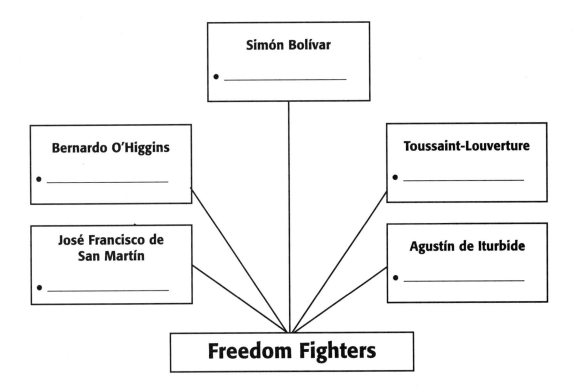

EVALUATING INFORMATION Mark each statement *T* if it is true or *F* if it is false.

_____ **1.** Spain and Portugal used their colonies in Latin America as sources of wealth for the mother country.

_____ **2.** The Spanish and the Portuguese imported slaves from Africa to replace the Indians who were wiped out by European diseases.

_____ **3.** The rights of the non-Europeans in colonial Latin America were carefully protected by law.

_____ **4.** Simón Bolívar was a member of the lower class who became an important general and liberator in South America.

_____ **5.** Charles III angered colonists because he forced them to pay heavy taxes to support Spain's wars in Europe.

_____ **6.** The first successful colonial revolt against the mother country took place in Chile.

_____ **7.** The states of Latin America never had the opportunity to unite as a single country.

_____ **8.** By 1825, almost all of South America was free from colonial rule.

REVIEWING FACTS Choose the correct items from the following list to complete the statements below.

Gran Colombia	*caudillos*	Monroe Doctrine
Haiti	creoles	slavery

1. In 1804, _____ became the first independent country in Latin America.

2. The independence movements of Hidalgo and Morelos favored the lower-class peasants against the upper-class Mexican _____.

3. The present-day countries of Colombia, Venezuela, Ecuador, and Panama were once part of a single country called _____.

4. According to the _____ of 1823, the United States would oppose the attempt of any European country to take back a former colony.

5. By 1888, _____ was abolished throughout Latin America.

6. Military leaders called _____ ruled as dictators and gave the people stability but not freedom.

CHAPTER **25** | Main Idea Activities 25.1

Modern Chapter **16** | **The Unification of Italy**

VOCABULARY Some terms to understand:

- **reactionary (632):** preferring to return to an earlier, usually more conservative, time
- **clerical (632):** referring to members of the clergy
- **dominate (633):** control; rule by strength or power
- **annexed (633):** added to a larger or more important thing
- **armistice (633):** temporary peace, agreement to stop fighting
- **overwhelmingly (636):** to an overpowering degree

ORGANIZING INFORMATION Complete the diagram by writing the letter of each item where it belongs.

A. "Red Shirts" army

B. Ruler of Sardinia

C. A republic government for Italy

D. Alliance with France against Austria

E. Secret meeting with Napoléon III

F. Young Italy movement

G. "Expedition of the Thousand"

H. Victor Emmanuel's chief minister

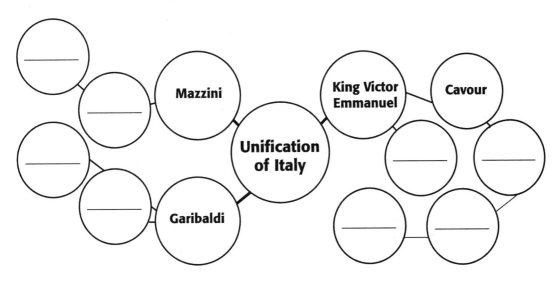

EVALUATING INFORMATION Mark each statement *T* if it is true or *F* if it is false.

_____ **1.** The Italian nationalist movement became known as *risorgimento*.

_____ **2.** The Carbonari was a secret society that advocated unification.

_____ **3.** The only kingdom in Italy that ever remained a completely independent state was Lombardy.

_____ **4.** One of the important aims of the unification movement was to lessen the influence of the church.

_____ **5.** Cavour's intention was to unify and industrialize Italy, starting with Sardinia.

_____ **6.** Napoléon III and Cavour successfully tricked Austria into going to war with Sardinia.

_____ **7.** After Napoléon III signed an armistice with Austria, the Italian states put under Austrian control rebelled against Austria.

_____ **8.** Garibaldi invaded the kingdom of the Two Sicilies to start a country of his own.

_____ **9.** Plebiscites all over Italy found little support for unification.

_____ **10.** Italy was eventually unified, with Garibaldi as its king.

REVIEWING FACTS Choose the correct items from the following list to complete the statements below.

| liberals | Austria | Garibaldi | Italy |
| Cavour | Rome | French Revolution | neither pope nor king |

1. The unification of Italy was inspired by the ideals of the

_____.

2. Mazzini believed that "_____" should rule Italy.

3. Italian _____ and nationalists both believed in the goals of national unity.

4. The person who actually governed the kingdom of Sardinia was not the king, Victor Emmanuel II, but _____.

5. The country that most stood in the way of Italian unification was

_____.

6. Napoléon III sided with Cavour because he felt that he could dominate a united

_____.

7. Cavour feared that _____ might turn Italy into a republic with himself as its leader.

8. _____ became the capital of the united Italy.

Main Idea Activities 25.2

Modern Chapter **16**

The Unification of Germany

VOCABULARY Some terms to understand:

- **patchwork (637):** a miscellaneous collection, a jumble
- **reserves (637):** soldiers not on active duty but ready when needed
- **standing army (637):** a permanent army
- **nationalism (638):** desire and plans for national independence
- **uniform (638):** all alike
- **cabinet (639):** group of advisors
- **confederation (639):** a group of countries joined together for a special purpose
- **duchies (639):** territories ruled by a duke or duchess
- **indemnity (640):** money demanded at the end of a war as a condition of peace

ORGANIZING INFORMATION Use the following items to complete the chart below.

- Prussian troops forced to fight for the French
- Helps defeat the French at Leipzig in 1813
- Bismarck unites Germany under Prussia in 1871
- French seize Prussian territory
- Helps defeat the French at Waterloo in 1815
- Conquered by Napoléon I in 1806

THE RISE OF PRUSSIA	
From Defeat	**To Victory**

EVALUATING INFORMATION Mark each statement *T* if it is true or *F* if it is false.

_____ **1.** Prussia was one of the four great powers at the Congress of Vienna in 1815.

_____ **2.** After the French defeat at Waterloo, Prussia's main rival was Austria.

_____ **3.** The Zollverein kept taxes artificially high to encourage competition between the German states.

Chapter 25, Main Idea Activities 25.2, continued

_____ **4.** Despite liberal reforms in France after 1848, the government of Prussia remained absolutist.

_____ **5.** One of Otto von Bismarck's first accomplishments in Prussia was to increase the strength of the army.

_____ **6.** Prussia and Austria combined forces to defeat Denmark and win the states of Schleswig and Holstein.

_____ **7.** A seven-year-long war between Prussia and Austria in the 1860s ended with the ultimate victory of Prussia.

_____ **8.** As a result of the Treaty of Prague in 1866, the king of Prussia became the absolute ruler of the German states.

_____ **9.** King William of Prussia intentionally provoked France to declare war on Prussia in 1870.

_____ **10.** The German emperor was known as the *kaiser.*

UNDERSTANDING MAIN IDEAS For each of the following, write the letter of the best choice in the space provided.

_____ **1.** Before the rise of Prussia, Germany was
   a. a united country.
   b. a province of France.
   c. the dominant power in Europe.
   d. a collection of independent states.

_____ **2.** The kind of government that Otto von Bismarck favored was
   a. liberal and democratic.
   b. dominated by France.
   c. autocratic.
   d. based on the equality of all the German states.

_____ **3.** The German empire, founded in 1871, was
   a. dominated by Prussia, whose king was also the emperor.
   b. dominated by the Austrians.
   c. weak and powerless in the face of stronger enemies, especially France.
   d. democratic.

 **CHAPTER 25**

Modern Chapter **16**

Main Idea Activities 25.3

Opposition to Bismarck

VOCABULARY Some terms to understand:

- **compromise (643):** give up part of what is demanded
- **confiscated (643):** seized for the public treasury
- **restrictive (645):** limiting
- **tactics (645):** methods for gaining success
- **grievances (645):** wrongs

ORGANIZING INFORMATION Select the five items from the choices below that complete the diagram correctly. Write the letters of the items inside the ovals.

A. Promoted atheism

B. Caused by strained relations with Italy

C. Broke relations with the Vatican

D. Laws controlled Catholic clergy and schools

E. Ended in failure

F. Socialist dominated

G. Church property confiscated

H. Anti-Catholic

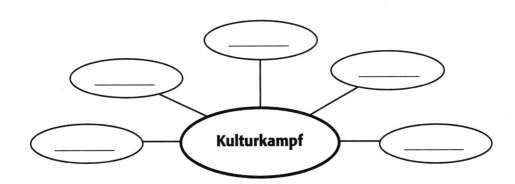

EVALUATING INFORMATION Mark each statement *T* if it is true or *F* if it is false.

_____ **1.** In the Prussian legislature of the 1870s, political power was in the hands of the conservative upper class.

_____ **2.** The Kulturkampf ended when Bismarck realized that he needed the support of the socialists.

_____ **3.** Industrialization happened earlier in Germany than in Great Britain.

_____ **4.** One way that Bismarck helped German industries was to standardize the way banking and postal services were handled.

_____ **5.** Germany used high tariffs to protect its industries from foreign competition.

_____ **6.** German workers were paid artificially high wages to keep socialism from spreading.

_____ **7.** In 1877, the Social Democratic Party won a majority of the seats in the Reichstag and the Bundesrat.

_____ **8.** When the emperor's life was threatened, Bismarck took it as a chance to dissolve the Reichstag.

_____ **9.** The would-be assassins who threatened the emperor were lifelong socialists.

_____ **10.** Bismarck resigned from his office at the death of William I.

UNDERSTANDING MAIN IDEAS For each of the following, write the letter of the best choice in the space provided.

_____ **1.** One reason why Bismarck began the Kulturkampf was that
   a. he was a socialist and did not trust nationalists.
   b. he believed that Italy was planning to go to war with Germany.
   c. he was a Protestant and did not trust Catholics.
   d. he thought it was the best way to begin the process of industrialization.

_____ **2.** Because its industrialization happened much later than that of France or Great Britain, Germany
   a. had time to plan.
   b. had no need to borrow resources.
   c. could take advantage of the latest advances.
   d. could improve on machinery made elsewhere.

_____ **3.** Bismarck decided to adopt many of the social changes that the socialists advocated because
   a. he believed deeply in workers' rights.
   b. that way he could take away people's reasons for supporting socialism.
   c. he learned that governments do not have as much power as they think.
   d. he was secretly a socialist.

_____ **4.** Bismarck became an obstacle to the new emperor, William II, because
   a. William believed in the absolute authority of the emperor.
   b. William believed in democratic reforms.
   c. William was weak and wanted no one stronger in charge.
   d. Bismarck refused to increase the size of the army.

 **CHAPTER 25**   Main Idea Activities 25.4

Modern Chapter **16**   **Reform and Revolution in Russia**

VOCABULARY Some terms to understand:

• **extensive (647):** large, vast

• **autocracy (648):** state of absolute rule

• **obstructed (649):** blocked

• **tracts (649):** areas or parcels of land

• **levy (649):** assess, charge

• **radical (650):** favoring extreme changes or reforms

• **intervene (651):** step in

ORGANIZING INFORMATION Select the five items from the choices below that complete the diagram correctly. Write the letters of the items inside the ovals.

A. Power of secret police curtailed

B. Rural areas allowed to elect their own governments

C. The Orthodox Church denounced

D. Court system reformed

E. More freedom of the press

F. Dominated by socialists

G. Serfs freed

H. Upper class persecuted

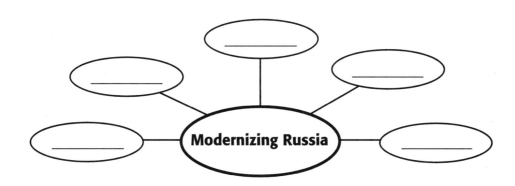

EVALUATING INFORMATION Mark each statement *T* if it is true or *F* if it is false.

_____ **1.** In the mid-1800s, the European country with the largest territory and population was Russia.

_____ **2.** The Russian Empire consisted of people from a single ethnic group.

_____ **3.** An autocrat is a ruler whose powers are set and limited by law.

_____ **4.** Russia struggled with the influence of the West because from the West came the winds of nationalism and liberalism.

_____ **5.** Czar Nicholas's program of Russification meant sending vast armies to conquer neighboring countries.

_____ **6.** Pan-Slavism promoted the union of all Slavic peoples under Russia's leadership.

_____ **7.** During the Crimean War of the 1850s, Russia expanded its territory considerably with lands from the Ottoman Empire.

_____ **8.** Despite a few differences, serfdom closely resembles slavery.

_____ **9.** The serfs were freed because Russian factories needed workers.

_____ **10.** *Zemstvos* were part of a new system of local government that began after 1864.

REVIEWING FACTS Choose the correct items from the following list to complete the statements below.

terrorism	repression	Duma
Revolution of 1905	poverty	Emancipation Edict
nobles	Nihilists	

1. The _____ of 1861 freed the Russian serfs.

2. Despite having their freedom, the serfs still lived in conditions of great

_____ .

3. Despite the reforms that new systems of local governments promoted, most of the

power remained in the hands of the _____ and the rich.

4. The _____ believed that Russia could be reformed only by throwing out the old system entirely and beginning anew.

5. The radical movement called People's Will used _____ to accomplish its aims.

6. After Alexander II was assassinated, his successors instituted programs of

_____ to stamp out liberalism.

7. The _____ began when soldiers shot a group of unarmed strikers.

8. The Russian parliament of the period is called the _____ .

 **CHAPTER 25**

Modern Chapter **16**

Main Idea Activities 25.5

Unrest in Austria-Hungary

VOCABULARY Some terms to understand:

• **obscurity (653):** remoteness, uncertainty

• **general (653):** widespread

• **nomadic (653):** wandering from place to place

• **abdication (654):** resignation, stepping down from power

• **strategically (655):** in a useful position for military purposes

ORGANIZING INFORMATION Use the following items to complete the Venn diagram below.

• Parliament in Budapest

• Francis Joseph I

• Strongly industrial

• A market for manufactured products

• Three ministries for empire's affairs

• A market for farm products

• Mostly agricultural

• Parliament in Vienna

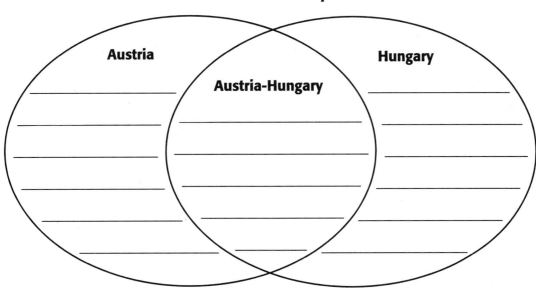

Dual Monarchy

Austria

Austria-Hungary

Hungary

EVALUATING INFORMATION Mark each statement *T* if it is true or *F* if it is false.

_____ **1.** The Magyars are descendants of nomadic warriors from Russia and Romania.

_____ **2.** Russia helped put down a revolt in Hungary in 1848 because the Czar feared that revolution could spread to Russia if it were not stopped.

_____ **3.** The Dual Monarchy was another name for Austria-Hungary.

_____ **4.** The Balkans are strategically located where Europe and North America meet.

_____ **5.** In the Balkans, Russia supported Balkan nationalists because they were fellow Slavs and Orthodox Christians.

_____ **6.** Great Britain supported the Russians in the Balkans as a way to control the Ottoman Empire.

_____ **7.** The Treaty of San Stefano of 1878 ended a war between Russia and the Ottoman Empire.

_____ **8.** Bulgaria, Serbia, Greece, and Montenegro were known together as the Balkan League.

UNDERSTANDING MAIN IDEAS For each of the following, write the letter of the best choice in the space provided.

_____ **1.** Prince Metternich of Austria claimed, "When France sneezes,
  a. the world sneezes."
  b. Austria turns away."
  c. all Europe catches cold."
  d. Russia covers its face."

_____ **2.** A typical representative of the nationalist movement spreading through Europe was
  a. Prince Metternich of Austria.
  b. Emperor Francis Joseph I of Austria-Hungary.
  c. Czar Nicholas I of Russia.
  d. the Hungarian patriot Lajos Kossuth.

_____ **3.** Austria-Hungary was formed
  a. to resolve Hungary's demands for independence.
  b. to counterbalance Germany.
  c. only as a practical economic relationship.
  d. to fight the Ottoman Empire.

_____ **4.** The Balkans underwent a period of unrest for every reason below except for
  a. the rise of nationalist movements in Greece, Serbia, and other countries.
  b. Turkish attempts to suppress nationalism.
  c. the decline of the Ottoman Empire.
  d. political intrigue on the part of the French.

CHAPTER 26

Modern Chapter **17**

Main Idea Activities 26.1

The Roots of Western Imperialism

VOCABULARY Some terms to understand:

• **spurred (663):** encouraged

• **raw materials (663):** materials before they are processed or prepared

• **exclusive (664):** not divided or shared with others

• **phenomenon (664):** event that can be observed

• **imposing (665):** forcing onto another

• **hygiene (665):** science of maintaining health

ORGANIZING INFORMATION Use the following items to complete the web below.

• Settlement colonies   • Protectorates

• Need for raw materials   • "The White Man's Burden"

• Dependent colonies   • Establish new markets

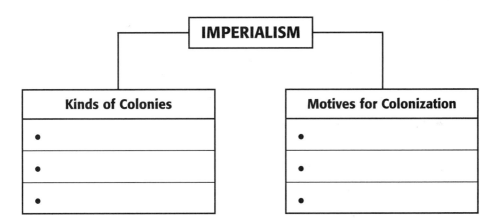

EVALUATING INFORMATION Mark each statement *T* if it is true or *F* if it is false.

_____ **1.** From the very start, the European nations planned to create empires.

_____ **2.** Merchants and explorers from Europe were always welcomed in foreign lands.

_____ **3.** Europeans developed foreign lands, but only for their own benefit.

_____ **4.** In a dependent colony, large groups of European settlers went to live in a new place.

_____ **5.** In a protectorate, Europeans controlled the policies of a local ruler.

_____ **6.** Colonies were sometimes a source of soldiers to serve in European armies.

_____ **7.** Islands were important colonies because they became refueling stations for a country's ships.

_____ **8.** The industrialized nations had all the raw materials they needed inside their own country's borders.

_____ **9.** Asia, Africa, and Latin America became markets for the industrialized nations' goods.

_____ **10.** Lack of jobs at home motivated many Europeans to emigrate to other lands.

REVIEW FACTS Choose the correct items from the following list to complete the statements below.

improving	India	raw materials	West Africa
Australia	immigrants	Rudyard Kipling	create new markets

1. _____ is an example of a settlement colony.

2. _____ is an example of a dependent colony.

3. Soldiers from _____ served in the French army.

4. European countries sought colonies in places that had the

_____ that their factories needed.

5. Some nations thought that they could _____ for their goods by changing people's habits or customs.

6. North America, South America, and Australia grew because great numbers of

_____ from Europe moved there.

7. The phrase "The White Man's Burden" is the title of a poem by the British poet

_____.

8. Europeans believed that they were _____ people's lives by imposing their own values and cultural ideals on them.

Modern Chapter **17**

Main Idea Activities 26.2

European Claims in North Africa

VOCABULARY Some terms to understand:

• **heartening (666):** encouraging

• **intervention (667):** a stepping in

• **extravagant (668):** lavish

• **bankruptcy (668):** running out of money; financial ruin

ORGANIZING INFORMATION Use the following names to complete the chart below.

• Libya   • Egypt

• Sudan   • Morocco

• Tunis   • Algiers

	Colonies in North Africa	
France	**Great Britain**	**Italy**

EVALUATING INFORMATION Mark each statement *T* if it is true or *F* if it is false.

_____ **1.** Algiers was originally a Muslim state and part of the Ottoman Empire.

_____ **2.** Algiers welcomed French rule, and people never rebelled against it.

_____ **3.** Tunis became a French protectorate ruled by its Turkish governor.

_____ **4.** Morocco's location deep inside the Sahara Desert made it an unlikely choice for a colony.

_____ **5.** By agreement, France would not interfere with Great Britain's plans in North Africa if Great Britain would not interfere with France's plans.

_____ **6.** French rule was imposed on Morocco by military force.

_____ **7.** The people of Morocco treated Sultan Moulay Abd al-Hafid as a national hero for saving the nation from its greatest enemies.

_____ **8.** To raise money, the ruler of Egypt decided to sell stock in the Suez Canal.

_____ **9.** The Suez Canal is important because it gave ship captains a direct route from the Atlantic Ocean to the Pacific Ocean.

_____ **10.** The Italians wanted to take over Sudan and make it into a protectorate.

UNDERSTANDING MAIN IDEAS For each of the following, write the letter of the best choice in the space provided.

_____ **1.** Algiers became a French colony as a result of
   a. a twenty-year war with the Otoman Empire.
   b. the need for a protective barrier around France.
   c. imperialism.
   d. the will of the people of Algiers.

_____ **2.** The French colonies in North Africa
   a. peacefully submitted to French rule.
   b. frequently rebelled against French rule.
   c. conspired with the British to change sides.
   d. became Italian colonies after a major war.

_____ **3.** Great Britain gained control of the Suez Canal
   a. by buying it from the French company that built it.
   b. by buying up the land through which the canal had to be dug.
   c. by buying the stock that the Egyptian government owned.
   d. by military force.

_____ **4.** Although Egypt appeared to be an independent country,
   a. it was under control of the Mahdi.
   b. it was ruled by Great Britain for many years.
   c. it was the capital of the Ottoman Empire.
   d. it was the personal property of 'Urabi Pasha.

_____ **5.** As a result of the Fashoda crisis,
   a. Great Britain and Egypt controlled the Sudan.
   b. General Kitchener captured Algiers.
   c. the army of the Mahdi controlled Egypt.
   d. France and Great Britain went to war.

Name _____ Class _____ Date _____

VOCABULARY Some terms to understand:

• **fueled (670):** acted as a driving force

• **forced labor (671):** slave labor

• **thriving (673):** flourishing, prosperous

• **mineral (673):** natural substances such as gold or coal that are obtained from the ground

ORGANIZING INFORMATION Use the following items to complete the chart below.

• French	• Samory Touré	• Zulu
• British	• King Leopold II	• Shaka
• Boers	• Ashanti	• British
• Belgium		

	West Africa	**Central and East Africa**	**Southern Africa**
Colonizers			
Opponents			

EVALUATING INFORMATION Mark each statement *T* if it is true or *F* if it is false.

_____ **1.** Places along the West African coast that had once been involved in the slave trade turned to trade other kinds of products.

_____ **2.** During the late 1800s, Europeans started to move inland in order to control the sources of the products they traded.

_____ **3.** The only French colony in Africa was Senegal.

_____ **4.** The Gold Coast became a Portuguese colony.

Chapter 26, Main Idea Activities 26.3, continued

_____ **5.** Liberia became a German colony in 1847.

_____ **6.** Henry Stanley explored large portions of central Africa during his search for the lost missionary, Dr. Livingston.

_____ **7.** King Leopold II of Belgium created an enormous colony in the Congo that was his personal territory.

_____ **8.** A disease called rinderpest killed off many European colonists in East Africa.

_____ **9.** The first Europeans to colonize South Africa were the Dutch.

_____ **10.** South Africa became a British colony when the Boers took over.

UNDERSTANDING MAIN IDEAS For each of the following, write the letter of the best choice in the space provided.

_____ **1.** According to the map of Africa in 1914,
  a. most of West Africa was independent.
  b. most of the major European countries had colonies in Africa.
  c. Angola was a Spanish colony.
  d. Libya was independent.

_____ **2.** When the Boers moved into new territories during the Great Trek, they
  a. fought with the Africans for control.
  b. sent Shaka to fight the British invaders.
  c. lost control of Natal to the French.
  d. fought the Zulu for control of the region.

_____ **3.** By 1890, all diamond production in South Africa was controlled by
  a. Cecil Rhodes.
  b. the Orange Free State.
  c. Zimbabwe.
  d. Cape Colony.

_____ **4.** The Boer War was fought between the Boers and
  a. the Zulu.
  b. the Dutch.
  c. the British.
  d. Rhodesia.

_____ **5.** Emperor Menelik II of Ethiopia
  a. entered a long-term alliance with Italy.
  b. gave up Ethiopian culture and imitated Italian culture.
  c. refused to be taken in by Italy's trickery.
  d. went to war with South Africa over slavery.

Main Idea Activities 26.4

Modern Chapter **17**

Expansion in Asia

VOCABULARY Some terms to understand:

- **tight rein (676)**: close control
- **samurai (676):** members of the warrior class in feudal Japan
- **shogunate (676):** government. Shoguns were hereditary military chiefs who were the real rulers of Japan
- **interests (679):** business dealings
- **nibbled (679):** eat with quick, small bites

ORGANIZING INFORMATION Use the following items to complete the chart below.

- Built bridges, roads, and railroads
- Felt themselves a superior race
- Did not ease religious hatreds
- Made India their permanent home
- Improved schools
- Treated Muslims and Hindus equally
- Principle of "divide and rule"
- No social contact with Indian people

Great Britain in India	
As rulers	**Socially**

EVALUATING INFORMATION Mark each statement *T* if it is true or *F* if it is false.

_____ **1.** The British East India Company once controlled a large portion of India.

_____ **2.** When the British government finally took control of India, it united the entire country under its direct rule.

_____ **3.** British settlers never intended to remain in India; they came solely for business reasons.

_____ **4.** The educational system that Britain set up in India was for Europeans only.

_____ **5.** The Muslim population of India feared that the end of British rule would mean a loss of protection from violence at the hands of the majority.

_____ **6.** The Meiji Restoration meant the end of the shogunate and a return to rule by the emperor.

_____ **7.** After the Meiji Restoration, the government improved education and almost completely wiped out illiteracy.

_____ **8.** According to the new Japanese constitution of 1899, every Japanese man and woman had the right to vote in national elections.

_____ **9.** Japan actively sought to bring back new ideas and machinery from the West.

_____ **10.** Japan was the second Asian country to industrialize; China was the first.

REVIEWING FACTS Choose the correct items from the following list to complete the statements below.

major world power	coaling stations	win
Liliuokalani	Korea	French Indochina
imperialists	Siam	

1. Fear of imperialism made the Japanese become _____ themselves.

2. Japan feared that the Western nations wanted to push China aside and control

_____.

3. The Japanese were not expected to _____ the Sino-Japanese War.

4. After the Sino-Japanese War, Japan became a _____.

5. Laos, Cambodia, and Vietnam were part of _____.

6. King Mongkut of _____ maintained his country's independence from France and Great Britain.

7. The Pacific Islands were useful to the Western powers as

_____ for their navies.

8. Queen _____ tried without success to keep foreigners from controlling Hawaii.

CHAPTER **26**

Modern Chapter **17**

Main Idea Activities 26.5

Imperialism in Latin America

VOCABULARY Some terms to understand:

- **pressure (682):** force, influence
- **stable (683):** not likely to fall or be overturned
- **lease (684):** rent
- **merchant ships (684):** ships that carry cargo; freighters
- **corollary (685):** natural consequence or result
- **effective (687):** producing the desired results
- **concerned (687):** troubled, worried

ORGANIZING INFORMATION Complete the diagram below by using the following items. Write the letter of the item where it belongs.

A. Ended the war

B. Platt Amendment

C. Spain gave up claims to Cuba

D. Rough Riders

E. A fight for Cuban Independence

F. Explosion of battleship *Maine*

G. New Cuban constitution

H. Spanish fleet defeated in the Philippines

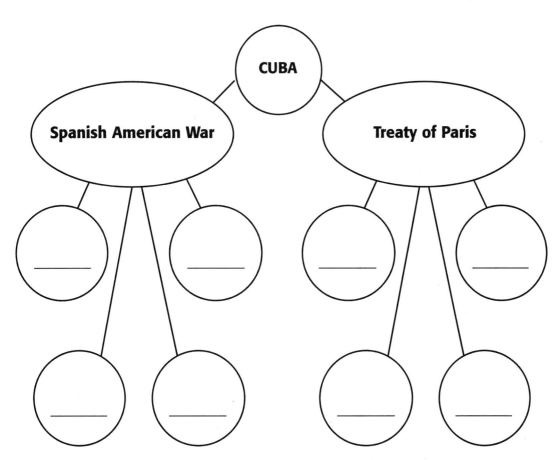

Chapter 26, Main Idea Activities 26.5, continued

EVALUATING INFORMATION Mark each statement *T* if it is true or *F* if it is false.

_____ **1.** Latin American countries had great difficulty finding markets in the industrialized nations for their products.

_____ **2.** Cuba was happy under Spanish rule until foreigners arrived to promote rebellion.

_____ **3.** The war with Spain included military actions in the Philippine Islands as well as in Cuba.

_____ **4.** The Platt Amendment to the Cuban constitution gave the United States the right to intervene in Cuba.

_____ **5.** America assisted Panama's revolution for independence in order to win the right to build a canal through its territory.

_____ **6.** Part of the Roosevelt Corollary involved the repayment of loans.

UNDERSTANDING MAIN IDEAS For each of the following, write the letter of the best choice in the space provided.

_____ **1.** The rule of Porfirio Díaz brought unrest to Mexico because
a. he supported the poor rather than the rich.
b. he favored land reform.
c. he allowed the rich and foreign investors to control Mexico.
d. he challenged the power of the North Americans.

_____ **2.** During the revolt against Huerta, the leader who spoke for the peasants was
a. Woodrow Wilson
b. Emiliano Zapata
c. Venustiano Carranza
d. Francisco Madero

_____ **3.** The Mexican guerrilla leader Pancho Villa
a. raided towns in the United States.
b. protected the rights of the large landowners.
c. fought to protect the Carranza government.
d. killed American general John Pershing in battle.

_____ **4.** At the end of the 1800s, Latin American countries were used mainly as
a. sources of profit for foreign investors.
b. stations for troops.
c. bases for the naval fleet.
d. sources of raw materials.

CHAPTER 27

Modern Chapter 18

Main Idea Activities 27.1

Setting the Stage for War

VOCABULARY Some terms to understand:

- **shattered (698):** smashed, broken
- **harmonious (698):** friendly, congenial
- **glorification (698):** presenting something as wonderful or splendid
- **ambitious (699):** guided by a desire to rise to a position of great influence or power
- **isolated (699):** separate, left by itself
- **recognize (699):** acknowledge
- **"powder keg" (701):** something dangerous and ready to explode
- **implicated (701):** involved
- **neutrality (702):** the position of being on neither side in a war or conflict

ORGANIZING INFORMATION Use the following items in the chart below to choose the correct countries in each alliance. Some countries do not belong in the chart.

- Poland
- Great Britain
- Austria-Hungary
- Secret understanding with Italy
- Russia
- Italy
- Germany
- Rumania
- United States
- France

Alliances	
Triple Alliance	**Triple Entente**

EVALUATING INFORMATION Mark each statement *T* if it is true or *F* if it is false.

_____ **1.** In the century before the start of World War I, some countries contained many nationalities ruled by a single government.

_____ **2.** The spirit of militarism encouraged finding peaceful solutions to disputes.

_____ **3.** Germany and Great Britain engaged in a race to build up their navies.

_____ **4.** The unification of Germany made the new Germany a weaker nation than it had been before it was united.

_____ **5.** Forming the Three Emperors' League was Bismarck's way of protecting Germany from going to war with neighboring states.

_____ **6.** After 1894, Germany was sandwiched between two enemies when France and Russia signed an alliance.

_____ **7.** Germany did not take part in the international race to claim overseas colonies.

_____ **8.** Obtaining Bosnia and Herzegovina was important to Serbia because they would give Serbia access to the sea.

_____ **9.** A Serbian nationalist assassinated the heir to the throne of Austria-Hungary.

_____ **10.** Germany sent Serbia an ultimatum, which Serbia quickly rejected.

REVIEWING FACTS Choose the correct items from the following list to complete the statements below.

France	Gavrilo Princep	Dardanelles
Pan-Slavism	Bulgaria	Belgium
Great Britain	Italy	

1. The unity of all Slavic peoples under Russian leadership is known as

_____.

2. Archduke Francis Ferdinand was assassinated by _____.

3. Germany declared war on _____ two days after declaring war on Russia.

4. Even though the great powers agreed to guarantee its neutrality, Germany sent

troops into _____ on August 14, 1914.

5. Japan entered the war on the side of _____ and France.

6. After remaining neutral for many months, _____ finally entered the war on the side of Great Britain and France.

7. The _____ connects the Black Sea and the Mediterranean Sea.

8. In October 1915, _____ entered the war as Germany's ally.

CHAPTER 27

Modern Chapter **18**

Main Idea Activities 27.2

World War I: A New Kind of War

VOCABULARY Some terms to understand:

• **blockade (705):** controlling access to a place by military means

• **extensive (705):** large, massive

• **artillery (705):** large guns manned by crews

• **trenches (706):** long, narrow ditches with mounds of earth in front to protect soldiers

• **treads (706):** a continuous band of metal tracks

• **drafted (706):** conscripted; compelled by law to serve in the army

• **humiliating (707):** embarrassing, humbling

• **bombard (708):** shell

• **stalemate (709):** deadlock, standoff

• **munitions (709):** military supplies

ORGANIZING INFORMATION Fill in the web by writing the letter of the answer where it belongs.

A. Machine guns

B. Trench warfare

C. Tanks

D. Airplanes

E. U-boats

F. Drafted civilians

G. Long-range artillery

H. War industry at home

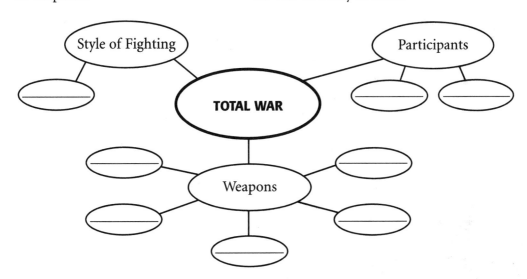

EVALUATING INFORMATION Mark each statement *T* if it is true or *F* if it is false.

_____ **1.** The Central Powers and the Allies expected a short war.

_____ **2.** Germany had the largest, most powerful navy in the world.

Chapter 27, Main Idea Activities 27.2, *continued*

_____ **3.** Germany by itself had a greater industrial capacity than France, Great Britain, Russia, and Italy combined.

_____ **4.** Submarines were ineffective weapons of war during World War I.

_____ **5.** Both sides outlawed the use of poison gas.

_____ **6.** The use of machine guns caused many casualties in attacks on well-defended positions.

_____ **7.** Protective trenches offered soldiers some safety from artillery fire.

_____ **8.** Baron von Richtofen was a famous flying ace of World War I.

_____ **9.** Heavily armored tanks were easily trapped in barbed wire and destroyed.

_____ **10.** War did not touch the lives of the civilian population of Europe.

UNDERSTANDING MAIN IDEAS For each of the following, write the letter of the best choice in the space provided.

_____ **1.** Innovations in the kinds of weapons that armies used
  a. caused fewer casualties than in earlier wars.
  b. were limited by each nations' inability to mass produce goods.
  c. were limited only to the Allies.
  d. had a significant effect on how the war was fought.

_____ **2.** "Total War" meant that
  a. only professional armies did the fighting.
  b. the civilian population was deeply involved both at home and in uniform.
  c. battles were fought in the air and on the ground.
  d. everyone paid attention to the latest war news.

_____ **3.** The attack on Gallipoli was
  a. one of Great Britain's greatest victories of the war.
  b. an attempt to bring the Ottoman Empire into the war.
  c. a reprisal for submarine raids on shipping.
  d. a major Allied defeat.

_____ **4.** By the end of 1915, the fighting in the west had reached the point of
  a. victory at sea but not on land.
  b. victory everywhere.
  c. stalemate.
  d. enjoyment.

Main Idea Activities 27.3

Modern Chapter **18**

The Russian Revolution

VOCABULARY Some terms to understand:

- **defiance (711):** standing up against authority and refusing to give in
- **disband (711):** break up, disperse
- **factions (712):** opposing sides
- **restore (713):** bring back
- **symbolic (713):** used to represent an idea or quality

ORGANIZING INFORMATION Use the following items to complete the time line below.

- Formation of Communist Party
- Strikes and demonstrations in Petrograd
- Czar's family imprisoned
- Menshevik-Bolshevik quarrels
- Czar abdicates the throne
- October Revolution
- Duma demands reforms
- Petrograd Soviet formed

The Russian Revolution

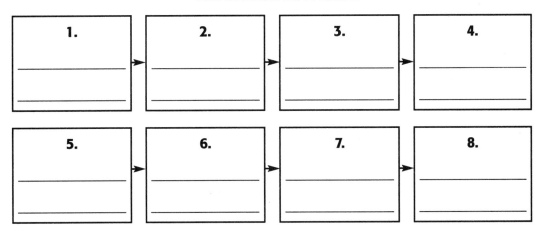

EVALUATING INFORMATION Mark each statement *T* if it is true or *F* if it is false.

_____ **1.** Russia's army lacked proper equipment, supplies, and leaders.

_____ **2.** The Allies never counted much on Russian help, even though Russia was on their side.

_____ **3.** By spring 1917, Russian morale was at its highest point of the war.

_____ **4.** Petrograd was the scene of demonstrations and great social unrest.

_____ **5.** When the Duma demanded reforms, the Czar disbanded it.

_____ **6.** The Czar abdicated his throne after the Duma and demonstrators defied his authority, and the army refused to support him.

_____ **7.** Radical socialists ran the first provisional government after the Czar was overthrown.

_____ **8.** Vladimir Lenin was an important leader of the radical Bolsheviks.

_____ **9.** Lenin created a version of Marxism that could take hold in Russia.

_____ **10.** The October Revolution brought the new Communist Party into power.

UNDERSTANDING MAIN IDEAS For each of the following, write the letter of the best choice in the space provided.

_____ **1.** By early 1917, Russia was
    a. still able to field a formidable army.
    b. considering changing sides and joining Germany.
    c. on the edge of collapse.
    d. ready to be conquered by the Ottoman Empire.

_____ **2.** The Czar was forced to give up the throne because
    a. German armies had occupied Petrograd.
    b. the economic power of the serfs had increased.
    c. his family and the Russian aristocracy no longer supported him.
    d. he was no longer able to put down demonstrations and control the Duma.

_____ **3.** The Petrograd Soviet of Workers and Soldiers' Deputies believed that
    a. new rulers of Russia should slowly restore order.
    b. political equality must be coupled with economic equality.
    c. economic power should be in the hands of the aristocracy.
    d. the czar should be restored to power.

_____ **4.** "Peace, bread, and land" was the slogan of the
    a. Mensheviks.
    b. Bolsheviks.
    c. Communists
    d. Duma.

_____ **5.** The civil war that broke out in Russia in 1918 was
    a. won by the Red Army.
    b. won by the White forces.
    c. an attempt to return the dead czar's family to power.
    d. encouraged by the Allies, who wanted Communism to spread.

Name _____ Class _____ Date _____

CHAPTER **27**

Modern Chapter **18**

Main Idea Activities 27.4

The Terms of Peace

VOCABULARY Some terms to understand:

- **idealistic (714):** high-minded, visionary
- **delegation (715):** group of representatives
- **dictating (716):** order in clear, definite terms
- **brink (716):** edge
- **conflicting (717):** opposing
- **kindle (717):** cause, ignite, set off

ORGANIZING INFORMATION Use the following items to complete the chart below.

- Border moved to Rhine River
- Tirol
- Germany's Pacific colonies
- Cities of Fiume and Trieste
- Germany's colonies in Africa
- Return of Alsace-Lorraine
- Coal-rich Saar valley
- Destruction of the German navy

Allied Demands			
France	**Italy**	**Great Britain**	**Japan**
• _____	• _____	• _____	• _____
• _____	• _____	• _____	
• _____			

EVALUATING INFORMATION Mark each statement *T* if it is true or *F* if it is false.

_____ **1.** President Woodrow Wilson claimed that the United States entered World War I to safeguard democracy.

_____ **2.** Wilson's Fourteen Points were an attempt to take the greatest revenge on Germany for its brutality during the war.

_____ **3.** One of Wilson's Fourteen Points urged the establishment of a general association of nations.

_____ **4.** The Treaty of Brest-Litovsk declared Russia the victor in the war against Germany.

_____ **5.** In May 1918, before American troops arrived in France, German soldiers were 37 miles from Paris.

_____ **6.** Château-Thierry was an important battle that the Allies lost.

_____ **7.** The Austro-Hungarian Empire collapsed, and separate governments were formed in each country.

_____ **8.** In November 1918, Germany signed an armistice that halted World War I.

_____ **9.** Germany was forced to cancel the harsh Treaty of Brest-Litovsk.

_____ **10.** Germany was allowed by the terms of the armistice to keep all its weapons.

UNDERSTANDING MAIN IDEAS For each of the following, write the letter of the best choice in the space provided.

_____ **1.** Kaiser William was forced to give up his throne because
   a. the British demanded that he go into exile.
   b. many Germans considered him an obstacle to peace.
   c. he was ashamed that his country had lost the war.
   d. radical socialists wanted him replaced.

_____ **2.** The losses on both sides were enormous, including
   a. $1 billion in goods and property.
   b. the release of millions of war prisoners.
   c. every nation's submarine fleet and fighter planes.
   d. 10 million soldiers dead and 21 million more wounded.

_____ **3.** The Allies at the Paris Peace Conference
   a. placed many severe demands on Germany.
   b. invited Russia to take part as one of the victors.
   c. worried only about territories and colonies in Europe.
   d. wanted to create a just peace.

_____ **4.** Many Allied leaders believed that the only way to guarantee a lasting peace was
   a. to disarm Germany and every country in Europe.
   b. to keep Germany from ever becoming powerful again.
   c. to treat Germany as an equal economically and socially.
   d. to keep Germany a monarchy with an absolute ruler.

Name _____ Class _____ Date _____

 **Main Idea Activities 27.5**

Modern Chapter **18**   **Creating a "New" Europe**

VOCABULARY Some terms to understand:

• **negotiations (718):** formal discussions

• **self-determination (721):** the decision by a people regarding the kind of government they will have

• **deported (721):** sent out of the country

• **commission (722):** a group of people given authority to do something

• **sanctions (723):** prohibitions, restrictions

• **ratify (723):** formally vote on and accept

ORGANIZING INFORMATION From the following list, choose the ten things that Germany was forced to do at the end of World War I.

• Pay reparations
• Destroy all its factories
• Admit guilt
• Give up territory to the victors
• Agree not to fortify the Rhineland
• Free Poland

• Destroy all its crops
• Make Danzig a free city
• Make its army smaller
• Allow Allied troops in the Rhineland
• Establish a "Polish Corridor" to the sea
• Not manufacture war materials

Treaty of Versailles	

EVALUATING INFORMATION Mark each statement *T* if it is true or *F* if it is false.

_____ **1.** At Versailles, a single peace treaty was signed with all the Central Powers.

_____ **2.** The Treaty of Versailles forced Germany to accept blame for the war.

Copyright © by Holt, Rinehart and Winston. All rights reserved.

Holt World History: The Human Journey   (233)   **Main Idea Activities**

Chapter 27, Main Idea Activities 27.5, continued

_____ **3.** Germany alone had to pay an unspecified amount of financial reparations to the victorious nations.

_____ **4.** As a result of the Treaty of Versailles, France and Belgium received territory from Germany.

_____ **5.** Germany was allowed to maintain only a small army and a small navy.

_____ **6.** Boundaries of new nations formed after World War I respected the natural ethnic divisions within Europe.

_____ **7.** The Armenians were accused of genocide in their treatment of the Turks.

_____ **8.** As a result of the Treaty of Versailles, the Ottoman Empire was stripped of all its territory except for Turkey.

_____ **9.** The League of Nations awarded German colonies in Africa and the Pacific as mandates to Great Britain alone.

_____ **10.** The United States never ratified the Treaty of Versailles.

UNDERSTANDING MAIN IDEAS For each of the following, write the letter of the best choice in the space provided.

_____ **1.** As a result of the Treaty of Versailles,
   a. Germany was allowed to keep its colonies in Africa.
   b. Poland was left in a very weakened state.
   c. there were no political or territorial changes.
   d. many new nations were established in Europe.

_____ **2.** The Polish Corridor would be "the root of the next war" because
   a. Foch said so.
   b. many civilians lived there.
   c. Poland was given land that more naturally would belong to Germany.
   d. nations do not need access to the sea.

_____ **3.** In the United States, many people believed that the League of Nations
   a. would drag the United States into another war.
   b. was the best hope for a peaceful future for the world.
   c. was the only force that kept countries from building new empires.
   d. was part of a French plan to make Germany a colony.

Main Idea Activities 28.1

Modern Chapter **19**

The Postwar Era

VOCABULARY Some terms to understand:

- **disconnection (728):** separation
- **irrational (728):** not explainable by reason
- **moral relativism (729):** belief that values depend on human agreement and not on any objective norm
- **disintegrate (729):** fall apart
- **random (731):** picked for no specific reason
- **mechanization (732):** industrialization
- **flocked (732):** went in large numbers
- **revenue (732):** income

ORGANIZING INFORMATION Use the following names to complete the chart below.

- Louis Sullivan
- Georges Braque
- F. Scott Fitzgerald
- Franz Kafka
- Salvador Dali
- Gertrude Stein
- Frank Lloyd Wright
- Igor Stravinsky
- Marcel Proust
- Pablo Picasso
- Louis Armstrong
- Ernest Hemingway
- Piet Mondrian
- Wassily Kandinsky

Literature	Music	Painting
	Architecture	

EVALUATING INFORMATION Mark each statement *T* if it is true or *F* if it is false.

_____ **1.** The influenza pandemic of 1918–1919 killed more than 20 million Americans.

_____ **2.** Sigmund Freud and Albert Einstein were important figures in the development of the science of psychoanalysis.

_____ **3.** Some important writers of the day were disillusioned and believed that European society would disappear.

_____ **4.** Writers such as James Joyce and T. S. Eliot used nontraditional techniques in their works.

_____ **5.** Jazz never became very popular outside of New Orleans.

_____ **6.** Frank Lloyd Wright's Imperial Hotel in Tokyo was able to withstand an earthquake because of the novel way Wright designed its foundation.

_____ **7.** Lindbergh's solo trans-Atlantic flight in 1927 impressed only fellow pilots.

_____ **8.** Movies often offered escape and entertainment to viewers.

_____ **9.** The Olympic Games have been played every four years since ancient times.

_____ **10.** The cost of luxury goods went up sharply in the 1920s.

REVIEWING FACTS Choose the correct items from the following list to complete the statements below.

twelve-tone scale	credit	unconscious
money and prestige	pandemic	World Cup
Gertrude Stein	prohibition	

1. A _____ is an epidemic that occurs over a very wide area and affects many people.

2. Freud believed that the _____ often controlled people's actions.

3. _____ first used the term "the Lost Generation."

4. The composer Arnold Schoenberg used a novel _____ when he composed his music.

5. The _____ soccer tournament began in 1930.

6. The Olympics brought _____ to its host countries.

7. Buying goods on _____ meant that people did not have to save money to get what they wanted.

8. From 1920 to 1933, _____ made alcoholic beverages illegal.

Main Idea Activities 28.2

Modern Chapter **19**

Postwar Prosperity Crumbles

VOCABULARY Some terms to understand:

• **over cultivation (734):** planting crops too often or of the wrong kind

• **vulnerable (734):** defenseless against

• **overvalued (735):** costing more than the actual worth

• **sell-off (735):** changing into cash

• **productivity (735):** ability to make new goods

• **breadlines (736):** places where food and other necessities were given free to the poor

• **massive (737):** large, extensive

ORGANIZING INFORMATION Use the following items to complete the chart below.

• speculation	• breadlines
• no jobs	• overvalued stock
• New Deal	• poverty amid productivity
• sudden sell-off	• protectionism

Causes		Effect
	The Great Depression	

EVALUATING INFORMATION Mark each statement *T* if it is true or *F* if it is false.

_____ **1.** Much of the prosperity of the 1920s came from advances in farming and agriculture.

_____ **2.** Farmers fell into debt when they bought land and machinery that they could not pay for.

_____ **3.** Protectionism involved putting high tariffs on foreign-made goods.

_____ **4.** If Europe could not sell its goods in the United States, Europe could not get money to pay off its war debts.

_____ **5.** Stock prices remained low throughout the 1920s.

_____ **6.** On Black Tuesday, investors panicked and sold off their stocks.

_____ **7.** Protective tariffs made it difficult to recover from the Great Depression.

_____ **8.** The New Deal was the plan of President Herbert Hoover.

_____ **9.** The New Deal created jobs and public works projects.

_____ **10.** The New Deal by itself was enough to restore prosperity to the United States after the Great Depression.

UNDERSTANDING MAIN IDEAS For each of the following, write the letter of the best choice in the space provided.

_____ **1.** The Great Depression followed World War I because
  a. the depression started only a year after the end of the war.
  b. there were not enough workers for all the available jobs.
  c. nations never fully recovered from the war.
  d. people lost hope in themselves.

_____ **2.** Economic nationalism, which attempted to protect domestic industry from foreign competition,
  a. was a successful method for Europeans and Americans.
  b. also kept American bankers from lending money to European nations.
  c. showed that the economies of the world's nations were not linked.
  d. also kept foreign nations from paying their debts.

_____ **3.** During the Great Depression, goods were not in short supply, but
  a. no one had money to buy them.
  b. no one needed manufactured goods anymore.
  c. people were too busy at work to need them.
  d. nations destroyed them rather than sell them to the poor.

_____ **4.** The New Deal was not fully successful because
  a. farmers resented government involvement in their lives.
  b. the economic collapse in the nation was so massive.
  c. there was no social security system in place.
  d. President Roosevelt did not support it.

CHAPTER 28

Modern Chapter **19**

Main Idea Activities 28.3

Political Tensions After Wrold War I

VOCABULARY Some terms to understand:

• **habitable (738):** able to be lived in

• **devastated (738):** totally destroyed

• **pact (739):** formal agreement

• **republican (739):** having the characteristic of a citizen-elected government

• **dictator (739):** a person exercising absolute authority

• **disrupted (741):** upset, disturbed, interrupted

• **destiny (742):** future

ORGANIZING INFORMATION Complete the web by writing the letter of the correct answers where it belongs.

A. Czechoslovakia

B. Maginot Line

C. Rumania

D. fear of Germany

E. 200 miles long

F. Poland

G. Yugoslavia

H. along border with Germany and Luxembourg

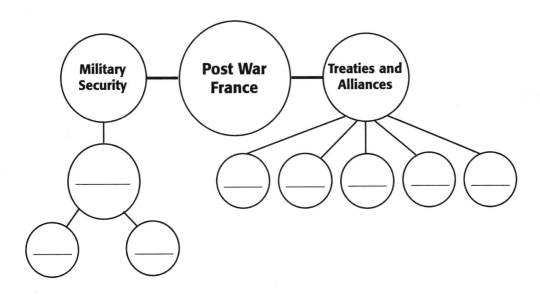

EVALUATING INFORMATION Mark each statement *T* if it is true or *F* if it is false.

_____ **1.** Rebuilding Europe after World War I was a short and easy process.

_____ **2.** French agriculture and industry were intact and ready to resume production.

_____ **3.** The Maginot Line was built to provide work for French youth.

_____ **4.** According to the Locarno Pact, the nations of Europe agreed to settle their disputes by peaceful means.

_____ **5.** Léon Blum, the leader of the Popular Front, became the premier of France.

_____ **6.** France remained a democracy despite pressure from the conservatives and the failure of socialist policies.

_____ **7.** Britain was able to avoid most of the social unrest that beset France after World War I.

_____ **8.** In 1922, the southern part of Ireland became the Irish Free State.

_____ **9.** Austria became a rich and successful nation after World War I.

_____ **10.** By 1926, Poland, Bulgaria, Romania, and Yugoslavia had replaced their democratic governments with monarchies or military dictatorships.

UNDERSTANDING MAIN IDEAS For each of the following, write the letter of the best choice in the space provided.

_____ **1.** After World War I, France built the Maginot Line because
   a. French generals feared that Luxembourg would invade.
   b. Great Britain was France's traditional enemy.
   c. Germany had invaded France twice in fifty years.
   d. construction costs were low.

_____ **2.** The nations of Europe after World War I
   a. turned against Italy.
   b. refused to make any alliances with Russia.
   c. only wanted to lose themselves in good times.
   d. felt a general mistrust of Germany.

_____ **3.** One of the major social difficulties facing Great Britain after World War I was
   a. the increase in unemployment.
   b. the lack of labor unions.
   c. the abdication of its king.
   d. the destruction of its factories.

_____ **4.** The word that best describes the political situation in eastern Europe was
   a. democratic.
   b. unstable.
   c. hopeful.
   d. peaceful.

Name _____ Class _____ Date _____

   Main Idea Activities 28.4

Modern Chapter **19**   **Fascist Dictatorships in Italy and Germany**

VOCABULARY Some terms to understand:

- **aftermath (743):** events that happened afterward
- **opposition (743):** conflict with
- **martial law (744):** military rule replacing civil rule in time of trouble
- **coalition (744):** alliance of leaders for some special purpose
- **figurehead (744):** a leader in name only
- **police state (744):** a state strictly controlled by the government
- **putsch (745):** (German) sudden attempt to overthrow a government
- **ideology (746):** belief system
- **legality (747):** accordance with the law

ORGANIZING INFORMATION Choose the five items below that correctly complete the following chart.

- appealed to the upper and middle classes
- believed in a society without social classes
- relied on dictatorship and totalitarianism
- name chosen by Benito Mussolini of Italy
- made Italy into a police state
- the opposite in philosophy from Nazism
- won support in Germany during the Great Depression

Fascism

EVALUATING INFORMATION Mark each statement *T* if it is true or *F* if it is false.

_____ **1.** Adolf Hitler was the first to develop the doctrine of fascism.

_____ **2.** Fascism is designed to appeal to rich and poor alike.

_____ **3.** Communism and fascism have the same set of beliefs and principles.

_____ **4.** Mussolini became premier of Italy as a result of violent demonstrations by his Black Shirts.

_____ **5.** The German people hated the Weimar government because its social policies were flawed.

_____ **6.** The Beer Hall Putsch helped bring Hitler and the Nazis to power.

_____ **7.** Hitler's book, *Mein Kampf*, stated Hitler's plans for establishing racial purity.

_____ **8.** Hitler used the burning of the Reichstag building to make himself dictator.

_____ **9.** Unlike fascist Italy, Nazi Germany had no secret police force.

_____ **10.** In 1936, Hitler legally stationed German troops in the Rhineland.

REVIEWING FACTS Choose the correct items from the following list to complete the statements below.

master race	figurehead	Nazi party
Treaty of Versailles	der Führer	Third Reich
Rome-Berlin Axis	nationalistic and militaristic	

1. Fascism is _____.

2. With Mussolini in charge, the king ruled as a _____.

3. In many Germans' minds, the _____ humiliated Germany.

4. The National Socialist German Workers' Party was the _____.

5. According to Hitler's ethnic policies, the Germans were the

_____.

6. Hitler took the title _____ after he took power.

7. The empire Hitler formed was called the _____.

8. Hitler and Mussolini formed the _____.

Modern Chapter **19**

Main Idea Activities 28.5

Dictatorship in the Soviet Union

VOCABULARY Some terms to understand:

- **nationalized (745):** taken over and run by the state
- **strict (750):** exact, precise
- **surplus (751):** amount over and above what is needed
- **ruthless (751):** stopping at nothing

ORGANIZING INFORMATION Use the following items to complete the chart below.

- divorce easier
- nationalized industries
- collective farms
- Leon Trotsky
- no emphasis on basic education

- women's pay lower than men's
- Joseph Stalin
- new economic policy
- five-year plans
- Vladimir Lenin

The Soviet Union		
Names	**Economic Policies**	**Lifestyle**

EVALUATING INFORMATION Mark each statement *T* if it is true or *F* if it is false.

_____ **1.** In 1922, Russia was renamed the Union of Soviet Socialist-Fascist Republics.

_____ **2.** In 1920, Russian farmers produced far more grain than they did during World War I.

_____ **3.** The Nepmen were the Soviet secret police.

_____ **4.** The Soviet government encouraged farmers to form collective farms.

_____ **5.** The lives of women were quickly and dramatically improved by the rise of Communism.

_____ **6.** The Communists hoped to raise the literacy rate, but many schools lacked books and other basic supplies.

_____ **7.** Leon Trotsky and Joseph Stalin were in total agreement about how Communist governments needed to work.

_____ **8.** Trotsky was murdered in Mexico on Lenin's orders.

_____ **9.** Five-year plans detailed military growth only.

_____ **10.** Farm output decreased when farmers moved onto collective farms.

UNDERSTANDING MAIN IDEAS For each of the following, write the letter of the best choice in the space provided.

_____ **1.** Joseph Stalin emerged as the leader of the Communist Party after
    a. losing to Mussolini in elections.
    b. replacing the czar.
    c. the failure of his first Five-Year Plan.
    d. a major struggle against Leon Trotsky.

_____ **2.** In Stalin's command economy, the government
    a. controlled all economic decisions.
    b. ruled by the consent of the people.
    c. burned crops and destroyed bridges.
    d. took full responsibility for recent economic failures.

_____ **3.** The second Five-Year Plan, starting in 1933, was
    a. the reason for the success of communism in Russia.
    b. beneficial only to people who worked in big farms.
    c. a cause of even greater hardship for the Russian people.
    d. of use only to the military.

_____ **4.** In the Soviet system on government under Stalin,
    a. the Red Army ruled the country under martial law.
    b. the Politboro of the Communist Party had the most power.
    c. the Supreme Soviet and the Politboro shared power.
    d. the Red Army workers met every year to determine national policies.

CHAPTER 29

Modern Chapter **20**

Main Idea Activities 29.1

The British Empire in the Postwar Era

VOCABULARY Some terms to understand:

- **forged (758):** formed
- **imposed (760):** put on
- **confronted (760):** encountered, faced
- **castes (760):** the officially recognized classes in a social order
- **revered (760):** highly respected
- **boycotting (761):** refusing to use
- **autonomy (761):** independence, self-rule

ORGANIZING INFORMATION Use the following items to complete the chart below.

- sponsors Egypt in League of Nations
- by Anglo-Egyptian Treaty
- may station soldiers in Egypt
- controls Suez for 20 years
- gets support in case of Mideast war
- controls Sudan
- oversees Egyptian foreign policy
- by declaration of British government

	Egyptian Independence	
Year	1922	1936
How won		
Terms		

EVALUATING INFORMATION Mark each statement *T* if it is true or *F* if it is false.

_____ **1.** When the Ottoman Empire allied itself with Germany during World War I, Egypt became a British protectorate.

_____ **2.** The Egyptians were happy as a protectorate and never revolted against British rule.

(**Chapter 29, Main Idea Activities 29.1, continued**)

_____ **3.** According to the terms of the Anglo-Egyptian Treaty, Egypt was given immediate control over the Suez Canal.

_____ **4.** Arabs in the Middle East were upset with Britain and France when those countries imposed control on them after World War I.

_____ **5.** In exchange for Jewish support for the war effort, Great Britain agreed to support a Jewish homeland in Palestine.

_____ **6.** In 1937, the British recommended dividing Palestine between the Arabs and the Jewish settlers who were living there.

_____ **7.** India refused to send troops to fight for Britain during World War I.

_____ **8.** The people of both Great Britain and India disagreed about whether India should be an independent nation.

_____ **9.** Mohandas Gandhi was a revolutionary speaker who preached a doctrine of bloody revolt.

_____ **10.** The Statute of Westminster of 1931 created the British Commonwealth of Nations.

REVIEWING FACTS Choose the correct items from the following list to complete the statements below.

Zionism	troops	autonomy
Wafd Party	Nazi	Balfour Declaration

1. In 1919, the _____ led a revolt against British rule in Egypt.

2. After 1936, despite being independent, Egypt still had British _____ stationed on its soil.

3. _____ promoted a Jewish homeland in Palestine.

4. The _____ shaped British policies in Palestine.

5. When _____ persecution increased, Jewish immigration to Palestine also increased.

6. The Commonwealth granted political _____ to Canada, Australia, New Zealand, and South Africa.

Main Idea Activities 29.2

Modern Chapter **20**

Turkey, Persia, and Africa

VOCABULARY Some terms to understand:

- **remnants (762):** leftovers
- **exert (763):** exercise, wield
- **repression (764):** holding down, subjugation

ORGANIZING INFORMATION Use the following items to complete the chart below.

- Modernized country
- Secularized society
- Kemal Atatürk
- Reza Shah Pahlavi
- Gave women the vote
- Held most of the power
- Renamed the nation Iran
- Mustafa Kemal
- Sought ties with Germany
- Forced adoption of Western ways
- Imposed civil and social reforms
- Reza Khan

	Turkey	**Persia**
Founder		
New Name		
Accomplishments		

EVALUATING INFORMATION Mark each statement *T* if it is true or *F* if it is false.

_____ **1.** After World War I, the Ottoman Empire lost all of its territory except for Turkey.

_____ **2.** In 1923, Turkey became a republic, with its capital at Constantinople.

_____ **3.** As president of Turkey, Mustafa Kemal made Turkey into a secular state rather than a religious state under Islam.

_____ **4.** Kemal required all Turkish males to take English last names.

_____ **5.** Modern Iran is ancient Persia.

_____ **6.** Persia went to war with Great Britain and Russia to gain its freedom.

_____ **7.** The new governments of both Turkey and Iran granted women more freedom.

_____ **8.** The Shah of Iran was a limited monarch in name only.

_____ **9.** Most Africans believed the colonial powers treated Africans with equality and respect.

_____ **10.** In Africa, the loudest proponents of independence were young men who had been educated in the West.

UNDERSTANDING MAIN IDEAS For each of the following, write the letter of the best choice in the space provided.

_____ **1.** After World War I, nationalist movements occurred
  a. only in lands that were allies of the victors.
  b. in colonies and in the remnants of fallen empires.
  c. only in colonies that were left poor by colonists.
  d. only in countries that were the first to be colonized.

_____ **2.** Kemal Atatürk wanted to westernize Turkey because he
  a. was an agent of Great Britain.
  b. knew that all his people supported him.
  c. believed in the importance of traditional ways.
  d. believed in Western ideas and technology.

_____ **3.** Among the accomplishments of Reza Shah Pahlavi is
  a. the weakening of the military.
  b. the start of massive industrialization.
  c. the building of a major canal.
  d. the building of many hospitals and roads.

_____ **4.** Africa was restless under colonial rule because
  a. colonial governments weakened tribal authority.
  b. no one could travel to Europe or the United States for schooling.
  c. Western ideals and colonial practices often did not agree.
  d. missionaries forced Africans to learn English.

Main Idea Activities 29.3

Modern Chapter **20**

Unrest in China

VOCABULARY Some terms to understand:

- **vague (765):** unclear
- **secondary (765):** of second rank or importance
- **dowager (765):** widow who rules with the power of her dead husband
- **imperialist (765):** someone who believes in the right of a country to rule an empire
- **dynasty (767):** series of related rulers
- **warlords (767):** local rulers whose authority is based on force
- **virtual (768):** in everything but name
- **assaults (768):** attacks
- **charismatic (768):** energetic and appealing

ORGANIZING INFORMATION Use the following items to complete the chart below.

- led Nationalist party
- attacked Communists
- once studied medicine
- encouraged Boxer Rebellion
- wanted China to be industrialized
- left China under foreign domination
- fought the warlords
- wanted constitutional government
- imprisoned Emperor Qing

Empress Dowager Tz'u-Hsi	Sun Yixian	Chiang Kai-Shek

EVALUATING INFORMATION Mark each statement *T* if it is true or *F* if it is false.

_____ **1.** The United States urged an Open Door Policy in China because it feared that its businesses would not get a fair share of Chinese markets.

_____ **2.** By the end of the 1800s, Western commercial interests dominated China.

_____ **3.** Emperor Qing was imprisoned by his aunt, who ruled China in his place.

_____ **4.** The Boxer Rebellion was an attempt to bring Western sports to China.

_____ **5.** Soldiers from many nations, including the United States, were sent to China to put down the Boxer Rebellion.

_____ **6.** One of the key leaders of the Chinese Nationalist Party was Sun Yixian.

_____ **7.** The rich merchants and the powerful rural families of China wanted to keep Emperor Qing in power.

_____ **8.** When the Guomindang came to power, Sun Yixian was executed.

_____ **9.** The Nationalist government hoped to subdue the warlords and set up a strong central government.

_____ **10.** Chiang Kai-shek was the legal head of the Nanjing government.

UNDERSTANDING MAIN IDEAS For each of the following, write the letter of the best choice in the space provided.

_____ **1.** The Boxer Rebellion
   a. failed to drive foreigners from Chinese soil.
   b. failed to defeat the Kuomintang.
   c. was directed by the deposed Emperor Qing.
   d. took place only in remote parts of China far from the coast.

_____ **2.** The Nationalists believed that China could control foreign domination
   a. only if it kept in contact with its rural population.
   b. only if it kept in contact with its imperial past.
   c. only if it became a modern, industrialized nation.
   d. only if they raised a large army.

_____ **3.** Chiang Kai-shek had to fight the warlords because the warlords
   a. received technical, political and military advice from the Soviets.
   b. controlled most of the country with their private armies.
   c. were in the pay of Great Britain and other colonial powers.
   d. controlled the all-important coastal cities.

_____ **4.** The hero of the Communist Long March to Shaanxi province was
   a. Jiangxi.
   b. Tz'h-hsi.
   c. Yuan Shikai.
   d. Mao Zedong.

CHAPTER 29

Modern Chapter **20**

Main Idea Activities 29.4

Imperialism in Japan

VOCABULARY Some terms to understand:

• **lease (770):** permit in change for money

• **prestige (771):** fame and honor

• **stunned (771):** strongly surprised

• **strain (771):** severe pressure

• **ceded (771):** gave

• **stability (772):** solidness, firmness

ORGANIZING INFORMATION Select the five items about Japan from the following list that correctly complete the chart below.

• could not dominate Korean government

• feared Russian presence in Manchuria

• signed an alliance with Great Britain in 1902 to protect their mutual interests

• not industrialized enough to be a modern country

• destroyed the Russian Baltic fleet at Tsushima

• lost land to China during the Boxer Rebellion

• Treaty of Portsmouth ended Russian competition in Manchuria

• attacked the Russian fleet at Port Arthur

Japan Against Russia
1.
2.
3.
4.
5.

EVALUATING INFORMATION Mark each statement *T* if it is true or *F* if it is false.

_____ **1.** Japan was colonized by the Western powers during the late 1800s.

_____ **2.** Japan needed to expand its influence because it needed new sources of raw materials and new markets for its products.

_____ **3.** Japan feared that Russia would try to dominate neighboring Manchuria.

_____ **4.** In 1902, Japan entered into an alliance with Great Britain that was clearly aimed at protecting Japan from Korea.

_____ **5.** Japan won the Russo-Japanese War.

_____ **6.** Japan took over Korea in 1910.

_____ **7.** One serious problem that Japan faced after 1905 is that its food supply was not enough for its growing population.

_____ **8.** The United States eventually limited the number of immigrants it would accept from Asian countries.

_____ **9.** The center of Japanese society never shifted from its rural roots.

_____ **10.** In the 1930s, military needs and values had no influence over Japanese life.

REVIEWING FACTS Choose the correct items from the following list to complete the statements below.

fifty years	militarism	Treaty of Portsmouth
fleet	Monroe Doctrine	tariffs

1. Japan surprised the world by defeating the Russian _____ at the Battle of Tsushima.

2. The _____ recognized Japanese power in Korea and Manchuria.

3. It took Japan _____ to become a major industrial and military power.

4. Many countries imposed _____ to protect their industries from less expensive Japanese products.

5. In the 1920s and 1930s, _____ became an important force in Japanese society.

6. The Japanese claimed the same right to exclude outsiders from Asia as the

_____ gave the United States in the Western Hemisphere.

CHAPTER 29

Modern Chapter **20**

Main Idea Activities 29.5

Latin America Between the Wars

VOCABULARY Some terms to understand:

• **professions (775):** doctor, lawyer, and similar occupations

• **sweeping (775):** large-scale

• **enacted (775):** put into place

• **transition (775):** shift from one person's or party's rule to another's

• **intervene (776):** step in

ORGANIZING INFORMATION Use the following items to complete the web below.

• Rafael Trujillo Molina   • Anastasio Somoza   • Fulgencio Battista

• Lázaro Cárdenas   • Gerardo Machado

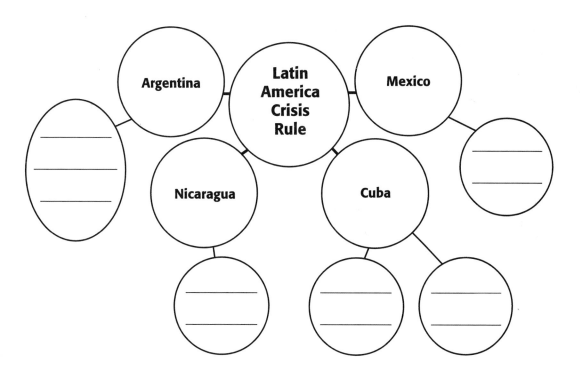

EVALUATING INFORMATION Mark each statement *T* if it is true or *F* if it is false.

_____ **1.** Latin America after World War I was highly industrialized and urbanized.

_____ **2.** Even though oil was discovered in Mexico, Venezuela, and other countries, foreigners owned the oil companies.

_____ **3.** Growth in the production of electricity in the 1920s helped Latin America produce more goods.

Chapter 29, Main Idea Activities, 29.5, continued

_____ **4.** Labor unions and labor unrest were never features of Latin American life.

_____ **5.** Mexico had a single-party political system in the hope of promoting stability.

_____ **6.** Chile's economy was hurt badly when Germany developed a way to make synthetic nitrates.

_____ **7.** Falling prices for farm products made it very difficult for Latin American nations to pay their debts during the Great Depression.

_____ **8.** Rafael Trujillo Molina brought democracy to Argentina.

_____ **9.** At the Pan-American Conference of 1933, the United States agreed not to interfere in the internal affairs of Latin America.

_____ **10.** The United States maintained the right to interfere in the affairs of Panama because of the importance of the canal to the world at large.

UNDERSTANDING MAIN IDEAS For each of the following, write the letter of the best choice in the space provided.

_____ **1.** By 1935, Mexico City, Rio de Janeiro, São Paulo, and Buenos Aires
  a. were the scenes of major labor unrest and violence.
  b. were torn down and replaced as part of land reform.
  c. each had a population of one million or more.
  d. were governed by socialist mayors.

_____ **2.** A sign of political crisis during the Great Depression was that
  a. landowners willingly agreed to land reform.
  b. many governments long in power were overthrown.
  c. politicians fled to Germany.
  d. foreign debt was low.

_____ **3.** The Good Neighbor Policy
  a. was a trick to control the labor movement.
  b. stressed cooperation and noninterference in Latin American affairs.
  c. improved diplomatic relations between the United States and England.
  d. was immediately suspended because of war in Brazil.

_____ **4.** When Lázaro Cárdenas of Mexico nationalized the oil companies,
  a. the world boycotted Mexican products.
  b. the people rebelled against him.
  c. Mexicans regarded it as an economic independence day.
  d. the United States sent troops to occupy Mexico.

CHAPTER 30

Modern Chapter 21

Main Idea Activities 30.1

Threats to World Peace

VOCABULARY Some terms to understand:

• **aggressor (784):** attacker

• **sanctions (784):** restrictions placed on a nation to get it to follow international law

• **bolster (784):** equip, reinforce

• **head of state (785):** head of the government

• **divisive (785):** causing disagreement

ORGANIZING INFORMATION Show the threats to world peace by writing the letters of the correct answer in the space provided.

A. invades Ethiopia

B. fascist dictatorship

C. withdraws from League

D. Loyalists

E. Franco

F. outbreak of civil war

G. Nationalists

H. attacks Manchuria

I. League of Nations sanctions not enforced

J. Communists

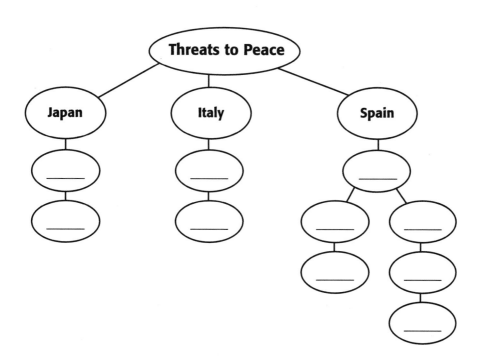

EVALUATING INFORMATION Mark each statement *T* if it is true or *F* if it is false.

_____ **1.** The Kellogg-Briand Pact gave Japan the right to capture territory in Asia.

_____ **2.** The Chinese attack at Mukden was faked.

Chapter 30, Main Idea Activities 30.1, continued

_____ **3.** The League of Nations voted to take military action against Japan for its activities in Manchuria.

_____ **4.** By 1939, Japan controlled all of China's seaports.

_____ **5.** Ethiopia attacked Italy in 1934.

_____ **6.** Because no country would enforce League of Nations sanctions, Japan and Italy felt free to continue their acts of aggression.

_____ **7.** The Civil War in Spain was fought between the Catholics and the Loyalists.

_____ **8.** The Loyalists were supported by Russia, and Franco's forces were supported by Germany.

_____ **9.** The International Brigade took no part in the fighting.

_____ **10.** General Franco was assassinated soon after the Nationalists captured Madrid.

REVIEWING FACTS Choose the correct items from the following list to complete the statements below.

| Manchuria | Ethiopia | Nationalists | fascist |
| League of Nations | dictator | another war | Osachi Hamaguchi |

1. Chaos followed the murder of Premier _____ of Japan.

2. Japan's first military conquest was _____.

3. Japan withdrew from the _____ because it condemned Japan's actions in China.

4. Mussolini ruled Italy as a _____.

5. _____ was one of the few nations left in Africa not controlled by a colonial power.

6. Memories of World War I made Great Britain and the United States unwilling to risk

_____.

7. The rebels in Spain led by Franco called themselves _____.

8. The kind of government the Nationalists proposed was

_____.

Main Idea Activities 30.2

Modern Chapter **21**   **Hitler's Agression**

VOCABULARY Some terms to understand:

- **dragged on (789):** lasted a long time
- **have a free hand (789):** be able to act without opposition
- **relentlessly (790):** again and again

ORGANIZING INFORMATION Put the boldfaced words in the box in the correct time order in the top row of the chart. Then use the remaining items to complete the chart.

Poland	Sudetenland	Austria

- violation of Treaty of Versailles
- League of Nations did nothing
- Czechoslovakia left defenseless
- strong local Nazi party
- Germans live in Polish Corridor

- German riots led to invasion
- Nonaggression pact gave it to Germany
- invasion on September 1, 1939
- annexed in 1938

World War II		
Place: _____	**Place:** _____	**Place:** _____
• _____ _____	• _____ _____	• _____ _____
• _____ _____	• _____ _____	• _____ _____
• _____ _____	• _____ _____	• _____ _____

EVALUATING INFORMATION Mark each statement *T* if it is true or *F* if it is false.

_____ **1.** In 1933, German troops occupied the Rhineland in violation of the Treaty of Versailles.

_____ **2.** The Axis powers signed the Anti-Comintern Pact, in which they agreed to halt the spread of fascism.

_____ **3.** Austria became a member of the German Third Reich by a vote of the Austrian people.

_____ **4.** Capturing the Sudetenland was an important German objective because the Sudetenland was heavily industrialized.

_____ **5.** Hitler announced that he would invade the Sudetenland in order to protect the Czechoslovakian people from the Germans who lived there.

_____ **6.** Giving in to the Nazi's demands became known as appeasement.

_____ **7.** Russia wanted to create a military alliance with Estonia and the other Baltic countries that would give Russia the right to move troops into those countries.

_____ **8.** According to the German-Soviet nonaggression pact, Germany and Russia agreed not to attack each other.

_____ **9.** The Western democracies expected Stalin to make the German-Soviet nonaggression pact with Hitler.

_____ **10.** The Polish army had no hope of defeating Hitler's far stronger army.

UNDERSTANDING MAIN IDEAS For each of the following, write the letter of the best choice in the space provided.

_____ **1.** Germany and Italy hid their intention to conquer Europe
   a. from an all-powerful League of Nations.
   b. under the mask of fighting Communism.
   c. from their own citizens.
   d. before Europe united to attack Germany.

_____ **2.** The philosophy behind appeasement was that
   a. the other nations of Europe were Nazi sympathizers.
   b. war, if it came, should be started on France's terms, not Germany's.
   c. war had been outlawed by the Kellogg-Briand pact.
   d. it was important to keep the peace at all costs.

_____ **3.** Stalin and Hitler signed a nonaggression pact because
   a. they trusted each other.
   b. they shared a belief in world domination.
   c. they were buying time from each other.
   d. they wanted to unite against the Western democracies.

_____ **4.** Regaining the Polish Corridor was an important German objective because
   a. the land was once Prussian territory.
   b. Poland already had access to the sea in other ways.
   c. many Poles lived in German territory.
   d. it was good terrain in which to use tanks.

CHAPTER **30**

Modern Chapter **21**

Main Idea Activities 30.3

Axis Gains

VOCABULARY Some terms to understand:

- **expel (791):** throw out
- **armored units (792):** units equipped with tanks
- **outflank (792):** get the better of something by going around it
- **boost (793):** lift
- **campaigns (793):** large-scale military actions
- **undermined (793):** hurt from inside
- **sabotage (793):** damage done by civilians
- **munitions (794):** war materials

ORGANIZING INFORMATION Use the following items to complete the chart below. Put the events in order by time.

- lands soldiers in France
- captures Estonia, Latvia, and Lithuania
- invades Denmark and Norway
- blockades German ports
- invades Netherlands and Belgium
- invades eastern Poland
- outflanks the Maginot Line
- evacuates its forces from Dunkirk
- captures Finland
- captures France

Great Britain	Soviet Union	Nazi Germany
1.	1.	1.
2.	2.	2.
3.	3.	3.
		4.

EVALUATING INFORMATION Mark each statement *T* if it is true or *F* if it is false.

_____ **1.** The German word *blitzkrieg* means "lightning war."

_____ **2.** People spoke of a "phony war" because there was little actual fighting despite much movement of troops.

_____ **3.** The League of Nations was powerless to take military action against the Soviet Union after it had invaded Finland.

_____ **4.** It took German forces more than a year to capture Norway.

_____ **5.** German tanks could not break through France's Maginot Line despite three major attempts.

_____ **6.** Great Britain successfully evacuated troops from Dunkerque.

_____ **7.** France's armies and generals were well prepared to fight the swift-paced modern style of warfare that Germany fought.

_____ **8.** The Vichy government refused to sign a peace treaty with Germany.

_____ **9.** The *maquis* was the anti-Nazi French underground.

_____ **10.** During World War II, Winston Churchill led Great Britain as prime minster.

UNDERSTANDING MAIN IDEAS For each of the following, write the letter of the best choice in the space provided.

_____ **1.** A chief reason why Hitler's armies were successful at the start of the war was
a. the speed at which they fought.
b. the flatness of the ground on which they fought.
c. the tanks they received from the Soviet army.
d. the weather, which turned battlefields to mud.

_____ **2.** The strategic advantage that Germany got from capturing Norway and Denmark was
a. it helped Germany defeat Norwegian collaborators.
b. it kept these countries from turning socialist.
c. it gave Germany bases for submarines and aircraft.
d. it allowed the Germans to fight a "phony war."

_____ **3.** The Battle of Britain was
a. an air war.
b. a ground war.
c. a sea war.
d. an undersea war.

_____ **4.** The Lend-Lease Act of 1941
a. let the United States sell munitions to Germany.
b. let the United States take responsibility for the fall of France.
c. let Great Britain receive much-needed war supplies.
d. left the Soviet Union alone to fight the Germans single-handed.

Main Idea Activities 30.4

Modern Chapter **21**   **The Soviet Union and the United States**

VOCABULARY Some terms to understand:

• **liberated (796):** freed

• **soundly (797):** totally and completely

• **front (798):** battlefront

• **scorched-earth method (798):** a method of defense where retreating soldiers destroy everything on the land they lose

• **embargo (799):** an order by a government that forbids trade with another country

ORGANIZING INFORMATION Tell when each action happened. Use the following items to complete the chart below.

• makes Netherlands East Indies a protectorate

• joins Germany and Italy as an Axis power

• captures New Guinea and Solomon Islands

• cuts British sea route to Hong Kong and Singapore

• captures Guam

• makes Indochina a protectorate

• attacks Philippines

• captures Burma, Thailand, and Malaya

Japan		
Before		**After**
• _____ _____		• _____ _____
• _____ _____	**Attack on Pearl Harbor** **December 7, 1941**	• _____ _____
• _____ _____		• _____ _____
• _____ _____		• _____ _____

(Chapter 30, Main Idea Activities 30.4, continued)

EVALUATING INFORMATION Mark each statement *T* if it is true or *F* if it is false.

_____ **1.** Spain remained neutral during Word War II but let German submarines use its ports.

_____ **2.** Japan allied itself with Germany and Italy after Great Britain and the United States refused an alliance with Japan.

_____ **3.** Italy's hope to build a Mediterranean empire for itself failed.

_____ **4.** Germany wanted to gain control of the Balkan nations because of the rich oil fields in the region.

_____ **5.** The forces of German General Erwin Rommel kept British troops out of North Africa for the entire war.

_____ **6.** Germany made a formal declaration of war against Russia before invading it.

_____ **7.** The scorched-earth methods that the Russians used against the Germans involved destroying anything that they could not carry away.

_____ **8.** Japan targeted the Netherlands East Indies as a military objective because of the oil reserves there.

_____ **9.** General Tojo headed a pacifist government that came to power in 1941.

_____ **10.** Japan's intention at Pearl Harbor was to destroy the ability of the United States to fight a war against Japan.

REVIEWING FACTS Choose the correct items from the following list to complete the statements below.

El Alamein   Guam   Stalingrad
Russia   battleships   Ethiopia

1. In 1940, Italian troops were driven from _____.

2. The Battle of _____ in North Africa was an important British victory.

3. Germany's invasion of _____ created a huge new front in Eastern Europe.

4. Stalin demanded that the city of _____ be held at all cost.

5. Japan captured _____ on the same day Japanese aircraft bombed Pearl Harbor.

6. At Pearl Harbor, many American _____ were heavily damaged or sunk.

CHAPTER 30 Main Idea Activities 30.5

Modern Chapter **21** **The Holocaust**

VOCABULARY Some terms to understand:

• **genocide (801):** the intentional extermination of a whole people

• **cremate (802):** burn the bodies of

• **ghetto (803):** the only portion of the city in which the Jews were allowed to live

ORGANIZING INFORMATION Complete the web by writing the letter of the correct answer where it belongs.

A. Dachau **G.** Danes

B. superiority of Aryan race **H.** Wannsee Conference

C. Raoul Wallenberg **I.** Treblinka

D. Heinrich Himmler **J.** Oskar Schindler

E. racial inferiority of Slavs **K.** anti-Semitism

F. Buchenwald **L.** Auschwitz

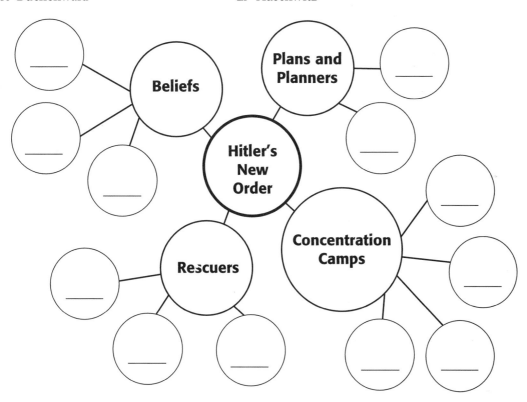

EVALUATING INFORMATION Mark each statement *T* if it is true or *F* if it is false.

_____ **1.** Hitler's plan in Eastern Europe was to provide living space for the Aryan race.

_____ **2.** It was acceptable to Hitler if tens of millions of Russians starved to death.

_____ **3.** Hitler pointed to the genocide of the Turkish people as a model for the elimination of the Jewish people.

_____ **4.** The SS was the military branch of the Nazi Party.

_____ **5.** The plan to use concentration camps to exterminate Jews was set at the Wannsee Conference.

_____ **6.** Only a few thousand Jews were taken to the concentration camps; most were killed in their homes.

_____ **7.** The Nazi concentration camps were also used as sources of forced labor.

_____ **8.** Ovens were used in the concentration camps to burn the bodies of the dead.

_____ **9.** Jewish people were the only ones killed by the Nazis during the Holocaust.

_____ **10.** Jews had to identify themselves by wearing the Star of David on their clothes.

UNDERSTANDING MAIN IDEAS For each of the following, write the letter of the best choice in the space provided.

_____ **1.** In the "New Order," Soviet territory was supposed to supply Germany with
    a. a large captive work force.
    b. a place for its troops to practice fighting.
    c. moral support for a New Germany
    d. only food and raw materials.

_____ **2.** The word that best describes the Wannsee Conference's plans for exterminating Jews is
    a. occasional.
    b. systematic.
    c. economic.
    d. merciful.

_____ **3.** In the concentration camps, people who could not work were
    a. sent to gas chambers.
    b. given other tasks.
    c. kept well-fed.
    d. forced to write books.

_____ **4.** The number of European Jews killed during the Holocaust was
    a. 60,000
    b. 600,000
    c. 6 million
    d. 6 billion

 **Main Idea Activities 30.6**

Modern Chapter **21**   **The End of the War**

VOCABULARY Some terms to understand:

- **sonar (805):** a device for locating objects underwater
- **turn the tide (805):** change to the opposite direction
- **unconditional (807):** total, absolute
- **radiation sickness (807):** illness caused by exposure to an atomic blast
- **staggering (808):** overwhelming, great
- **endurance (808):** ability to hold on or continue
- **atrocities (809):** acts of great outrage and inhumanity

ORGANIZING INFORMATION Use the following items to complete the chart below.

- Battle of the Coral Sea
- Guadalcanal
- Stalingrad
- D-Day and France
- Battle of Leyte Gulf
- bombing of Hiroshima and Nagasaki
- Sicily
- Battle of the Bulge
- Battle of Midway
- Tunisia

Allied Victory	
Major German and Italian Defeats	**Major Japanese Defeats**

EVALUATING INFORMATION Mark each statement *T* if it is true or *F* if it is false.

_____ **1.** The Battle of Stalingrad is considered a turning point of World War II.

_____ **2.** When General Eisenhower defeated General Montgomery, the Allies captured North Africa.

Chapter 30, Main Idea Activities 30.6, continued

_____ **3.** The "soft underbelly of the Axis" referred to the coast of France, where an important invasion was set to take place.

_____ **4.** Italy fought the Allies to the bitter end in defense of Mussolini and fascist plans for Europe.

_____ **5.** Many important battles against Japan in the Pacific were naval and air battles.

_____ **6.** After the Battle of Midway, Japan was no longer the likely victor in the war.

_____ **7.** The strategy of island hopping meant that every island in the Pacific had to be fought for, one at a time.

_____ **8.** The Allies controlled the Philippine islands after the Battle of Leyte Gulf.

UNDERSTANDING MAIN IDEAS For each of the following, write the letter of the best choice in the space provided.

_____ **1.** The importance of the D-Day invasion of Normandy in June 1944 was that
  a. it was the strongest blow yet to the Japanese army.
  b. it was the long planned-for major invasion of Europe.
  c. it took Germany's attention away from the true invasion site.
  d. it was fought only in the air without any loss of life.

_____ **2.** When Soviet and American armies met in East Germany in 1945,
  a. the war was soon over.
  b. the Germans broke through their lines and started the Battle of the Bulge.
  c. Russia was planning to rejoin the war on Germany's side.
  d. Great Britain was upset.

_____ **3.** An unconditional surrender means that
  a. the loser has to make a secret treaty with the other side.
  b. the loser has the right to appeal the conditions of the peace.
  c. the loser surrenders totally and completely.
  d. the loser is entitled by law to rearm itself in five years.

_____ **4.** Winston Churchill was an important symbol of wartime Britain because
  a. he made excuses for British losses.
  b. he hated and feared the French.
  c. he symbolized the country's determination and valor.
  d. he was a bully and Great Britain needed a bully.

Main Idea Activities 31.1

Modern Chapter 22

Aftermath of the War in Europe

VOCABULARY Some words to understand:

- **zones (820):** distinct areas created for a particular purpose
- **spheres (821):** a field or range of influence or significance
- **approach (821):** a preliminary step, the first step toward an end
- **acquitted (822):** set free or discharged completely
- **charter (823):** an official document granting or defining rights and duties of a body
- **skepticism (824):** an attitude of doubt, suspicion or uncertainty
- **despite (824):** in spite of or even though

ORGANIZING INFORMATION Use the following decisions to fill in the graphic organizer.

- establish the United Nations
- demilitarize Germany and outlaw the Nazi party
- defeat Germany by attacking it from two fronts
- divide Austria and Germany into zones of military occupation

Decisions at Conferences	
Conference	**Decisions**
"Big Three" meeting in Tehran, 1943	
Meeting at the Black Sea resort in Yalta, 1945	
Meeting of allied leaders in Potsdam, 1945	
Meeting of 51 nations in San Francicso, 1945	

EVALUATING INFORMATION Mark each statement *T* if it is true or *F* if it is false.

_____ **1.** Stalin agreed to grant the Eastern European nations free elections even without their learning Socialist principles.

_____ **2.** Roosevelt believed that peace can be achieved through collective security among nations.

_____ **3.** The Potsdam Conference decided on what to do with Germany.

_____ **4.** France agreed with the United States and Great Britain to revive German industries.

Chapter 31, Main Idea Activities 31.1, continued

_____ **5.** War reparations instead of recovery was more important to the Soviet Union.

_____ **6.** The Nürnberg trials declared the Nazi party a criminal organization.

_____ **7.** Americans readily accepted the idea of the United Nations.

_____ **8.** Italy refused to give up the countries it gained during the war.

REVIEWING FACTS Choose the correct item from the following list to complete each statement.

China	veto power	concentration camp
East and West Germany	Yalta	Eleanor Roosevelt
Harry Truman	Sudeten	Big Three
three		

1. Churchill, Roosevelt and Stalin led the allied countries called the

_____.

2. The meeting in _____ decided on zones of military occupation in Germany and Eastern Europe.

3. After the death of Roosevelt, _____ represented the United States at the postwar settlement in Potsdam.

4. Czechoslovakia evicted the _____ Germans, who had supported Hitler's invasion in 1938.

5. The Nazi leaders were brought to trial after horrors of racial purification and the

_____ were exposed.

6. Only _____ of the 22 Nazi leaders charged with crimes against peace and humanity were acquitted.

7. When the division of Germany became formal, Germany became two countries

initially known as _____.

8. _____ a famous First Lady, helped make Americans support the newly-organized United Nations.

9. The five members of the UN Security Council are Great Britain, France, the Soviet

Union, the United States, and _____.

10. Each member of the Security Council can prevent action by using a single vote called

_____.

CHAPTER 31

Modern Chapter **22**

Main Idea Activities 31.2

Origins of the Cold War

VOCABULARY Some words to understand:

- **dissolve (825):** bring to an end
- **buffer zone (825):** area between two rival powers that can lessen impact of invasion or attack
- **intervene (825):** come between in order to stop, settle or change something
- **subjugation (826):** force to submit to control
- **denounced (827):** informed against, put it down
- **consequence (325):** point of view

ORGANIZING INFORMATION Fill in the graphic organizer by using the items below. Add them in correct time order.

- The alliance between the Soviet and the Western allies dissolved.
- The Truman Doctrine considered the spread of communism a threat to democracy.
- The Marshall Plan put Europe on the road to prosperity.
- The Soviets established the Cominform to oppose the Marshall Plan.

EVENTS THAT LED TO THE COLD WAR

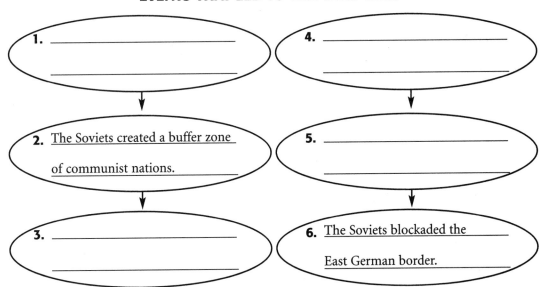

1. _____

2. The Soviets created a buffer zone of communist nations.

3. _____

4. _____

5. _____

6. The Soviets blockaded the East German border.

EVALUATING INFORMATION Mark each statement *T* if it is true or *F* if it is false.

_____ 1. Each side in the Cold War believed its own system should serve as model for European recovery and reconstruction.

_____ **2.** The Truman Doctrine only helps a country if it asks to prevent a communist takeover.

_____ **3.** Marshall Tito, a devoted communist, allowed the Soviets to dominate Yugoslavia.

_____ **4.** Western leaders feared that the poverty in Europe after the war could lead to communism.

_____ **5.** The Soviet Union accepted the offer of the United States for assistance through the Marshall Plan.

_____ **6.** The Berlin blockade is given as the official beginning of the Cold War.

_____ **7.** Because of the split in Germany, the Western nations formed the North Atlantic Treaty Organization (NATO) and the Eastern bloc nations formed the Warsaw Pact.

_____ **8.** The NATO ground troops outnumbered those of the Warsaw Pact.

UNDERSTANDING MAIN IDEAS For each of the following, write the letter of the best choice in the space provided.

_____ **1.** Right after the war that led the Western nations to believe he hoped to expand the Soviet Union and one day dominate all of Europe, Stalin
   a. invaded Austria.
   b. blockaded Poland.
   c. created a buffer zone along the Soviet Union's western frontier.
   d. insisted joint control of the Black Sea to the Aegean with the Turkish.

_____ **2.** Under the Marshall Plan, European nations were encouraged to
   a. share costs in production.
   b. determine their needs and remove trade barriers.
   c. set up farm and industrial factories.
   d. tighten up defense against communism.

_____ **3.** The Cold War worsened in Asia during the 1950s when
   a. the Soviets took over China.
   b. the Soviets formed a new military alliance.
   c. North Korea invaded South Korea.
   d. Stalin invaded Taiwan.

_____ **4.** The member nations of NATO agree to
   a. help each other in times of economic crisis.
   b. dissolve all barriers to unity.
   c. reinforce ground troops.
   d. take united action if one nation is attacked.

Main Idea Activities 31.3

Modern Chapter **22**

Reconstruction, Reform and Reaction in Europe

VOCABULARY Some words to understand:

- **commitment (831):** something pledged
- **interfere (832):** meddle in the affair of others
- **ravaged (833):** suggests violent, often repeated, or continuing destruction
- **offset (833):** make up for, compensate
- **entrenched (834):** established solidly
- **rifts (836):** divisions, estrangments

ORGANIZING INFORMATION Fill in the Venn Diagram by using the items below.

- economic rise
- outdated factories
- too reliant on coal reserves
- few labor troubles
- won the war
- economic downturn
- anti-communist
- technical innovaton
- lost the war
- slow industrial growth
- lost overseas colonies
- anti-Soviet

Two Economies

Great Britain   **In Common**   **West Germany**

_____   _____   _____

_____   _____   _____

_____   _____

_____   _____

_____   _____

_____

Name _____ Class _____ Date _____

EVALUATING INFORMATION Mark each statement *T* if it is true or *F* if it is false.

_____ **1.** West Germany prospered from Ludwig Erhard's free market policies and achieved an "economic miracle" in the 1960s.

_____ **2.** The East Germans built the Berlin Wall to stop escapees from the communist side to West Germany.

_____ **3.** Great Britain progressed in its economic recovery like the rest of Europe.

_____ **4.** A welfare state such as Great Britain expects its citizens to take care of themselves.

_____ **5.** Under Charles de Gaulle, the French empire became the French community, or an association of free nations.

_____ **6.** The French accepted Charles de Gaulle's reforms to meet labor and student demands during the unstable decade of the sixties.

_____ **7.** Portugal and Spain ended their autoritarian governments and turned democratic like the rest of postwar Europe.

_____ **8.** Nikita Kruschev's primary economic goal was to make more consumer goods available to the people.

_____ **9.** Soviet controlled governments gained economically from collective farming.

_____ **10.** Dissatisfaction with communism became widespread in Europe during the 1960s.

REVIEWING FACTS Choose the correct items from the following list to complete the statements below.

Common Market   Konrad Adenauer
Prague Spring   Fifth Republic

1. _____ encouraged those from the Eastern bloc to escape to West Berlin.

2. The new constitution de Gaulle wrote gave birth to France's

_____ .

3. The European Economic Community is also called the _____ .

4. Alexander Dubcek's short-lived period of freedom in Czechoslovakia is known as the

_____ .

CHAPTER 31

Modern Chapter 22

Main Idea Activities 31.4

The United States and Canada

VOCABULARY Some words to understand:

- **foreshadow (837):** have a hint before something happens
- **hysteria (837):** emotional excess, unmanageable fear
- **affluent (838):** wealthy, rich
- **boycott (838):** jointly refuse to deal with someone or to force a settlement
- **emulate (838):** try to equal or excel
- **perspective (840):** view or outlook
- **undermine (840):** weaken or wear away slowly and secretly

ORGANIZING INFORMATION Complete the chart by filling in solutions to America's problems with the following items.

- United States Supreme Court orders integration in schools.
- Eisenhower faces spread of communism in Southeast Asia.
- Joseph McCarthy leads anti-communist hysteria.
- Martin Luther King leads civil rights movement.
- Senate Committee investigation finds claims groundless.
- Creates Southeast Asian Treaty Organization (SEATO).

Postwar United States	
Problems	**Solutions**

EVALUATING INFORMATION Mark each statement *T* if it is true or *F* if it is false.

_____ **1.** The United States economy continued to grow after the war but Americans felt anxious and insecure.

_____ **2.** Sen. Joseph McCarthy led some Americans to believe that certain people in the United States were siding with communism.

_____ **3.** President John F. Kennedy's term ended before Congress could pass his proposed legislations.

_____ **4.** Before 1954, black children went to school with white children.

_____ **5.** Martin Luther King, Jr., won the Nobel Peace Prize for his nonviolent methods to bring about change.

_____ **6.** The Eisenhower Doctrine's aim was to help non-communist nations in Europe from a takeover.

_____ **7.** The United States invaded Cuba by air during John F. Kennedy's presidency.

_____ **8.** The Soviet Union built nuclear missile sites to support Cuba in its fight with the United States

_____ **9.** The United States and Canada built the Distant Early Warning Line, or DEW Line, to detect early signs of air attacks.

_____ **10.** There are no groups in Canada that want to form a separate nation.

REVIEWING FACTS Choose the correct items from the following list to complete the statements below.

Quebecois	Fidel Castro	Kurds
refugees	Chicago	missiles

1. A Marxist named _____ took over the Cuban government in 1959.

2. The real threat of a war using _____ came during the Cuban crisis.

3. The turning point in the American protests against United States involvement in the Vietnam War happened at the Democratic Party Convention in

_____.

4. Like the United States after World War II, Canada accepted

_____ from other parts of the world.

5. The _____, a people with its own language and culture, have been trying to separate from Canada.

6. The _____ in the Middle East and the Basque people of Spain both want their own nation.

CHAPTER 32

Modern Chapter **23**

Main Idea Activities 32.1

South Asia After the Empire

VOCABULARY Some terms to understand:

- **resist (845):** to withstand the force or its effect
- **chaos (847):** state of utter confusion
- **tragedy (847):** a disastrous event like a calamity
- **back (849):** give support
- **torn apart (850):** separated painfully, forcibly
- **barely managed (850):** scarcely made it, almost did not make it

ORGANIZING INFORMATION Use the following items to complete the chart below.

- Mohandas Gandhi starts "Quit India"
- Britain sends Sir Stafford Cripps
- India and Pakistan are born
- Gandhi and Jinnah fail to resolve differences
- Lord Louis Mountbatten sets deadline for Independence

Events that Led to the Independence of India and Pakistan

1. National Congress resigns; calls for self-rule

↓

2. _____

↓

3. _____

↓

4. _____

5. Riots break out

↓

6. _____

↓

7. Independence declared; borders defined

↓

8. _____

Evaluating Information Mark each statement *T* if it is true or *F* if it is false.

_____ **1.** India agreed to serve as base for the Allies when Japan sided with Germany.

_____ **2.** The Indian National Congress accepted the terms of independence from Sir Stafford Cripps.

_____ **3.** The British colonial government considered Mohandas Gandhi's non-violent campaign for self-rule as rebellion.

Chapter 32, Main Idea Activities 32.1, continued

_____ **4.** Muhammad 'Ali Jinnah led the Indian Muslims to demand a separate state.

_____ **5.** India's declaration of independence was peaceful, a sign that the Indians were ready for it.

_____ **6.** Under Jawaharlal Nehru, India was an ally of both the United States and the Soviet Union.

_____ **7.** Nehru's socialist ideas worked for India's economy.

_____ **8.** By the end of the 1980s, India had solved its population problems.

_____ **9.** Many countries followed India's policy to stay neutral in hope of aid from both the communist countries and the West.

_____ **10.** When Pakistan was separated from India, it became a united country.

REVIEWING FACTS Choose the correct items from the following list to complete the statements below.

Khalida Zia	Bangladesh	two percent	three-quarters
Dalai Lama	Sikhs	Benazir Bhutto	

1. Indihra Gandhi's most difficult problem was the _____ from Punjab who were fighting for self-rule.

2. India's growing population of one billion by 2050 live on just

_____ of the world's land area.

3. Tibet's religious and political leader, the _____ fled to India and formed a government in exile after China invaded his country.

4. India and Pakistan have been fighting over the northern state of Kashmir because

_____ of its inhabitants are Muslims.

5. After East Pakistan defeated West Pakistan in the 1971 civil war, it became

_____ .

6. The first woman prime minister of Bangladesh, _____, faced problems of floods and political unrest.

7. _____ who was elected prime minister of Bangladesh in 1988 was the first woman to head a Muslim nation.

Main Idea Activities 32.2

Modern Chapter **23**   **Communist China and Its Influence**

VOCABULARY Some terms to understand:

- **resumed (852):** started again
- **furnaces (853):** enclosed structure in which heat is produced
- **rampage (854):** to rush wildly about, to destroy any which way
- **disastrous (854):** a natural event or calamity that comes with misfortune or suffering
- **treason (854):** betrayal of a trust
- **stunned (855):** taken by surprise

ORGANIZING INFORMATION Use the following items to complete the chart below.

- Five-Year Plan for economic growth
- Violent Attempt at Social Change
- Four Modernizations
- Great Leap Forward
- Cultural Revolution
- A shift toward an open society

The Rise of China	
The Plan	**The Purpose**

EVALUATING INFORMATION Mark each statement *T* if it is true or *F* if it is false.

_____ **1.** The United States supported the Chinese nationalists in their fight for power.

_____ **2.** Mao Zedong modeled his economic recovery plan after the Soviet Union and succeeded.

_____ **3.** Mao's goal to match the West in industrial output was reached in the Great Leap Forward.

_____ **4.** The Cultural Revolution attempted to retain old customs, habits, and thoughts.

_____ **5.** Jiang Qing, Mao's widow, and her group were found innocent of their crimes.

Chapter 32, Main Idea Activities 32.2, continued

_____ **6.** As a result of the Tiananmen Square incident, international aid agencies stopped or lessened loans to China.

_____ **7.** The United States maintains diplomatic relations with both the People's Republic of China and Taiwan.

_____ **8.** Taiwan is a province of China.

_____ **9.** Since 1950, South Korea was never lead by a dictator or a leader with dictatorial powers.

_____ **10.** China and the United States formally declared war on one another because of Korea.

UNDERSTANDING MAIN IDEAS For each of the following, write the letter of the best choice in the space provided.

_____ **1.** Part of the plan to turn China into a modern industrialized nation was land reform which was carried out by
　　　a. organizing peasants into communities.
　　　b. taking large tracts of idle land and farming them.
　　　c. forcing landowners to give their land to the peasants.
　　　d. buying out landowners and distributing the land to peasants.

_____ **2.** Encouraged by Deng Xiaoping's "fifth modernization," or democracy, students staged hunger strikes at Tiananmen Square and were
　　　a. rounded up and imprisoned.
　　　b. expelled by the universities.
　　　c. shot at and killed or wounded.
　　　d. heard by the government officials.

_____ **3.** Korea remained divided long after the war because
　　　a. communist Korea's idea of unification was invasion.
　　　b. Soviet Russia attacked South Korea.
　　　c. China threatened to expand its borders to Korea.
　　　d. the United States did not want to bomb China.

_____ **4.** This event in June 30, 1997 was a time of national pride for China because
　　　a. the United States signed a new trade agreement with the communist government.
　　　b. Hong Kong, a British colony since 1840, was returned to China.
　　　c. Chinese artists and business leaders returned home with honors.
　　　d. the United States ended recognition of Taiwan as an independent country.

CHAPTER **32**

Modern Chapter **23**

Main Idea Activities 32.3

The Japanese Miracle

VOCABULARY Some terms to understand:

- **demilitarize (859):** to strip of military forces
- **disarm (859):** disband or reduce the size of a country's armed forces
- **pace (860):** rate of movement
- **renounce (861):** give up; abandon or resign usually by verbal declaration
- **stance (861):** attitude or way of standing or being placed
- **coalition (862):** a temporary alliance of persons or countries for joint action

ORGANIZING INFORMATION Complete the graphic organizer by filling in answers that match given items by using the following items:

- Land reform
- Break up of zaibatsu
- Women in workforce
- Higher standard of living
- More factories

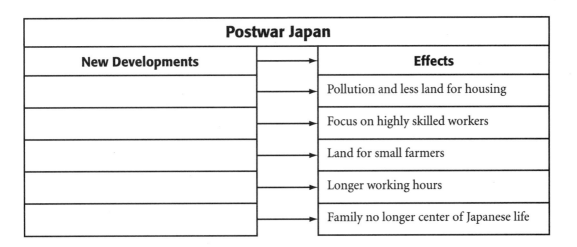

Postwar Japan		
New Developments		**Effects**
		Pollution and less land for housing
		Focus on highly skilled workers
		Land for small farmers
		Longer working hours
		Family no longer center of Japanese life

EVALUATING INFORMATION Mark each statement *T* if it is true or *F* if it is false.

_____ **1.** General McArthur's first task after World War II was to demilitarize Japan.

_____ **2.** The Allied Powers wanted to give the Japanese the chance to provide for themselves.

_____ **3.** After the war, the Japanese emperor remained divine and powerful.

Chapter 32, Main Idea Activities 32.3, continued

_____ **4.** War was kept as a natural right of Japan under the McArthur Constitution.

_____ **5.** By the 1980s, Japan had become Asia's leading economic power.

_____ **6.** In General McArthur' plan, raising an army in postwar Japan was as important as raising the standard of living.

_____ **7.** The Japanese did not like United States troops stationed in their country.

_____ **8.** According to an agreement between the United States and Japan, Japan would not provide the United States with armed forces in case of a conflict near Japan.

UNDERSTANDING MAIN IDEAS For each of the following, write the letter of the best choice in the space provided.

_____ **1.** One important reason why Japan made a surprisingly rapid recovery from a badly damaged economy after the war was
a. the resistance of the allied powers.
b. the personal authority and influence of the emperor.
c. the break up of zaibatsu controlled by powerful families.
d. the large number of factories untouched by allied bombing.

_____ **2.** Because of economic growth that resulted in a higher standard of living, the Japanese of today
a. work longer hours.
b. have more time for recreation.
c. can spend more time with their families.
d. can afford to buy bigger homes on large plots of land.

_____ **3.** The main cause of tension between the United States and Japan was
a. the financial scandal in government.
b. political turmoil that continued after recovery.
c. the pressure to increase Japanese armed forces.
d. the aid Japan gives to other countries.

_____ **4.** Japan and the Soviet Union have an ongoing dispute over
a. technical aid required by Japan.
b. the four small Kuril islands.
c. Japanese ties with the United States.
d. the return of a militaristic government.

CHAPTER 32   Main Idea Activities 32.4

Modern Chapter **23**   **Independence Struggles in Southeast Asia**

VOCABULARY Some terms to understand:

• **dissension (864):** disagreement in opinion

• **bribes (864):** money or favor given or promised to put improper influence on the judgment or conduct of a person in a position of trust

• **faction (864):** a group acting together within and usually against a larger body

• **standstill (866):** a complete stop

• **genocide (869):** deliberate or systematic destruction of a racial or cultural group

• **disputes (869):** quarrels, irritable arguments

• **installed (869):** to set up for use or service

ORGANIZING INFORMATION Complete the web by writing the letters of the correct answer in the space provided.

A. 1960s: Dictator created own parliament.

B. 1974: President placed country under martial law for 12 years.

C. 1962: Leader took control of the economy and almost destroyed it.

D. 1950s: Guerilla leader built a communist zone after the French freed his country.

E. 1975: Guerilla leader set up a government that enforced a brutal plan.

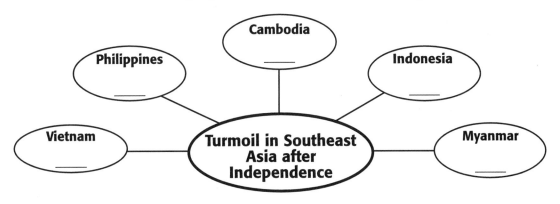

EVALUATING INFORMATION Mark each statement *T* if it is true or *F* if it is false.

_____ **1.** U.S. officials continued to support Philippine president Ferdinand Marcos because he put a new constitution in place.

_____ **2.** Corazon Aquino who replaced Marcos brought back democracy but failed to revive the economy.

_____ **3.** Burmese authorities freed Aung San Suu Kyi when she won the Nobel Prize.

_____ **4.** Sukarno and Suharto of Indonesia both ended up as dictators.

Chapter 32, Main Idea Activities 32.4, continued

_____ **5.** Because American leaders wanted to prevent the spread of communism, the U.S. became involved in the Vietnam War.

_____ **6.** North and South Vietnam were reunited under a democratic, western-style government.

_____ **7.** The Pathet Lao in Laos maintained its nonalignment policy and succeeded.

_____ **8.** Cambodia sided with North Vietnam and allowed the Ho Chi Minh trail to cross its borders.

_____ **9.** The Khmer Rouge took advantage of the Viet Nam War to attack China.

_____ **10.** Pol Pot of Cambodia brought years of freedom and prosperity to his country.

REVIEWING FACTS Choose the correct item from the following list to complete each statement below.

Khmer Rouge	Saigon	Paris Peace Accords
Tet Offensive	Myanmar	domino theory
Pol Pot	boat people	

1. Burma's new leaders renamed their country _____ in 1988.

2. The idea that caused U.S. involvement in the Vietnam War is the

_____.

3. Named for the New Year, the North Vietnamese attack that triggered American

opposition to the war was the _____.

4. The 1973 document that ended American involvement in the Vietnam War was the

_____.

5. Vietnamese refugees who faced dangerous sea voyages in search of freedom were

called _____.

6. Today's Ho Chi Minh City was once named _____.

7. The Cambodian communist group who took Phnom Penh and enforced a brutal

plan that turned into genocide was the _____.

8. Under _____ and his communist regime, one fifth of the Cambodian population died between 1975 and 1977.

CHAPTER **32**

Modern Chapter **23**

Main Idea Activities 32.5

Asian Paths to Prosperity

VOCABULARY Some terms to understand:

- **restrain (870):** prevent an action
- **reverse (870):** opposite or contrary to a previous condition
- **downturn (871):** decline especially referring to a business activity
- **reformed (872):** made changes to fit present needs
- **diffusion (872):** spread out freely, intermingling of parts

ORGANIZING INFORMATION Match the following items with the problems to complete the graphic organizer.

- army and police forces to control citizens
- unrestrained anti-communist violence
- government control at the expense of rights

How Asia Copes with Problems	
Problems	**Solutions**
desire for rapid economic growth	
continuing internal conflicts between ethnic groups	
worries about national security	

EVALUATING INFORMATION Mark each statement *T* if it is true or *F* if it is false.

_____ **1.** Most Asian countries have populations made up of different races and cultures.

_____ **2.** Asians still live in poverty, but the continent is home to some of the fastest growing economies in the world.

_____ **3.** Both democratic and communist countries use violence to stop opponents.

_____ **4.** Because Lee Kuan Yew strictly controlled labor unions, political activity and the media, Singapore remains one of the most backward countries in the world.

_____ **5.** Reliance on foreign investment has helped Asian economic growth in the 1990s.

_____ **6.** Loose economic groups among Asian countries have helped them get better loan terms and higher prices for exports.

_____ **7.** To speed up economic growth, Indonesia allowed big companies to manage its oil industry.

_____ **8.** Experts predict that by 2050, China may surpass the United States and become the largest economy in the world.

UNDERSTANDING MAIN IDEAS For each of the following, write the letter of the best choice in the space provided.

_____ **1.** Asian countries started postwar growth slowly because
    a. they suffered in the war.
    b. many of their leaders died in the war.
    c. most of them emerged from colonial rule with no wealth.
    d. no country in the West could loan them enough money.

_____ **2.** South Korea, Taiwan, Singapore and Hong Kong are called "Four Tigers"
    a. because of their important role in the world market.
    b. because of the modernized structures in their capital cities.
    c. because their population has multiplied beyond land capacity.
    d. because of the growing gap between the rich and poor.

_____ **3.** The Association of Southeast Asian Nations (ASEAN) aims to
    a. help member countries keep their culture.
    b. promote growth and social progress in the region.
    c. help choose the best leaders for each country.
    d. assist governments of member nations pass economic laws.

_____ **4.** Of these aspects of Asian culture, the one that would seem the least exotic and unfamiliar to most Westerners is its
    a. ancient religions, philosophies and martial arts.
    b. ancient manuscripts, carpets, arts and crafts.
    c. centuries-old traditions, values and work habits.
    d. modernized cities, transportation and lifestyles.

_____ **5.** One reason given for the success of Japanese products in the marketplace is that
    a. the Japanese people expect themselves to be more successful than their neighbors.
    b. Japanese schools stress writing and literature.
    c. the Japanese government provides low-interest business development loans.
    d. Japanese workers never go out on strike.

CHAPTER 33

Modern Chapter **24**

Main Idea Activities 33.1

African Independence After World War II

VOCABULARY Some terms to understand:

• **civil disobedience (879):** non-violent acts against a government

• **commemorate (879):** to remember or honor through ceremony or action

• **expel (879):** to force a person or group to leave an area or place

• **radical (881):** being extremely different from what is considered normal

• **mutiny (883):** overthrow of a rightful leader by subordinates

• **coup (884):** the overthrow of a government by a small group, usually from inside

ORGANIZING INFORMATION Use the items below to complete the diagram.

• Jomo Kenyatta
• Kwame Nkrumah
• Robert Mugabe

• voted to withdraw from federation of multi-racial state
• began a campaign of civil disobediance
• Mau Mau organization, fought a four-year guerilla campaign

Struggles for Independence

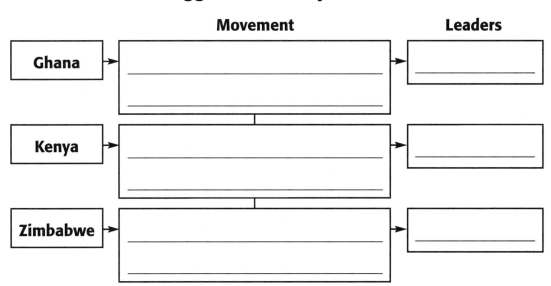

EVALUATING INFORMATION Mark each statement *T* if it is true or *F* if it is false.

_____ **1.** The Italian invasion of Ethiopia was one of the final triggers of the African nationalist movement.

_____ **2.** Ghana achieved its independence from Britain through purely peaceful means.

_____ **3.** Kenyans fought to achieve their independence from white settlers who owned the majority of profitable farmland.

_____ **4.** The Mau Mau organization lobbied for peace in Kenya by debating with the British government.

_____ **5.** Prime Minister Ian Smith of Southern Rhodesia broke from British rule to set up the African state of Zimbabwe.

_____ **6.** French President de Gaulle allowed the African colonies to choose between independence without French aid and continued status as a French colony.

_____ **7.** Belgium was the European power most friendly toward African self-rule.

_____ **8.** The Portuguese colonies gained their independence only after bloody conflicts.

REVIEWING FACTS Choose the correct items from the following list to complete the statements below.

apartheid	Ghana	Portugal
Kwame Nkrumah	Nelson Mandela	Prime Minister Ian Smith
Jomo Kenyatta	France	Congo

1. One of the early supporters of the Pan-African movement who went on to lead a

liberation effort was _____.

2. _____ was a British colony and was the first African nation to gain its independence.

3. Under pressure to allow a democratic system of majority rule,

_____ declared Southern Rhodesia an independent state.

4. The colonies of _____ only gained their independence after a military coup took place in the nation's European capital.

5. The people of Kenya mobilized and gained their independence under the leadership

of _____.

6. _____ attempted to appease its colonies by giving many blacks the right to vote and hold office within the nation's government.

7. The Belgian colony of _____ received its independence too quickly and suffered from a lack of skilled workers and leaders.

8. _____ became the first South African president after serving over 25 years in prison.

Main Idea Activities 33.2

Modern Chapter **24**

Africa Since Independence

VOCABULARY Some terms to understand:

• **prosperity (886):** the condition of being successful or thriving

• **junta (887):** a group of people who control a government immediately after a revolution

• **world market (888):** trade done on a global scale which impacts many nations

• **drought (889):** a long period of extreme dryness without sufficient rain for normal life

ORGANIZING INFORMATION Use the following items to complete the chart below. Place the names of the nations under each item that adversely affected that nation. A name can be used more than once.

• Ghana
• Somalia
• Nigeria

• Angola
• Rwanda
• Zaire

Affected Nations		
Colonial Economics	**Cold War**	**Cultural Differences**

EVALUATING INFORMATION Mark each statement *T* if it is true or *F* if it is false.

_____ **1.** Because the people of the newly independent African nations were unprepared to run a nation, violence often broke out.

_____ **2.** Ghana fell into trouble when the price of their primary export, cocoa, dropped on the world market.

_____ **3.** Nigeria developed and maintained a strong sense of national unity.

_____ **4.** Fierce conflict in Rwanda has led to the massacre of hundreds of thousands of Hutus and Tutsis.

_____ **5.** Many African nations enjoyed thriving industries that helped stabilize their economies.

_____ **6.** African nations were helped significantly by the World Bank.

_____ **7.** A rebel army allied with the Tutsi people claimed the capital of Zaire and renamed it the Democratic Republic of the Congo.

_____ **8.** The United States and the Soviet Union helped opposing armies in Angola fight a bloody civil war.

_____ **9.** African nations, in appealing to communist or capitalist nations for aid, did so because they cared about the ideological standpoints of the United States and the USSR.

_____ **10.** Independence in Africa has led to a revival of interest in the traditions of the African peoples.

UNDERSTANDING MAIN IDEAS For each of the following, write the letter of the best choice in the space provided.

_____ **1.** A common political pattern in Africa after independence involved
  a. a cash crop selling at a high price.
  b. an elected leader becoming a dictator.
  c. a constitution setting up a monarchy.
  d. sacrificing national identities

_____ **2.** Long-term ethnic violence occurred in Rwanda and Burundi between
  a. Nigeria and Ghana.
  b. the eastern region and the military.
  c. Zaire and Congo.
  d. Hutu and Tutsi.

_____ **3.** The civil war in Angola became
  a. a test of strength of the superpowers.
  b. a war between Cuba and the Soviet Union.
  c. an opportunity to use nuclear weapons.
  d. an opportunity for a lasting peace.

_____ **4.** The revival of African culture
  a. involved literature alone.
  b. was a revival of the Bantu language
  c. involved literature, music, sculpture, and other arts.
  d. was a sign of weakness and political unrest.

CHAPTER 33

Modern Chapter **24**

Main Idea Activities 33.3

Nationalism in the Middle East and North Africa

VOCABULARY Some terms to understand:

• **mandate (891):** instruction or obligation, in this case, to govern a nation

• **atrocity (892):** an act which is extremely wicked, brutal, or cruel

• **protectorate (892):** a nation's status of being governed by a larger nation

• **kibbutz (893):** a type of communal farm settlement in Israel

ORGANIZING INFORMATION Use the following items to complete the chart below.

• Reza Shah Pahlavi

• Mohammad Mosaddeq

• Mohammad Reza Pahlavi

• Gamal Abdel Nasser

• Mustafa Kemal

• King Farouk

• Mohammad Reza Pahlavi

• Ismet Inönü

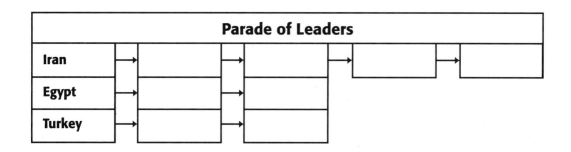

EVALUATING INFORMATION Mark each statement *T* if it is true or *F* if it is false.

_____ **1.** Syria and Lebanon were the first protectorates to gain their independence from France in the 1940s.

_____ **2.** Other nations, such as Algeria, took their example from Syria and Lebanon and waged wars for independence.

_____ **3.** Tunisia is the last remaining protectorate of France today.

_____ **4.** Britain had occupied Iran during World War II in an effort to protect Soviet supply lines.

Name _____ Class _____ Date _____

_____ **5.** Only the Jews have historical ties to Palestine.

_____ **6.** Britain created the Jewish nation of Israel.

_____ **7.** Immediately after the creation of Israel, Muslim forces moved against it.

_____ **8.** The Jews forcefully expelled the Palestinians who lived in the lands that were given to Israel, without compensating them for their losses.

_____ **9.** Muslim governments resettled the Palestinian refugees within their own borders.

_____ **10.** Britain and France attempted to regain control of the Suez Canal back from Egypt but failed.

MATCHING Place the letter of the description in the right-hand column next to the appropriate name or term in the left-hand column.

_____ **1.** Egypt

_____ **2.** Ba'athism

_____ **3.** kibbutz

_____ **4.** Lebanon

_____ **5.** FLN

_____ **6.** Menachem Begin

_____ **7.** the Suez Crisis

_____ **8.** *colons*

_____ **9.** Iran

_____ **10.** Charles de Gaulle

_____ **11.** Gamal Abdel Nasser

_____ **12.** CIA

_____ **13.** Turkey

a. leader of Irgun, which bombed a hotel

b. government agency that put a dictator into power in Iran

c. French president who chose to negotiate rather than fight

d. conflict over control of a major waterway

e. nation that nationalized its oil companies

f. first Arab nation to become independent from France

g. Middle Eastern nation threatened by Soviet territorial advances

h. European minority in Algeria

i. Algerian liberation army

j. leader of Egypt

k. political ideology which started out as a Pan-Arab movement

l. nation in which revolution preceded independence

m. communal farms in Israel

CHAPTER **33**

Modern Chapter **24**

Main Idea Activities 33.4

War, Revolution, and Oil in the Middle East and North Africa

VOCABULARY Some terms to understand:

- **desalinization plant (901):** factories which remove salt from sea water to make it usable for drinking and irrigation

ORGANIZING INFORMATION Use the following items to complete the graphic organizer below.

- Six-Day War
- OPEC cuts off the United States from oil
- Iran seizes American embassy

- bombing of Lebanon
- Gulf War
- Iraq-Iran War

Arab-Israeli Disputes	Islam in the Arab World	Inter-Arab Aggressions

EVALUATING INFORMATION Mark each statement *T* if it is true or *F* if it is false.

_____ **1.** Nasser chose to lead a strike against Israel in 1967 to maintain his role as leader of the Arab world.

_____ **2.** The Israelis launched an attack on Arab forces but were badly beaten.

_____ **3.** Palestinians began to take matters into their own hands after the Six-Day War.

_____ **4.** Egypt and Syria attacked Israel again in 1973.

_____ **5.** President Jimmy Carter of the United States threatened to attack both Israel and Egypt if they could not control their differences.

_____ **6.** Regardless of diplomatic efforts for peace, individuals on both sides of the Arab-Israeli dispute have repeatedly instigated terrorist-style violence that has halted peace efforts.

_____ **7.** Until the 1960s most of the oil in the Middle East was owned by western businesses.

_____ **8.** Oil-producing countries joined forces to claim ownership of their oil.

_____ **9.** OPEC ceased selling oil to the United States in 1973 because of religious differences.

_____ **10.** The Ayatollah Khomeini was an Islamic religious leader who opposed the Iranian dictator put into power by the CIA.

REVIEWING FACTS Choose the correct items from the following list to complete the statements below.

Tehran	Saddam Hussein	Mohammad Reza Pahlavi
Iraq	Kuwait	Ariel Sharon
Syria	Yasir Arafat	OPEC
Arab Fundamentalism		

1. The leader of the Palestinian Liberation Organization is _____.

2. _____ became the new power in the Arab world once Egypt lost its standing.

3. The United States embassy in _____ was taken hostage by Iranians who wanted the United States to turn over their shah to stand trial.

4. _____ became prime minister of Israel in 2001 and was known as the "bulldozer" for his treatment of Palestinians.

5. Iraq attacked the small nation of _____ because it claimed they were taking Iraqi oil.

6. _____ is the leader of Iraq and is known for extreme violence against his own people.

7. _____ was the shah of Iran who was put into power by the United States because it disapproved of the democratically elected prime minister.

8. The organization of oil-producing nations is called _____.

9. _____ attacked Iran for control of a waterway in 1980 and began a war which lasted for 8 years.

10. The rise of _____ has reversed the trend in many Arab countries to improve the status of women.

CHAPTER 34

Modern Chapter 25

Main Idea Activities 34.1

Facing New Challenges

VOCABULARY Some terms to understand:

- **capital (910):** money
- **spur (910):** encourage
- **multinational (910):** with offices in many countries
- **pharmaceuticals (911):** drugs and medicines
- **interest rates (911):** money paid to a lender for borrowing money

ORGANIZING INFORMATION Use the following items to complete the chart below.

- NAFTA
- develop national industry
- population growth
- brought in multinationals
- environment/toxins/disease
- import substitution
- monoculture
- inflation
- debt

Problems and Solutions	
Problems Facing Latin America	**Efforts to Combat Problems**

EVALUATING INFORMATION Mark each statement *T* if it is true or *F* if it is false.

_____ **1.** Corporations that came into Latin America to run factories kept the money they earned and spent it in their own countries, thereby not helping the Latin American economies.

_____ **2.** Latin American countries tried to make and sell goods to their own people so that their money could stay in the country.

_____ **3.** The World Bank gave large monetary gifts called grants to many Latin American nations to help them stimulate their economies.

_____ **4.** Inflation is what happens when an economy begins to grow and improve very quickly.

_____ **5.** The Andean Pact was a military and defense agreement signed by several South American countries.

_____ **6.** As people move to cities, the death rate goes down because of access to better medicine, sanitation, nutrition, and living conditions.

_____ **7.** Latin American populations grew too fast during the second half of the twentieth century for the cities to accommodate the rising number of people.

_____ **8.** Like many other areas of the world, Central America has destroyed many of its natural habitats to make room for more and more people.

_____ **9.** The conditions for women in Latin America are very poor and most cannot vote.

_____ **10.** The Catholic Church has remained silent on ethical issues in Latin America.

UNDERSTANDING MAIN IDEAS For each of the following, write the letter of the best choice in the space provided.

_____ **1.** Many regions in Latin America found it difficult to become economically stable because of
a. government incompetence.
b. government corruption.
c. debt problems and monocultural economies.
d. war.

_____ **2.** The population of Latin America is expected to grow until
a. 2010.
b. 2020.
c. 2025.
d. 2030.

_____ **3.** The purpose of the Organization of American States was to
a. promote domestic violence.
b. control the Catholic Church.
c. use force against the Dominican Republic.
d. foster cooperation among the region's nations.

CHAPTER **34**

Modern Chapter **25**

Main Idea Activities 34.2

Mexico and Central America

VOCABULARY Some terms to understand:

• **entrenched (915):** to hold a strong, safe position; to be difficult to remove

• **free-trade (916):** trade between groups in which tariffs are kept to a minimum

• **death squad (919):** illegal right-wing groups who kill any political enemies

• **deteriorate (920):** to worsen

ORGANIZING INFORMATION Use the following items to complete the chart below.

FMLN   contras   El Salvador
Nicaragua   Sandanistas   death squads

Country	Left Wing	Right Wing

REVIEWING FACTS Choose the correct items from the following list to complete the statements below.

the Panama Canal   Manuel Noriega   Mexico City
Sandanistas   NAFTA   the FMLN
PEMEX   contras   the Contadora Principles

1. _____ was severely damaged during an earthquake in 1985.

2. Many Mexicans supported _____ because they believed it would stimulate foreign investment in their country.

3. _____ is the oil company of Mexico which fell into trouble in the 1980s, causing national financial instability.

4. The communist party in Nicaragua, called the _____, took control in 1979.

5. The U.S.-funded revolutionary group in Nicaragua was called the

_____.

6. Many United States citizens argued against giving _____ to Panama because they feared Panamanian control over such an important site.

7. _____ was the dictator of Panama whom the United States captured and sent to jail for drug trafficking.

8. _____ were the left-wing revolutionaries in El Salvador fighting against military dictatorship.

9. _____ is an agreement between several Central American countries that promotes peace and dialogue over violence.

EVALUATING INFORMATION Mark each statement *T* if it is true or *F* if it is false.

_____ **1.** The PRI controlled the Mexican government for over 70 years because it denied opportunities for opposition.

_____ **2.** Mexico's financial situation improved when it discovered oil reserves.

_____ **3.** Mexico's leaders profited from Mexico's situation while the nation grew worse.

_____ **4.** Mexicans cross the border into the United States because they feel oppressed in their country and believe America to be less oppressive.

_____ **5.** The PRI retained power through the twenty-first century.

_____ **6.** The people of Central America have an equal distribution of wealth, and there are few disproportionately rich landowners.

_____ **7.** Nicaragua started moving toward communism in the late 1970s, while United States-funded rebels called contras fought for democracy.

_____ **8.** After Nicaragua became democratic and elected a president, many of its economic and social problems began to improve.

_____ **9.** Right-wing death squads in El Salvador killed or hurt anyone who disagreed with their ideals, including, at one time, six Catholic priests.

_____ **10.** The United States has owned the Panama Canal since its creation, and, as of 2000, had no intentions of giving it over to Panama.

CHAPTER **34**

Main Idea Activities 34.3

Modern Chapter **25**

Nations of the Caribbean

VOCABULARY Some terms to understand:

• **exile (922):** the state of being barred from one's country

• **civil liberties (922):** rights and freedoms which the people of a nation possess by law

• **political asylum (924):** protection given to an individual who is not safe within his/her own country for political reasons

• **commonwealth status (925):** a self-governing territory under the control of the United States government

• **secede (928):** become an independent state

ORGANIZING INFORMATION Use the following information to complete the graphic organizer below.

• François Duvalier
• Rafael Trujillo
• Jean-Bertrand Aristide
• Fulgencio Batista

• Juan Bosch
• Fidel Castro
• René Préval

• Luis Muñoz Marín
• Jean-Claude Duvalier
• Che Guevara

Cuba				
Puerto Rico				
Dominican Republic				
Haiti				

EVALUATING INFORMATION Mark each statement *T* if it is true or *F* if it is false.

_____ **1.** Many of the Caribbean nations have enjoyed peace because of their isolation from the mainland.

_____ **2.** The United States enters into the affairs of other nations when it holds a strong enough opinion about the affairs of that nation.

_____ **3.** The Dominican Republic was ruled by Rafael Trujillo for over 30 years.

_____ **4.** Puerto Rico is not an actual state but is part of the United States.

_____ **5.** Pope John Paul II visited Cuba in 1998 to urge the United States to stop sanctions against Cuba.

Chapter 34, Main Idea Activities 34.3, continued

_____ **6.** Fidel Castro refused to execute people just because they disagreed with him.

_____ **7.** Castro allowed some private business in Cuba to stimulate the economy.

_____ **8.** The United States practice of using economic boycotts has let citizens of a nation starve in order to put pressure on that nation's leaders.

_____ **9.** During the Bay of Pigs invasion, help promised by the United States did not arrive, and the invaders were killed or captured.

_____ **10.** When Castro took power he enacted reforms, one of which raised literacy in Cuba to 96 percent.

MATCHING Place the letter of the description in the right-hand column next to the appropriate name or term in the left-hand column.

_____ **1.** Miami

_____ **2.** Angola

_____ **3.** Luis Muñoz Marín

_____ **4.** Che Guavara

_____ **5.** Jamaica

_____ **6.** Grenada

_____ **7.** President Eisenhower

_____ **8.** Bay of Pigs

_____ **9.** Fulgencio Batista

_____ **10.** Jean-Bertrand Aristide

_____ **11.** Haiti

_____ **12.** Lyndon Johnson

_____ **13.** Fidel Castro

a. lieutenant to Fidel Castro who was killed while aiding Bolivian revolutionaries

b. first nation to secede from the West Indies Federation

c. Puerto Rican leader who fought for improved status with the United States

d. United States president who punished Cuba for developing close ties with the Soviet Union

e. dictator of Cuba, overthrown by Fidel Castro

f. where most Cubans settled after leaving Cuba

g. first democratically elected president of Haiti

h. Cuba sent troops to this African nation

i. Cuban revolutionary who seized power and led Cuba into communism

j. nation formed when its slave population overthrew the French

k. unsuccessful invasion of Cuba

l. United States president who defended the military government of Haiti to prevent communist rule

m. The United States invaded this island country to restore order after a Communist coup.

VOCABULARY Some terms to understand:

- **oust (929):** to forcefully remove a person or group from power
- **armada (931):** a large fleet of warships

ORGANIZING INFORMATION Use the following items to complete the chart below.

- MRTA guerillas
- Medellín drug cartel
- Dirty War
- Falkland Islands
- "The Violence"
- Augusto Pinochet
- Shining Path guerillas
- Salvador Allende

Revolution and Political Crisis			
Argentina	**Peru**	**Chile**	**Columbia**

EVALUATING INFORMATION Mark each statement *T* if it is true or *F* if it is false.

_____ **1.** Argentinean president Juan Perón lost power shortly after Eva Perón's death.

_____ **2.** After Juan Perón was removed from power, the military government declared amnesty for political dissidents, and a new era of peace began.

_____ **3.** Peru was plagued by terrorist groups, oppressive military leaders, and dishonest conservative presidents.

_____ **4.** During a short period in Columbia's recent history, its politicians worked together and created a healthy democracy.

_____ **5.** In Columbia, rival drug cartels, the military, the government, and radical terrorist groups killed each other for power.

_____ **6.** No Marxist or communist president has ever come to power peacefully in the Western Hemisphere.

_____ **7.** Augusto Pinochet was a democratically elected president of Chile who lost his power in a military coup.

_____ **8.** The Chilean economy has prospered over the decade or so since Pinochet and by 2000 was among the strongest in Latin America.

_____ **9.** The war waged against drugs in Columbia and other countries, including the United States, has been successful in limiting the production of drugs.

_____ **10.** Nearly every major Latin American government has suffered from corruption and abuse of power.

UNDERSTANDING MAIN IDEAS For each of the following, write the letter of the best choice in the space provided.

_____ **1.** The political life of Argentina is characterized by
   a. 200 years of peace.
   b. 200 years of unending war and revolution.
   c. both dictatorships and democratically elected presidencies.
   d. strong regard for the rights of the poor.

_____ **2.** The Shining Path and the MRTA forces
   a. both helped protect the country's cocaine business.
   b. both declared frequent truces so that they could create jobs.
   c. both were anti-socialist and anti-Communist.
   d. both were headed by Japanese-born leaders.

_____ **3.** The two important cartels in Colombia
   a. are in charge of national defense.
   b. control anti-poverty programs funded by foreign governments.
   c. were founded by people from Peru.
   d. control the drug trade.

_____ **4.** The regimes of Allende and Pinochet in Peru were
   a. a general followed by another general.
   b. a Marxist followed by a dictator.
   c. a drug lord followed by a Marxist.
   d. a priest followed by a businessman.

Name _____ Class _____ Date _____

VOCABULARY Some terms to understand:

• **scandal (941):** action by an official, regarded as wrong, that outrages people

• **impeach (942):** to remove an official from power through legal means,

• **stagflation (942):** a word made from *stagnation* ("sluggishness," "standing still") and *inflation*

• **human rights (945):** rights to which all humans are entitled

ORGANIZING INFORMATION Use the information below to complete the chart.

• Gulf War
• Iran-contra
• United States recession
• increased military spending
• Watergate scandal

• Iran hostage situation in Tehran
• Vietnam
• sex scandal
• doctrine opposing Soviet control of Middle East
• lied to grand jury

Nixon	
Carter	
Reagan	
Bush	
Clinton	

EVALUATING INFORMATION Mark each statement *T* if it is true or *F* if it is false.

_____ **1.** President Nixon invaded Cambodia because he wanted to encourage the communists to desire peace with the United States.

_____ **2.** After United States withdrawal from Vietnam, the objectives of the United States were achieved through the efforts of the South Vietnamese.

_____ **3.** During anti-war demonstrations, government troops killed college students.

_____ **4.** Nixon was forced to resign his presidency after it was discovered that he was having a sexual affair with an office intern.

_____ **5.** In dealing with a recession, Reagan began borrowing heavily from foreign lenders, which drove up American debt.

Chapter 35, Main Idea Activities 35.1, continued

_____ **6.** The 1990s were a strong financial time for the United States, largely because of the rise of technology companies.

_____ **7.** Efforts to develop clean, cheap, and renewable sources of energy have had little support.

_____ **8.** SALT was a treaty that linked United States and Canadian economic interests.

_____ **9.** The United States and the Soviet Union pursued a course of international disarmament during the 1980s.

_____ **10.** Citizens of Quebec achieved independence from Canada in the 1990s.

REVIEWING FACTS Choose the correct items from the following list to complete the statements below.

détente	Kim Campbell	Carter Doctrine
separatism	NAFTA	Official Languages Act
Tiananmen Square	Meech Lake Accord	

1. _____ is the name for the efforts of certain citizens of Quebec to form an independent nation.

2. _____ is the name for the period in United States/Soviet relations when the Cold War was calmed by several agreements between the two nations.

3. _____ became the first woman prime minister of Canada.

4. Many Canadians feared _____ because they feared giving the United States too much control over their economy.

5. The _____ declares that any attempts by outside forces to control the Persian Gulf would be regarded as an assault to United States interests.

6. China was criticized heavily by United States citizens for the massacre in

_____ of thousands of citizens protesting for democracy.

7. Passed in 1969, the _____ made both French and English the official languages of Canada.

8. Canadian leaders agreed to accept Quebec as a "distinct society" within Canada

under the _____.

CHAPTER **35**   Main Idea Activities 35.2

Modern Chapter **26**   **Europe**

VOCABULARY Some terms to understand:

• **staged (949):** set up, arranged

• **fragility (952):** being breakable

• **accords (953):** agreements

• **deploying (954):** using in the field for military purposes

• **containing (954):** keeping something from expanding

ORGANIZING INFORMATION Use the information below to complete the chart.

• North Sea oilfields	• Ostpolitik	• Margaret Thatcher
• Georges Pompidou	• Helmut Kohl	• Arab immigration problems
• Tony Blair	• German reunification	• François Mitterand
• Northern Ireland	• Jacques Chirac	• Falkland Islands War
• nuclear weapons tests	• fall of Berlin Wall	• Willy Brandt

Great Britain	**France**	**Germany**

EVALUATING INFORMATION Mark each statement *T* if it is true or *F* if it is false.

_____ **1.** Margaret Thatcher increased government control and funding in an effort to combat Britain's economic problems.

_____ **2.** The economic shift from heavy industry to services led to financial problems in the industrial areas of Britain.

Chapter 35, Main Idea Activities 35.2, continued

_____ **3.** Margaret Thatcher reached her highest level of popularity when she replaced the property tax with the new poll tax.

_____ **4.** Catholics in Northern Ireland fought for independence from Britain.

_____ **5.** East and West Germany were reunited when Eastern Germans revolted and tore down the Berlin Wall.

_____ **6.** The Basque region of Portugal has used terrorism to fight for independence from Portugal.

_____ **7.** NATO became a strong international force because it was needed to organize western nations against communism.

_____ **8.** The Helsinki Accords were a binding set of rules for those nations involved.

MATCHING Place the letter of the description in the right-hand column next to the appropriate name or term in the left-hand column.

_____ **1.** Ostpolitik

_____ **2.** Berlin Wall

_____ **3.** Sweden

_____ **4.** IRA

_____ **5.** Margaret Thatcher

_____ **6.** Juan Carlos

_____ **7.** ETA

_____ **8.** Maastricht Treaty

_____ **9.** EEC

_____ **10.** NATO

_____ **11.** Helsinki Accords

_____ **12.** Antonio de Spinola

_____ **13.** Colonels

a. terrorist group fighting for independence from Spain

b. king of Spain who restored democracy

c. remained neutral during the Cold War

d. German policy of improved relations with eastern European countries

e. dividing barrier between the communist and non-communist halves of Germany

f. ousted Portuguese dictator Marcello Caetano

g. ruled Greece during the early 1970s

h. international agreements that pushed Europe towards greater cooperation

i. North Atlantic Treaty Organization

j. predecessor of the European Union

k. terrorist group fighting for the independence of Northern Ireland

l. treaty that created the European Union

m. prime minister of Britain

CHAPTER **35**

Modern Chapter **26**

Main Idea Activities 35.3

The Fall of Communism

VOCABULARY Some terms to understand:

- **hard-line (957):** unable to tolerate any change from established principles
- **privatized (958):** transferred from government control
- **flared (959):** burst into the open
- **repressive (960):** having the power to keep down or suppress

ORGANIZING INFORMATION Use the information below to complete the chart.

- *glasnost*
- black market goods
- Mikhail Gorbachev
- organized crime

- privatized industry
- Boris Yeltsin
- communist
- *perestroika*

- Yuri Andropov
- post-communist
- war in Chechnya
- coup attempt by hard liners

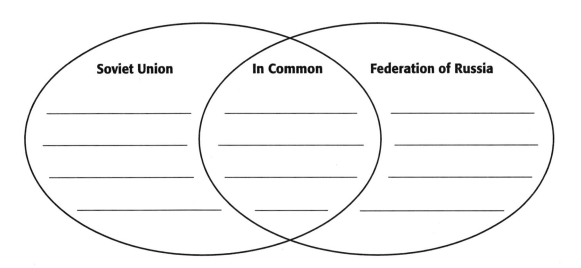

EVALUATING INFORMATION Mark each statement *T* if it is true or *F* if it is false.

_____ **1.** Communism led to a high standard of living in the Soviet Union.

_____ **2.** Brezhnev restricted the freedoms of speech and movement.

_____ **3.** Gorbachev personally profited from the illnesses of the Soviet Union and caused its final collapse.

_____ **4.** A military coup almost took control of the Soviet Union but failed when it did not receive sufficient support.

_____ **5.** *Glasnost* allowed for greater freedom of speech, which brought many tensions to the surface and helped pull apart the Soviet Union.

Chapter 35, Main Idea Activities 35.3, continued

_____ **6.** Chechnya achieved independence from Russia shortly after the fall of the Soviet Union.

_____ **7.** Czechoslovakia suffered a bloody civil war after gaining its independence.

_____ **8.** Serbia wanted to dominate the former Yugoslavia once the Soviet Union lost control.

REVIEWING FACTS Choose the correct items from the following list to complete the statements below.

Dayton Accord	*perestroika*	Solidarity
Yeltsin	Velvet Revolution	Brezhnev Doctrine
Yugoslavia	Afghanistan	

1. The Soviet Union under Brezhnev invaded _____ in the 1970s.

2. The _____ said that the Soviet Union would use force to stop any nation from leaving the Soviet Union.

3. _____ was the name for the new era of rebuilding that began in the Soviet Union during the late 1980s.

4. _____ became the first democratically elected leader of Russia in history in the early 1990s.

5. The political party in Poland that fought for the end of communism was called

_____.

6. The change of government from communism to democracy in Czechoslovakia was

called _____.

7. _____ fell into ethnic fighting after changing to a democratic style of government.

8. The _____ brought an end to war in Bosnia.

Name _____ Class _____ Date _____

Main Idea Activities 35.4

Modern Chapter **26**   **A Day That Changed the World**

VOCABULARY Some terms to understand:

• **hijack (964):** to take over a flying airplane

• **wreckage (965):** the remains of a wreck, ruins

• **mobilize (965):** to assemble and make ready for action

• **telethon (966):** a long television program usually to solicit funds

• **fundamentalism (967):** emphasis on the literal interpretation of a holy book

• **impoverished (969):** poor

• **humanitarian (969):** the promotion of social welfare

ORGANIZING INFORMATION Fill in the graphic organizer by writing the following items in the order that they happened.

• United Airlines Flight 93 crashed southeast of Pennsylvania.

• American Airlines Flight 77 hit the westside of the Pentagon.

• United Airlines Flight 175 slammed into the World Trade Center south tower.

• The south tower of the World Trade Center collapsed.

• An American Airlines passenger jet crashed into the World Trade Center north tower.

• World Trade Center north tower collapsed.

Sequence of Events

8:45	
9:00	
9:40	
10:00	
10:30	

EVALUATING INFORMATION Mark each statement *T* if it is true or *F* if it is false.

_____ **1.** People had been evacuated before the collapse of the World Trade Center's towers.

_____ **2.** Passengers in United Airlines Flight 93 failed to stop the terrorists.

_____ **3.** Very few survivors were admitted to New York hospitals.

_____ **4.** Republicans and Democrats displayed an unusual degree of cooperation to help the families of the victims.

_____ **5.** Sympathy and support came from all over the world except the traditional opponents of the United States, such as Cuba and Iran.

_____ **6.** The FBI found that suspects planned the attacks while living and training in the United States.

_____ **7.** Falling consumer confidence was one of the most difficult economic problems the government faced after the attacks.

_____ **8.** President Bush declared the United States would wage war not only on terrorist organizations, but also on governments that support and protect terrorist organizations.

_____ **9.** Osama bin Laden is an Afghan supported by wealthy Arabs.

_____ **10.** The United States and its allies air-dropped food and medicine to Afghanistan's population.

REVIEWING FACTS Choose the correct items from the following list to complete the statements below.

fundamentalist	Article 5	Office of Homeland Security
the Base	Tony Blair	Rudolph Giuliani

1. Of the final death toll, New York City mayor _____ said, "It will be more than we can bear."

2. British prime minister _____ called the terrorist acts "an attack on the free and democratic world everywhere."

3. Osama bin Laden's global terrorism network is known as the al Queda or "_____."

4. The Taliban is composed of splinter groups of _____ Muslims.

5. The _____ was created after the attacks to coordinate the domestic national security efforts of various government agencies.

6. For the first time since its existence, NATO members were required under _____ of its original treaty to help defend an alliance member.

CHAPTER **36**

Main Idea Activities 36.1

Modern Chapter **27**

The Arts and Literature

VOCABULARY Some terms to understand:

• **experimentation (974):** the act of trying out a new idea or activity

• **techniques (975):** ways of making

• **broke new ground (975):** began

• **satirical (977):** relating to a work that ridicules or mocks vice or folly

• **musical (978):** a movie or play that includes singing and dancing

• **controversy (979):** disagreement or conflict

ORGANIZING INFORMATION Complete the chart by placing the following names under the correct category.

• Andy Warhol   • John Cage

• The Beatles   • Jackson Pollock

• Toni Morrison   • Naguib Mahfouz

EVALUATING INFORMATION Mark each statement *T* if it is true or *F* if it is false.

_____ **1.** After 1945 there was a period of change and experimentation in the arts.

_____ **2.** Op art artists used everyday items such as soup cans, comic strips, or road signs in their art.

_____ **3.** Using reinforced concrete in buildings was a popular technique after 1945.

_____ **4.** Rock 'n' roll developed in the United States before 1945.

Chapter 36, Main Idea Activities 36.1, continued

_____ **5.** Russian ballet stars could not make new homes and careers in the West.

_____ **6.** A group of writers called Beats praised wealthy citizens and their values.

_____ **7.** Egyptian author Naguib Mahfouz was among the writers who provoked controversy.

_____ **8.** *West Side Story* is a postwar musical that focused on gangs.

_____ **9.** Protest was a theme that was important to many postwar writers.

_____ **10.** Postwar artistic and literary activity made people less interested in the arts.

REVIEWING FACTS Choose the correct items from the following list to complete the statements below.

modern	conceptual artists	engineering	op art
New Wave	technology	Beatles	visual effects
cultural	experimentation		

1. Since 1945 there has been a lot of _____ in the arts.

2. In _____ painters created optical illusions.

3. Artists who believe that the act of creating art is more important than the actual art object are called _____.

4. New _____ techniques made domed stadiums possible.

5. The universal themes of love and finding one's place in the world made the

_____ popular around the world.

6. A group of young French directors known as the _____ believed that a film should reflect one person's idea.

7. Films such as *Star Wars* and *Titanic* depended heavily on _____.

8. Dramatists like John Osborne and Arthur Miller wrote realistic plays that criticized

_____ society.

9. Excitement about new _____ inspired science fiction writers.

10. Education, more leisure time, and increasing _____ awareness have made people more interested in the arts.

Main Idea Activities 36.2

Modern Chapter **27**

Science and Technology

VOCABULARY Some terms to understand:

- **commonplace (981):** ordinary
- **convenient (981):** easy
- **shift (982):** to change
- **track movements (983):** follow
- **install (983):** to build and equip
- **process information (984):** put in order so that it can be understood
- **global network (985):** organized link all over the world

ORGANIZING INFORMATION Write each of these discoveries or inventions next to the name of the scientist or institution.

first automatic calculator   mapping of DNA
penicillin   first successful cloning

Scientist or Institution	Discoveries or Inventions
Human Genome Project	
Roslin Institute	
Blaise Pascal	
Alexander Fleming	

EVALUATING INFORMATION Mark each statement *T* if it is true and *F* if it is false

_____ **1.** Since 1972, space programs have shifted focus to manned space crafts.

_____ **2.** All advances that followed World War II involved physics or electronics.

_____ **3.** Scientists believe understanding the genetic code will lead to new cures for cancer, heart disease, drug addiction and mental illness.

_____ **4.** Plastics are substances that can be found in nature.

Chapter 36, Main Idea Activities 36.2, continued

_____ **5.** Population and industrialization increase the amount of waste that pollutes the environment.

_____ **6.** After the first jumbo jet began passenger service in 1970, travel around the world changed.

_____ **7.** The development of the transistor made possible the improvements on computers to be smaller and more efficient.

_____ **8.** Computers continue to increase both in power and in cost.

UNDERSTANDING MAIN IDEAS For each of the following items write the letter of the best choice in the space provided

_____ **1.** In the 1950s faster travel was made possible by
  a. jet airplanes.
  b. space exploration.
  c. landing on the moon.
  d. unmanned spacecrafts.

_____ **2.** After the moon landing, scientists learned about the solar system through exploration by
  a. satellites.
  b. unmanned spacecrafts.
  c. magnetic resonance imaging.
  d. self-focusing cameras.

_____ **3.** Miniaturization and computerization revolutionized ways of storing and processing
  a. diseases.
  b. airplanes.
  c. space stations.
  d. information.

_____ **4.** Computers, the Internet, cellular phones, and fiber-optic cables are
  a. communication tools.
  b. inventions made before 1945.
  c. examples of genetic engineering.
  d. delicate pieces of art.

_____ **5.** Developments in medical science and genetic research since 1945 has eliminated some
  a. scientists.
  b. humans.
  c. diseases.
  d. inventions.

_____ **6.** New products and sources of energy are examples of how people's lives are affected by
  a. industry.
  b. technology.
  c. travel.
  d. medicine.

Main Idea Activities 36.3

Human Rights and the Spread of Democratic Ideals

VOCABULARY Some terms to understand:

• **horrors (990):** frightening events or scenes
• **repressive (991:** dictatorial or controlling
• **pressure (991):** force; push
• **regimes (992):** governments
• **stepped aside (993):** resigned; quit

ORGANIZING INFORMATION Use the following items to complete the graphic organizer below.

• President Suharto left office.
• Most countries moved to a more democratic system.
• Autocratic rule by Marcos ended.
• Black majority elected Nelson Mandela.

DEMOCRATIC GAINS

Philippines: _____

South Africa: _____

Indonesia: _____

Latin America: _____

Chapter 36, Main Idea Activities 36.3, continued

EVALUATING INFORMATION Mark each statement *T* if it is true and *F* if it is false

_____ **1.** The UN can enforce the agreed-upon basic human rights in the Universal Declaration of Human Rights it adopted in 1948.

_____ **2.** Human rights violations often have political, ethnic, racial or religious roots.

_____ **3.** Terrorist acts in Northern Ireland protected the rights of innocent people.

_____ **4.** The trend toward democracy that began with the fall of communism in the Soviet Union continues in many parts of the world.

_____ **5.** International pressure promoted apartheid in South Africa.

_____ **6.** Different cultures have a uniform view of human rights.

_____ **7.** Spain returned to democracy under King Juan Carlos I.

_____ **8.** Cuba rejected communism when Soviet economic support dried up.

_____ **9.** Revolutionary dictatorships continued in Syria and Iraq.

_____ **10.** A military junta restored democracy in Burma.

INTERPRETING VISUAL IMAGES Examine the line graph below and answer the questions that follow.

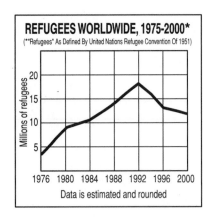

REFUGEES WORLDWIDE, 1975-2000*
(**"Refugees" As Defined By United Nations Refugee Convention Of 1951)

Millions of refugees

1976 1980 1984 1988 1992 1996 2000
Data is estimated and rounded

1. What year had the most number of refugees worldwide? _____

2. Has the number of refugees increased or decreased since 1996? _____

EPILOGUE

Main Idea Activities E.1

Revolution to Imperialism

VOCABULARY Some words to understand:

• **tyrant (451):** a ruler who exercises power in a brutal manner

• **resent (451):** to feel angered over something thought of as a wrong, insult or injury

• **antagonized (452):** provoked hostility or ill feelings

• **repealed (452):** to do away with by a legislative enactment

• **treaties (453):** agreements made by negotiation; contracts between two or more states

• **reshuffle (454):** to reorganize usually by redistributing what is existing

• **amended (455):** to change formally by taking out or adding something

• **endorsed (456):** to express approval publicly

• **scrambled (457):** to move or act urgently in trying to win or escape something

ORGANIZING INFORMATION Arrange the items below in sequence and fill in the graphic organizer

• Settlers founded Plymouth

• America gains independence

• British troops seize guns in Boston

• British colonizers establish Jamestown.

• Americans stage uprisings against taxes.

• Confederate states adopt federal system.

• Americans take to heart Rousseau's ideas

From British colony to United States of America

1. _____

2. _____

3. _____

4. _____

5. _____

6. _____

7. _____

Epilogue, Main Idea Activities E.1, continued

EVALUATING INFORMATION Mark each statement *T* if it is true or *F* if it is false.

_____ **1.** One of the changes in monarchy after 1500 is the successful expansion of power.

_____ **2.** Americans declared independence from England because they were not allowed to have lands.

_____ **3.** The Declaration of Independence included women and slaves.

_____ **4.** "Liberty, equality, and fraternity," the slogan of the French Revolution, was copied from the Americans.

_____ **5.** Discontent caused by economic crisis led to the French Revolution.

_____ **6.** The first ever coup d'etat, or taking government by force, made Napoléon Bonaparte a dictator.

_____ **7.** The Industrial Revolution that started in England was good for employees.

_____ **8.** Imperialism was born when powerful European nations wanted to dominate other nations or regions.

REVIEWING FACTS Choose the correct items from the following list to complete the statements below.

communism   Waterloo   internal combustible engine
guillotine   electricity   Articles of Confederation

1. The first American government was established after the American Revolution by the

_____.

2. The French Revolution ended the monarchy in France and the last king, Louis XVI,

was beheaded with a _____.

3. Napoleon's final defeat by the British and their Prussian allies happened in

_____.

4. _____ as a power source was one of the most important inventions during the Industrial Revolution.

5. The invention of the _____ made the automobile possible.

6. Karl Marx, advocated a system called _____ in which labor controlled production and profits.

(EPILOGUE)

Main Idea Activities E.2

World War in the Twentieth Century

VOCABULARY Some words to understand:

• **alliances (458):** associations of two or more nations as in a treaty to further common interests

• **spark as in a war (461):** to cause it

• **infuriated (458):** made violently angry

• **severe (459):** extreme; at its worst

• **trenches (459):** a long ditch protected by a bank of earth that is used to shelter soldiers

• **aggression (462):** an unprovoked attack

• **crash as in a stock market (460):** to decline or fall suddenly

• **spark as in a war (461):** to cause it

ORGANIZING INFORMATION Match leaders with their new type of government by filling in the graphic organizer.

• Josef Stalin
• Benito Mussolini
• Adolf Hitler

• fascism
• nazism
• communism

Area	Leaders	Type of Government
Italy		
Germany		
Soviet Union		

EVALUATING INFORMATION Mark each statement *T* if it is true or *F* if it is false.

_____ **1.** Serbian nationalists who fought to regain colonized Bosnia and Herzegovina from the Austria-Hungary rule sparked World War I.

_____ **2.** Russia was part of the Allied Powers that included France and Great Britain.

_____ **3.** World War I resulted in territorial and economic gains especially for Russia.

Epilogue, Main Idea Activities E.2, continued

_____ **4.** The Great Depression in America was followed by a period of prosperity around the world.

_____ **5.** Some European colonies such as Egypt, India and China gained their independence with nationalist movements after the war.

_____ **6.** The Boxer Rebellion in China failed to restore the Chinese emperor to power.

_____ **7.** Japan's problems after World War II were population growth and lack of raw materials.

_____ **8.** Some countries like those in Latin America supported military dictatorships because they wanted to go to war.

_____ **9.** Initially, the United States was only giving war materials to Great Britain when Germany started World War II.

_____ **10.** Japan, an ally of Germany, bombed Pearl Harbor because it wanted to stop United States modernization.

UNDERSTANDING MAIN IDEAS For each of the following, write the letter of the best choice in the space provided.

_____ **1.** What is the main reason for World War I?
  a. clash of ideas
  b. fight for the throne
  c. struggle for dictatorship
  d. contest for more territories

_____ **2.** What was the effect of the Great Depression on the United States?
  a. Every person went into debt.
  b. A long-term relief and reform program began.
  c. The government struggled with political conflicts.
  d. People voted for politicians who advocated socialism.

_____ **3.** Industrialization provided more jobs but it also
  a. set up colonial rule.
  b. caused military unrest.
  c. increased labor union activity.
  d. suppressed growth among the middle class.

_____ **4.** The United States ended World War II with
  a. the bombing of Hiroshima and Nagasaki.
  b. the signing of the Treaty of Versailles.
  c. troops invading Manchuria and Okinawa.
  d. an attack on all Japanese and allied territories.

(EPILOGUE)   Main Idea Activities E.3

Europe and the Americas Since 1945

VOCABULARY Some words to understand:

- **deter (464):** to discourage or prevent from acting
- **disputes (464):** quarrels, arguments
- **threat (464):** an expression of an intent to do harm
- **brink of (466):** edge, at the point of
- **smuggle (467):** to take, bring, or introduce secretly
- **dissent (467):** difference of opinion
- **crash as in a stock market (460):** to decline or fall suddenly

ORGANIZING INFORMATION Match the following items to complete the graphic organizer

- blockaded the East German border
- restricted spread of communism
- planned to unify Germany
- expanded the influence of communism

- assisted in rebuilding European economy
- established the German Democratic Republic
- combined troop strength in the Warsaw Pact
- formed the North Atlantic Treaty Organization

The Cold War	
The United States and Allies	**The Soviet Union**

EVALUATING INFORMATION Mark each statement *T* if it is true or *F* if it is false.

_____ **1.** The first challenge the United States and its European allies faced after World War II was how to end Nazi control and prevent future wars .

_____ **2.** The Cold War between Russia and the United States was a battle of troops and nuclear weapons

_____ **3.** In a market economy, government controls all economic decisions.

_____ **4.** Countries belonging to the Warsaw Pact outnumbered those of the NATO in terms of ground troops.

Epilogue, Main Idea Activities E.3, continued

_____ **5.** After the war, the Soviet Union no longer dealt with revolts in Eastern Europe.

_____ **6.** The United States enjoyed economic power and a lead role in international politics in the 60s but faced protests from African Americans demanding equality.

_____ **7.** The United States aimed to gain control of Cuba when it got involved with the communist takeover

_____ **8.** The North American Free Trade Agreement (NAFTA) between the United States, Canada and Mexico aims to stop the growth of communism.

_____ **9.** From 1945 until the 1990s, Central and South America have suffered from political instability.

_____ **10.** The major problem in Colombia is drug-related violence.

REVIEWING FACTS For each of the following, write the letter of the best choice in the space provided.

_____ **1.** The body of 51 nations established in 1945 to maintain peace and security, deter aggressors and protect international cooperation is the
  a. United Nations.
  b. Atomic Energy Community.
  c. European Economic Community.
  d. North Atlantic Treaty Organization.

_____ **2.** The communist version of the Western Allies' market economy is called
  a. common market.
  b. capitalist market.
  c. command economy.
  d. workers economy.

_____ **3.** Who led in civil rights non-violent protests to gain equality for African Americans?
  a. Harry Truman
  b. Manuel Noriega
  c. John F. Kennedy
  d. Martin Luther King

_____ **4.** In 1945, which Latin American country appeared to be one of the most stable in the region?
  a. Chile
  b. Mexico
  c. Argentina
  d. Nicaragua

EPILOGUE

Main Idea Activities E.4

Asia, Africa, and the Middle East Since 1945

VOCABULARY Some words to understand:

- **virtual (468):** being in essence or in effect but not in fact or name
- **symbolic (468):** something that stands for something else
- **devastate (468):** to reduce to ruin, lay waste
- **radicals (469):** a group that separates sharply from the usual or traditional
- **sanctions (469):** economic or military measure nations adopt against another violating international law
- **apparent (470):** suggests an appearance that on closer look might not be what it appears
- **hampered (471):** to restrict or interfere with an action or operation

ORGANIZING INFORMATION Use the following names to fill in the chart below.

- awaharlal Nehru
- Douglas MacArthur
- Mao Zedong
- Nelson Mandela
- Corazon Aquino
- Ho Chi Minh

Leader	Action
1.	demilitarized Japan
2.	launched the Cultural Revolution
3.	restored constitutional democracy after Marcos
4.	led a communist guerrilla movement
5.	As first prime minister, he hoped to create a democratic nation with a socialist economy.
6.	elected president in an all-race election

EVALUATING INFORMATION Mark each statement *T* if it is true or *F* if it is false.

_____ **1.** Japan recovered fast from its postwar ruins and became Asia's leading economic power.

_____ **2.** Japanese imports later caused a trade imbalance in the United States to the benefit of Japan.

_____ **3.** The Japanese still honor their traditions inspite of progress.

_____ **4.** Communist China's "Great Leap Forward" that encouraged backyard manufacturing resulted in economic gains.

Epilogue, Main Idea Activities E.4, continued

_____ **5.** Pro-democracy activists who massed up at Tiananmen Square were peacefully heard.

_____ **6.** Southeast Asian countries who gained independence from colonial rule have remained poor.

_____ **7.** Thailand is the only country in the Southeast Asian region that was not colonized.

_____ **8.** East and West Pakistan, both predominantly Muslim in population, separated from India after a bitter religious conflict with the Hindus.

_____ **9.** Apartheid in Africa allowed marriages between people of different races.

_____ **10.** Conflicts between Israel and the Arab states have been resolved with the signing of the Camp David Accords.

UNDERSTANDING MAIN IDEAS For each of the following, write the letter of the best choice in the space provided.

_____ **1.** The major effect of World War II on Asian countries was
   a. overpopulation.
   b. higher death rate.
   c. economic difficulties.
   d. greater consumption of goods.

_____ **2.** Which internal conflict still divided some Asian and African countries after they gained freedom from colonial rule?
   a. social discrimination
   b. racial segregation
   c. nationalist movements
   d. ethnic and religious differences

_____ **3.** Which form of government that began in Russia before World War I divided countries like China, Korea, and Vietnam?
   a. imperialism
   b. capitalism
   c. communism
   d. feaudalism

_____ **4.** Which commodity caused disputes and wars among Arab countries?
   a. oil
   b. water
   c. agricultural produce
   d. heavy machineries

(EPILOGUE) Main Idea Activities E.5
The Modern Era and Beyond

VOCABULARY Some words to understand:

- **disillusion (474):** lose of hope or illusion
- **integrity (474):** quality or state of being of being complete or undivided
- **sluggish (474):** slow and inactive
- **priority (475):** order of preference based on urgency, importance or merit
- **referendum (475):** the principle or practise of submitting to popular vote a proposed measure
- **barriers (475):** something immaterial that separates people like language
- **insight (476):** what is seen or understood from a situation

ORGANIZING INFORMATION Use the following items to fill in the graphic organizer below.

- longer lives
- easier movement
- large-scale production
- pollution; damage to the ozone layer
- population growth
- migrations

Advancements	Positive Results	Negative Results
Faster, more reliable transportation		
Medical advances		
Industrialization		

UNDERSTANDING MAIN IDEAS Choose the best answer and write the letter in the space provided.

_____ **1.** After the Cold War, tension between the United States and Russia remained due to
    a. nuclear weapons.
    b. communist revolts.
    c. ethnic cleansing.
    d. environmental issues.

_____ **2.** Overpopulation and industrialization have increased use of natural resources that has threatened destruction of
    a. solar energy.
    b. water supply.
    c. energy source.
    d. natural habitats.

_____ **3.** Some writers still explore this theme on Germany.
   a. the Berlin Wall
   b. impact of Hitler
   c. the First World War
   d. the independent nations

_____ **4.** Some moviemakers deal with this social issue still common in a few countries including the United States.
   a. rebellion and repression
   b. communism versus democracy
   c. racism and violence
   d. reformists versus fundamentalists

MATCHING   In the space provided, match each statement in the left column to the term or person it describes in the right column.

_____ **1.** The fall of this country into communist hands divided Americans in the 1970s.

_____ **2.** This scandal at the White House led to the resignation of President Richard Nixon.

_____ **3.** Signed in 1993, this enabled members of the European Economic Community to remove trade barriers and adopt a common currency.

_____ **4.** This series of reforms on restructuring and openness that Mikhail Gorachev implemented caused dramatic changes in the Soviet Union.

_____ **5.** This United Nations agency investigates and reports human rights violations.

_____ **6.** He is the second United States president to be impeached by the House of Represetatives.

_____ **7.** This first space satellite was launched into orbit in 1957.

_____ **8.** He is the first person to walk on the moon's surface.

_____ **9.** This branch of science studies the way chromosomes affect development and its findings are now being used for cancer research.

_____ **10.** This disease has been totally eliminated by vaccines.

a. polio

b. Neil Amstrong

c. genetics

d. Bill Clinton

e. Sputnik

f. perestroika/glasnost

g. Watergate

h. South Vietnam

i. Maastricht Treaty

j. Amnesty International

EPILOGUE | Main Idea Activities E.6

A Day That Changed the World

VOCABULARY Some terms to understand:

- **hijack (964):** to take over a flying airplane
- **wreckage (965):** the remains of a wreck, ruins
- **mobilize (965):** to assemble and make ready for action
- **telethon (966):** a long television program usually to solicit funds
- **fundamentalism (967):** emphasis on the literal interpretation of a holy book
- **impoverished (969):** poor
- **humanitarian (969):** the promotion of social welfare

ORGANIZING INFORMATION Fill in the graphic organizer by writing the following items in the order that they happened.

- United Airlines Flight 93 crashed southeast of Pennsylvania.
- American Airlines Flight 77 hit the westside of the Pentagon.
- United Airlines Flight 175 slammed into the World Trade Center south tower.
- The south tower of the World Trade Center collapsed.
- An American Airlines passenger jet crashed into the World Trade Center north tower.
- World Trade Center north tower collapsed.

Sequence of Events

8:45	
9:00	
9:40	
10:00	
10:30	

EVALUATING INFORMATION Mark each statement *T* if it is true or *F* if it is false.

_____ **1.** People had been evacuated before the collapse of the World Trade Center's towers.

_____ **2.** Passengers in United Airlines Flight 93 failed to stop the terrorists.

_____ **3.** Very few survivors were admitted to New York hospitals.

_____ **4.** Republicans and Democrats displayed an unusual degree of cooperation to help the families of the victims.

_____ **5.** Sympathy and support came from all over the world except the traditional opponents of the United States, such as Cuba and Iran.

_____ **6.** The FBI found that suspects planned the attacks while living and training in the United States.

_____ **7.** Falling consumer confidence was one of the most difficult economic problems the government faced after the attacks.

_____ **8.** President Bush declared the United States would wage war not only on terrorist organizations, but also on governments that support and protect terrorist organizations.

_____ **9.** Osama bin Laden is an Afghan supported by wealthy Arabs.

_____ **10.** The United States and its allies air-dropped food and medicine to Afghanistan's population.

REVIEWING FACTS Choose the correct items from the following list to complete the statements below.

fundamentalist	Article 5	Office of Homeland Security
the Base	Tony Blair	Rudolph Giuliani

1. Of the final death toll, New York City mayor _____ said, "It will be more than we can bear."

2. British prime minister _____ called the terrorist acts "an attack on the free and democratic world everywhere."

3. Osama bin Laden's global terrorism network is known as the al Queda or "_____."

4. The Taliban is composed of splinter groups of _____ Muslims.

5. The _____ was created after the attacks to coordinate the domestic national security efforts of various government agencies.

6. For the first time since its existence, NATO members were required under _____ of its original treaty to help defend an alliance member.

(PROLOGUE)   Main Idea Activities P.1

The First Civilizations

VOCABULARY Some terms to understand:

- **irrigation (4):** in agriculture, the way water is made to flow over lands for feeding plants
- **surplus (4):** amount that remains when use or need is satisfied
- **well-being (5):** the state of being happy or healthy
- **immortality (26):** unending life

ORGANIZING INFORMATION Use the following items to complete the chart below.

- first people to use coined money
- worshiped Yahweh as creator
- strong believers in polytheism
- developed cuneiform

- Canaan
- Asia Minor
- Tigris-Euphrates valley
- Nile valley

Civilization	Location	Distinguishing Characteristics
• Egyptians	•	•
• Sumerians	•	•
• Lydians	•	•
• Hebrews	•	•

EVALUATING INFORMATION Mark each statement *T* if it is true or *F* if it is false.

_____ **1.** There is unlimited evidence available about humans who lived before the development of writing.

_____ **2.** Initially, the early humans were nomads.

_____ **3.** It was during the New Stone Age that people first tamed the dog.

_____ **4.** A division of labor is one of the characteristics of a civilization.

_____ **5.** People in the early world developed calendars because they wanted to plan their religious celebrations.

_____ **6.** Egyptian architects and engineers were among the best in the world.

Prologue, Main Idea Activities P.1, continued

_____ **7.** The Egyptians strongly believed in an afterlife.

_____ **8.** City-states included the city itself, but not the lands, fields, and villages around it.

_____ **9.** The greatest traders in the ancient Mediterranean world were the Hittites.

_____ **10.** The code of the Torah set a higher value on human life than had earlier law codes.

REVIEWING FACTS Choose the correct items from the following list to complete the statements below.

prehistory	monotheism	Neolithic Revolution
Sumerians	Hammurabi	Judaism
Menes	coined money	

1. The period before the invention of writing is called _____.

2. Agriculture was developed and animals were domesticated during the

_____.

3. The king known as _____ united lower and Upper Egypt.

4. Amenhotep IV attempted to get his people to adopt _____ as their religious belief.

5. The first people to develop and use the wheel may have been the

_____.

6. The code of _____ is a collection of laws.

7. The Lydians were the first to use _____.

8. The Hebrew form of monotheism is _____.

(PROLOGUE)   Main Idea Activities P.2

Ancient India and China

VOCABULARY Some terms to understand:

- **shrine (8):** a case, box, or receptacle where sacred relics are deposited; a place in which devotion is paid to a saint or deity
- **dynasty (8):** a succession of rulers of the same line of descent
- **tradition (9):** an established pattern of thought, action, or behavior (as a religious practice or social custom)
- **mandate (9):** an authoritative command

ORGANIZING INFORMATION Use the following items to complete the chart below.

- Hinduism and Buddhism
- Daoism and Legalism
- Gobi Desert
- Gupta dynasty
- began in the Indus River valley
- began along the Huang River

Indian Civilization	Chinese Civilization
•	•
•	•
•	•

EVALUATING INFORMATION Mark each statement *T* if it is true or *F* if it is false.

_____ **1.** The first civilization to develop in India was the Harappan civilization.

_____ **2.** In the Indo-Aryan civilization, the merchants were at the top of the social system.

_____ **3.** Both Hinduism and Buddhism developed in ancient China.

_____ **4.** Hindus believe that the soul does not die with the body.

_____ **5.** Hindus believe that the karma determines a person's status in the next life.

_____ **6.** The Eightfold Path is part of the Buddhist religion.

_____ **7.** The Shang dynasty reunited most of northern India.

_____ **8.** The golden age of India was a time when society and the arts flourished.

_____ **9.** Indian doctors invented innoculation, which is the practice of infecting people with a mild form of a disease so that they do not get the more serious form of the disease.

_____ **10.** Because of unique land features, such as the Gobi Desert and the mountains of central Asia, Chinese culture developed without outside influences.

_____ **11.** Animism is the belief that spirits live in everything.

_____ **12.** Confucius was an ancient Indian philosopher.

_____ **13.** The philosophy of Legalism taught that people were basically good.

_____ **14.** The Five Classics are important pieces of Chinese literature.

UNDERSTANDING MAIN IDEAS For each of the following, write the letter of the best choice in the space provided.

_____ **1.** Who in ancient India and China developed some of the earliest civilizations?
a. people living in river valleys
b. Hindus and Buddhists
c. the Qin and Han dynasties
d. Siddhartha Gautama and Confucius

_____ **2.** Which of these characterized ancient Indian civilization?
a. advanced city planning and design
b. a belief in animism
c. limited art and literature
d. a central school system

_____ **3.** Which of these characteristics did the ancient Indian and Chinese civilizations share?
a. a strong central government
b. the caste system
c. production of luxury goods
d. written language

_____ **4.** What contribution did the Han dynasty make to Chinese civilization?
a. invention of paper
b. standardized weights
c. brick sewer system
d. uniform taxation

(PROLOGUE)

Main Idea Activities P.3

Civilizations of the Mediterranean World

VOCABULARY Some terms to understand:

- **epic (11):** a long poem, such as the Iliad and the Odyssesy, telling the deeds of an historical hero
- **harsh (11):** having a rough surface that is unpleasant to the touch; causing a disagreeable or painful reaction
- **myth (12):** a person or thing having an imaginary existence; a false idea
- **imperial (14):** related to an empire or emperor
- **magistrates (14):** a person who helps make sure the laws of the government are followed

ORGANIZING INFORMATION Complete the graphic organizer using the following items.

- impressive works of art
- logical explanations for natural events
- spread of Greek ideas to the world
- a republic government
- engineering marvels
- blend of different cultures

	Golden Age of Culture	
Greek	**Hellenistic**	**Roman**
• _____	• _____	• _____
• _____	• _____	• _____

Name _____ Class _____ Date _____

EVALUATING INFORMATION Mark each statement *T* if it is true or *F* if it is false.

_____ **1.** Greek civilization was one of the foundations of modern Western civilization.

_____ **2.** Usually Greek city-states were organized in river valleys.

_____ **3.** Around 600 B.C., a struggle began for control of the Greek city-states.

_____ **4.** Greeks held athletic contests to honor their governmental leaders.

_____ **5.** The Peloponnesian War was actually a war between Athens and Sparta, along with other city-states.

_____ **6.** The Parthenon was constructed during Greece's Hellenistic age

_____ **7.** By the 400s B.C. the unification of the Greek city-states was complete.

_____ **8.** Alexander the Great died at the age of 33.

_____ **9.** The expansion of the Roman Republic eventually weakened the Roman system of government and society.

_____ **10.** Julius Caesar died in battle in 44 B.C.

CLASSIFYING INFORMATION For each of the following, write the letter of the correct choice in the space provided.

_____ **1.** wrote the *Iliad* and the *Odyssey*

_____ **2.** king of the gods

_____ **3.** created a direct democracy

_____ **4.** sculptor who created the *Discus Thrower*

_____ **5.** belived that everything could be explained through numbers

_____ **6.** taught that disease comes from natural causes

_____ **7.** established a way of learning through questioning

_____ **8.** a great military leader

_____ **9.** dictator of the Roman Republic

_____ **10.** founder of Christianity

a. Myron

b. Hippocrates

c. Jesus

d. Socrates

e. Zeus

f. Cleisthenes

g. Pythagoras

h. Alexander the Great

i. Julius Caesar

j. Homer

(PROLOGUE)　　Main Idea Activities P.4

Africa and the Americas

VOCABULARY Some terms to understand:

• **elders (17):** older people; those who have authority because of age or experience

• **merchant (19):** a person who buys and sells things for profit; a storekeeper

• **nomadic (19):** describes people who move from place to place with no permanent home

• **totem pole (19):** a pole that is carved with symbols that represent the family or clan

• **anesthetic (21):** a substance that causes a loss of bodily feeling

• **fortresses (21):** permanent army posts; secure places

ORGANIZING INFORMATION Write each item where it belongs in the diagram.

A. Maya　　　　　**C.** Inca

B. Aztec　　　　　**D.** African city-states

merged African, Arabic, and Persian elements.

invented the only writing system in the Americas.

Civilizations in Africa and the Americas

developed a calendar and used mathematics.

advanced in the practice of medicine, using anesthetic.

UNDERSTANDING MAIN IDEAS For each of the following, write the letter of the best choice in the space provided.

_____ **1.** The ties that held early African societies together were
　　　a. trade agreements.
　　　b. organized government.
　　　c. family relationships.
　　　d. pacts among villages.

_____ **2.** What helped to promote city-states' economic development by creating good conditions for trade?
　　　a. spread of Islam
　　　b. development of the Swahili language
　　　c. advances in mathematics
　　　d. the rise of the Kush kingdom

Name _____ Class _____ Date _____

_____ **3.** The earliest Americans were
   a. farmers.
   b. fishers.
   c. merchants and traders.
   d. hunters and gatherers.

_____ **4.** Who was responsible for developing the only writing system in the Americas?
   a. Aztec
   b. Maya
   c. Inca
   d. Olmec

REVIEWING FACTS Choose the correct items from the following list to complete the statements below.

| King 'Ēzānā | Mali | Swahili | Egypt |
| coastal trade | gold | Aztec | Andes Mountains |

1. At first, the African kingdom of Kush kept close cultural and economic ties with

_____.

2. The Kush were finally conquered by _____ from the kingdom of Aksum.

3. The African city-states along the Red Sea and Indian Ocean depended on

_____ for their economic survival.

4. The _____ language developed as a result of a new society that had African, Arabic, and Persian influences.

5. Mansa Mūsā ruled the West African empire of _____.

6. At the edge of the Sahara desert, traders exchanged _____ for salt that had been mined in the Sahara itself.

7. The _____ took control of the central region of Mexico around A.D. 1200.

8. The Inca civilization developed in the _____ in South America.

Chapter 1

SECTION 1 ACTIVITIES
Organizing Information
Neanderthal—lived about 35,000 to 130,000 years ago, buried their dead, believed in an afterlife;
Both—*Homo sapiens*, made their own tools;
Cro-Magnon—appeared in Europe about 35,000 years ago, spear-throwing hunters; artwork found on cave walls

Evaluating Information
1. T
2. T
3. T
4. F
5. F

Reviewing Facts
1. anthropologists
2. archaeologists
3. Donald Johanson
4. Stone Age
5. fire
6. Neanderthal
7. Cro-Magnon
8. Middle
9. New
10. agricultural revolution

SECTION 2 ACTIVITIES
Organizing Information
The correct caption should be placed next to each illustration.

Evaluating Information
1. F
2. T
3. F
4. T
5. T
6. T
7. F
8. F

Understanding Main Ideas
1. d
2. a
3. b
4. b

Chapter 2

SECTION 1 ACTIVITIES
Organizing Information
1. The Middle Kingdom
2. The Old Kingdom
3. The New Kingdom

Evaluating Information
1. T
2. T
3. F
4. T
5. F
6. T
7. F
8. T

Reviewing Facts
1. hieroglyphics
2. Hatshepsut
3. pharaoh
4. Rosetta Stone
5. polytheism
6. papyrus
7. Menes
8. Ramses II

SECTION 2 ACTIVITIES
Reviewing Facts
1. Giza
2. Great Pyramid
3. decimal
4. herbs
5. Amon-Re
6. Osiris
7. scarab beetles
8. mummification

Evaluating Information
1. T
2. F
3. T
4. F
5. F
6. T

Understanding Main Ideas
1. b
2. c
3. c
4. c

ANSWER KEY

SECTION 3 ACTIVITIES
Organizing Information

Sumerian Civilization—built ziggurats, did not believe in rewards after death, often invaded by wandering tribes;

Both—had a system of writing, practised polytheism;

Egyptian Civilization—was geographically isolated, built pyramids, believed in an afterlife

Reviewing Facts
1. flood control
2. stylus
3. arch
4. ziggurats
5. wheel
6. circle

Understanding Main Ideas
1. a
2. c
3. c

SECTION 4 ACTIVITIES
Organizing Information
1. Akkadian
2. Babylonian
3. Hittite
4. Assyriran
5. Chaldean
6. Persian

Evaluating Information
1. T
2. F
3. T
4. F
5. F
6. T

Reviewing Facts
1. Semitic
2. Nineveh
3. Seven Wonders of the World
4. Assyrian
5. *Epic of Gilgamesh*
6. Royal Road
7. Zoroastrianism
8. Alexander the Great

SECTION 5 ACTIVITIES
Organizing Information

Phoenicians—invented the alphabet, invented the art of glassblowing, may have sailed as far as Britain, well known for their prized purple cloth, greatest traders in the ancient world;

Lydians—developed a money economy, once lived in what is now known as Turkey, first to use coins for exchange

Evaluating Information
1. F
2. T
3. F
4. T
5. T
6. F

Reviewing Facts
1. Tyre
2. murex
3. Carthage
4. Sicily
5. Babylon
6. Greece
7. Asia Minor
8. barter

SECTION 6 ACTIVITIES
Organizing Information
2. The Egyptians enslaved the Hebrews for 400 years.
4. Moses brought the Ten Commandments to the Hebrews.
5. After wandering in the desert, the Hebrews reached the "promised land."
7. King Saul united the 12 tribes of Israel.
8. The Hebrew kingdom was split into two, Israel and Judah.

Evaluating Information
1. T
2. F
3. T
4. T
5. F
6. T
7. F
8. T
9. T
10. F

Reviewing Facts
1. Abraham
2. Moses
3. David
4. Solomon

Chapter 3

SECTION 1 ACTIVITIES
Organizing Information
1. Himalayas
2. Ganges and Indus
3. Deccan
4. Western Ghats
5. monsoons
6. November through March
7. mid-June through October
8. Indo-Gangetic Plain

Evaluating Information
1. T	5. F
2. T	6. T
3. F	7. T
4. F	8. T

Understanding Main Ideas
1. b	3. c
2. d	4. c

SECTION 2 ACTIVITIES
Organizing Information
Religion—Sanskrit, Vedas, Brahmins;
Economy—farming, bartering, irrigation

Evaluating Information
1. F	5. F
2. T	6. T
3. T	7. F
4. T	8. T

Reviewing Facts
1. raja
2. "That One"
3. Brahmins
4. Vedas
5. Indo-Arayan
6. Sanskrit

SECTION 3 ACTIVITIES
Organizing Information
1. rulers and warriors
2. Brahmins
3. merchants, traders, and farmers
4. peasants
5. untouchables

Evaluating Information
1. T	5. F
2. T	6. T
3. F	7. T
4. T	8. F

Reviewing Facts
1. Four Noble Truths
2. nirvana
3. Ramayana
4. Eightfold Path
5. Right Intentions
6. maya
7. varnas
8. reincarnation

SECTION 4 ACTIVITIES
Organizing Information
Chandragupta Maurya—golden age of Indian
  civilization, Hinduism became the most
  popular religion in India;
Aśoka—became a Buddhist, ordered an end to
  killing and conquest;
Chandra Gupta—had an army of 600,000
  soldiers with chariots and elephants,
  standardized weights and measures

Evaluating Information
1. F	5. F
2. T	6. T
3. T	7. T
4. T	8. F

Understanding Main Ideas
1. b	3. c
2. b	4. c

SECTION 5 ACTIVITIES
Organizing Information
1. Science—astronomy, identified seven planets;
2. Medicine—inoculation, bone setting;
3. Mathematics—concept of zero, quadratic equations

Evaluating Information
1. F	5. F
2. T	6. F
3. T	7. F
4. T	8. T

Reviewing Facts
1. polygyny
2. stupa
3. Laws of Manu
4. suttee
5. Nalanda
6. *Panchatantra*

Chapter 4

SECTION 1 ACTIVITIES
Organizing Information
1. Chinese nicknamed the Huang River "The Yellow River."
2. Chinese nicknamed the Huang River "China's Sorrow."
3. The river began to flow more slowly.
4. China did not adopt many outside skills and ideas.

Evaluating Information
1. F	5. T
2. F	6. T
3. F	7. F
4. T	8. T

Understanding Main Ideas
1. a	3. b
2. c	4. a

SECTION 2 ACTIVITIES
Organizing Information
Fact:
1. Yu drained the floodwaters so people could live in China.
2. Markings on oracle bones had helped scholars.
3. Each Chinese pictograph represents a single word.
4. A Chinese king was popular if he could predict the harvest.

Legend:
1. Priests saw the future in oracle bones.
2. An all-powerful and friendly dragon lived in the seas.
3. Pangu awoke from 18,000 years of sleep to create the universe.
4. The moon told the people when to harvest.

Evaluating Information
1. T	5. F
2. T	6. T
3. F	7. T
4. F	8. T

Classifying Information
1. g	6. d
2. j	7. h
3. f	8. b
4. e	9. i
5. a	10. c

SECTION 3 ACTIVITIES
Organizing Information
Zhou
1. Rulers divided powers between family members.
2. Right to rule came from heaven.

Qin
1. Laborers were forced to build the Great Wall.
2. The word "China" was taken from this dynasty's name.

Han
1. Chinese today call themselves people of this dynasty.
2. Trade prospered along the Silk Road.

ANSWER KEY

Reviewing Facts

1. scholars
2. Liu Bang
3. Wu Ti
4. leveling
5. paper
6. Silk

Understanding Main Ideas

1. b   3. a
2. b   4. b

SECTION 4 ACTIVITIES
Evaluating Information

1. T   6. F
2. T   7. T
3. T   8. F
4. F   9. F
5. T   10. T

Understanding Main Ideas

1. a   3. d
2. d   4. a

Reviewing Facts

1. *Analects*
2. The Way
3. Mahayana
4. legalists
5. compassion

SECTION 5 ACTIVITIES
Organizing Information

Men—honored for strength, ruled the family, chose careers for the sons;

Women—honored for gentleness, had no property rights, had more power after giving birth to a son;

Both—held elders in great respect, lived with relatives in one house, accepted decisions from their superiors

Evaluating Information

1. T   5. T
2. F   6. T
3. T   7. F
4. T   8. T

Reviewing Facts

1. seismograph
2. acupuncture
3. sundial
4. hemp
5. genealogy
6. measures

Chapter 5

SECTION 1 ACTIVITIES
Organizing Information

1. Legendary King Minos built a great civilization.
2. Myceneans conquered central Crete.
3. Minoans traded through the Aegean Sea.
4. The Greeks formed independent city-states.

Evaluating Information

1. F   6. F
2. T   7. T
3. T   8. T
4. F   9. T
5. T   10. T

Classifying

1. Minoans
2. Myceneans
3. Greeks
4. Minoans
5. Greeks
6. Minoans
7. Mycenenas
8. Greeks

SECTION 2 ACTIVITIES
Organizing Information

1. Athena—goddess of wisdom and womanly goodness, daughter of Zeus
2. Zeus—ruler of Mount Olympus, king of the gods
3. Apollo—god of poetry, music, and light, a son of Zeus
4. Dionysus—god of wine and fertility, another son of Zeus
5. Odysseus—Mycenean king who was the hero of Homer's epic poem

Reviewing Facts

1. myths
2. Homer
3. epics
4. *Iliad*
5. Helen
6. *Odyssey*
7. Athens
8. Zeus
9. aristocracies
10. oracle

Evaluating Information

1. T
2. T
3. F
4. F
5. F
6. T

SECTION 3 ACTIVITIES
Organizing Information

Athens—recognized citizens, metics, and
   slaves; created the first real democracy;
Sparta—completely controlled citizens' lives;
   became a completely military society

Evaluating Information

1. T		5. F
2. T		6. F
3. F		7. T
4. T		8. T

Understanding Main Ideas

1. c		3. a
2. d		4. c

SECTION 4 ACTIVITIES
Organizing Information

Pedagogue—manners;
Elementary—reading, writing, and grammar;
   poetry, music and gymnastics;
Military—military skills;
Sophist—mathematics and rhetoric,
   government and ethics

Evaluating Information

1. T		5. T
2. F		6. F
3. F		7. T
4. T		8. T

Reviewing Facts

1. terraced
2. Black
3. agora
4. olive oil
5. Sophist
6. ethics
7. rhetoric
8. hoplites

SECTION 5 ACTIVITIES
Organizing Information

2. Persians invaded Greece.
3. the Battle of Marathon
4. the Battle of Thermopylae
5. The Persians marched towards Athens.
6. The Greeks sank much of the Persian fleet.
7. Athenians and Spartans defeated the
   Persians.

Evaluating Information

1. T		4. T
2. F		5. F
3. T		6. T

Understanding Main Ideas

1. d		3. b
2. d		4. a

Chapter 6

SECTION 1 ACTIVITIES
Understanding Main Ideas

1. b		3. a
2. d		4. d

Evaluating Information

1. T		5. T
2. F		6. T
3. T		7. T
4. T		8. F

Reviewing Facts
1. golden age
2. architecture
3. Egyptian
4. colonnade
5. Phidias
6. moderation
7. restraint
8. usefulness

SECTION 2 ACTIVITIES
Organizing Information
Tragedies
1. Some force always defeats the main character.
2. Heroes are punished for displaying hubris.

Comedies
1. Plays made fun of ideas and people.
2. Main characters solved their problems.

Reviewing Facts
1. philosopher
2. Thales of Miletus
3. Socratic Method
4. Plato
5. Aristotle
6. Pythagorean theorem
7. Hippocrates
8. Father of History

Evaluating Information
1. T   4. F
2. F   5. F
3. T   6. T

SECTION 3 ACTIVITIES
Organizing Information
Philip II of Macedon
1. defeated Thebes and Athens at the Battle of Chaeronea and united Greece
2. borrowed the Greek idea of the phalanx
3. restored order in Macedon

Alexander the Great
1. trained in the army and educated by Aristotle
2. conquered the huge Persian territory by 331 B.C.
3. his reign spread a new Hellenistic culture

Evaluating Information
1. F   5. F
2. T   6. F
3. F   7. T
4. T   8. T

Understanding Main Ideas
1. d   3. b
2. c   4. d

SECTION 4 ACTIVITIES
Organizing Information
1. The middle ranks thrived.
2. More people could afford an education.
3. New values changed people's lifestyles.
4. People turned to new religions and philosophies.
5. People felt more unity, security, and personal worth.
6. Four schools of philosophy became popular.

Evaluating Information
1. F   6. F
2. T   7. T
3. F   8. F
4. F   9. T
5. T   10. T

Classifying Information
1. Cynicism
2. Scepticism
3. Stoicism
4. Epicureanism
5. Cynicism
6. Scepticism
7. Scepticism
8. Epicureanism

Chapter 7

SECTION 1 ACTIVITIES
Organizing Information
Senate—controlled public funds, decided on foreign policy;

Magistrates—commanded the army, had power to veto (consuls), oversaw the moral conduct of citizens (censors), oversaw the Roman legal system (praetors);

Assemblies—had power over actions of the Senate or public officials (tribunes)

Evaluating Information

1. F		**5.** F	
2. T		**6.** T	
3. F		**7.** T	
4. T		**8.** F	

Reviewing Facts

1. Apennine
2. Etruscans
3. Tiber
4. Senate
5. checks and balances
6. Conflict of the Orders
7. plebeians
8. patricians
9. Twelve Tables
10. legionnaires

SECTION 2 ACTIVITIES
Organizing Information

1. captured a Carthaginian ship
2. used the captured ship as model
3. built "boarding bridges" inside the ship
4. used an army trained in land warfare
5. ship rammed into enemy ship
6. army stampeded across the bridge
7. army captured the enemy

Evaluating Information

1. T		**5.** T	
2. F		**6.** F	
3. T		**7.** T	
4. F		**8.** T	

Understanding Main Ideas

1. d		**3.** c	
2. d		**4.** a	

SECTION 3 ACTIVITIES
Organizing Information

First Triumvirate—Julius Caesar, Gnaeus
   Pompey, Licinius Crassus;
Second Triumvirate—Octavian, Marc Antony,
   Lepidus;
Julio-Claudian Emperors—Tiberius, Caligula,
   Claudius, Nero;
Flavian Emperors—Vespasian, Titus,
   Domitian;
Five Good Emperors—Nerva, Trajan, Hadrian,
   Antonino Pius, Marcus Aurelius

Evaluating Information

1. T		**5.** F	
2. T		**6.** T	
3. F		**7.** T	
4. F		**8.** T	

Matching

1. i		**6.** j	
2. f		**7.** a	
3. d		**8.** e	
4. h		**9.** c	
5. b		**10.** g	

SECTION 4 ACTIVITIES
Organizing Information

Men—made all the important family
   decisions, conducted religious ceremonies,
   taught sons the duties of citizenship;
Women—managed the households, taught
   daughters to manage the household, helped
   entertain guests;
Both—taught their children at home, could
   accept inheritances, could own property

Evaluating Information

1. T		**4.** F	
2. T		**5.** F	
3. F		**6.** T	

Classifying Information

1. G		**7.** C	
2. F		**8.** D	
3. E		**9.** A	
4. D		**10.** E	
5. T		**11.** F	
6. F		**12.** G	

SECTION 5 ACTIVITIES
Organizing Information

2. Jesus of Nazareth began teaching in
   communities outside the city.
3. Romans feared Jesus would lead an
   uprising.
4. Romans believed that followers of Jesus
   were attacking Roman religion and law.
5. Jesus was arrested, tried before Pontius
   Pilate, and then crucified.
6. Rome outlawed Christianity.

Evaluating Information

1.	T	**5.**	T
2.	T	**6.**	T
3.	F	**7.**	T
4.	T	**8.**	F

Understanding Main Ideas

1.	a	**3.**	a
2.	d	**4.**	b

SECTION 6 ACTIVITIES

Organizing Information

Diocletian's Solutions

1. He appointed a co-emperor and two assistants.
2. He drove out invading barbarians.
3. He tried to control prices and wages; He collected more taxes.

Evaluating Information

1.	T	**5.**	F
2.	T	**6.**	T
3.	F	**7.**	T
4.	T	**8.**	F

Reviewing Facts

1. inflation
2. Constantinople
3. Attila
4. Germans
5. transportation
6. Mediterranean

Chapter 8

SECTION 1 ACTIVITIES

Organizing Information

Sahara—covers one-fourth of the African continent;

Sahel—from the Arabic word for "shore";

The Savannas—vast stretches of dry grasslands;

The Tropical Rain Forests—areas of jungle

Evaluating Information

1.	F	**6.**	T
2.	T	**7.**	T
3.	F	**8.**	T
4.	T	**9.**	T
5.	F		

Reviewing Facts

1. plateau
2. Kalahari
3. Lake Victoria
4. Great Rift Valley
5. Mount Kilimanjaro
6. Bantu
7. griots
8. Asia

SECTION 2 ACTIVITIES

Organizing Information

Kush—ruled a unified Egypt in about 710 B.C., Meroë may have been a center of ironwork;

Aksum—lay in the rugged Ethiopian highlands, introduced Christianity into the region;

Both—located to the west of the Red Sea, controlled important trade routes between the Red Sea and Egypt

Understanding Main Ideas

1.	d	**3.**	c
2.	d	**4.**	a

Reviewing Facts

1. Nubia
2. Napata
3. Meroë
4. the Red Sea
5. Ethiopian Church

SECTION 3 ACTIVITIES

Organizing Information

Mohammed I Askia—built Songhai into a strong kingdom;

Sonni 'Alī—divided Songhai into several provinces, built a fleet of warships to patrol the Niger River;

Mansa Mūsā—made a pilgrimage to Mecca;

Tunka Manin—great ruler of Ghana, commanded an army of 200,000 warriors

Classifying Information

1.	E	**8.**	W
2.	D	**9.**	E
3.	F	**10.**	E
4.	W	**11.**	W
5.	W	**12.**	W
6.	W	**13.**	E
7.	W	**14.**	E

ANSWER KEY

Understanding Main Ideas

1. a   3. d
2. a   4. a

Chapter 9

SECTION 1 ACTIVITIES
Organizing Information

1. Early peoples from Asia migrated to the Americas.
2. The climate changed and large animals became extinct.
3. The early migrants had to rely on plants as a food source.
4. The earliest known farming communities began in Mexico.
5. Villages and towns began to grow.

Understanding Main Ideas

1. d   4. c
2. c   5. c
3. b

Evaluating Information

1. T
2. F
3. T
4. T

SECTION 2 ACTIVITIES
Organizing Information

The Northwest—held gatherings called potlatches, created totem poles;
The Southwest—included the Hohokam people, built irrigation systems in dry regions;
The Great Plains—people hunted buffalo, people lived in teepees;
The Eastern Woodlands—made animal-shaped mounds, Cahokia was a center of ceremony and trade.

Evaluating Information

1. T   4. T
2. T   5. T
3. F   6. F

Understanding Main Ideas

1. b   3. d
2. b   4. a

SECTION 3 ACTIVITIES
Understanding Main Ideas

1. d   3. d
2. d

Classifying Information

1. M   11. A
2. O   12. M
3. T   13. I
4. C   14. M
5. A   15. I
6. M   16. A
7. I   17. I
8. M   18. O
9. I   19. T
10. I   20. I

Chapter 10 (Modern Chapter 1)

SECTION 1 ACTIVITIES
Organizing Information

Significant contributions of the Byzantine Empire to civilization are: collection of Roman laws—Justinian code; liquid that bursts into flame—Greek fire; holy picture that inspires devotion—icon; alphabet created by the Eastern Orthodox church for the Slavs—Cyrillic alphabet; picture made from small pieces of enamel, glass, or stone—mosaic; a round dome over a rectangular building—Hagia Sophia

Evaluating Information

1. T   6. T
2. T   7. T
3. F   8. F
4. F   9. F
5. T   10. T

Reviewing Facts

1. Institutes
2. dowry
3. heresy
4. Father
5. Seljuq Turks

SECTION 2 ACTIVITIES
Organizing Information
Social classes in Kievan Russia in the order of
their importance are:
1. local princes and their families
2. boyars
3. town artisans and merchants
4. peasants

Evaluating Information
1. F   5. T
2. T   6. T
3. F   7. F
4. F   8. F

Matching
1. d   5. e
2. h   6. b
3. g   7. g
4. c   8. a

SECTION 3 ACTIVITIES
Organizing Information
The events that would lead to the rise of
Russia are:
1. The Polovtsy (a Turkish people) gained
   control of the area south of Kiev.
   (A.D. 1055)
2. Vladimir Monomakh regained Kiev and
   ruled it. (A.D. 1113 to A.D. 1125)
3. Groups of princes sacked Kiev. (A.D. 1169
   and A.D. 1203)
4. Mongols conquered and destroyed cities
   in Kievan Russia. (A.D. 1240)
5. Ivan the Great led Russia to independence
   from the Mongols. (A.D. 1480)
6. Ivan the Terrible became czar with
   absolute power. (A.D. 1547)
7. Moscow became the center of the Russian
   Orthodox Church. (A.D. 1589)

Evaluating Information
1. T   5. F
2. F   6. T
3. T   7. T
4. F   8. F

Understanding Main Ideas
1. a   3. b
2. c   4. b

Chapter 11
(Modern Chapter 2)

SECTION 1 ACTIVITIES
Organizing Information

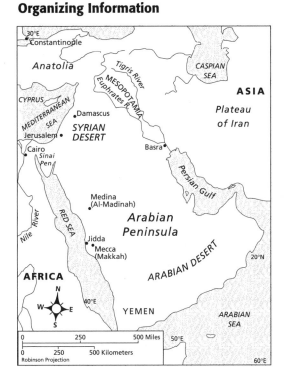

Evaluating Information
1. T   6. F
2. T   7. T
3. F   8. F
4. F   9. T
5. T   10. T

Reviewing Facts
1. shiekh
2. hiraj
3. Kaaba
4. jihad
5. Five Pillars of Islam
6. mosques

SECTION 2 ACTIVITIES
Organizing Information
1. d
2. b
3. d

Evaluating Information
1. F   4. F
2. T   5. T
3. T   6. F

Reviewing Facts
1. caliph
2. 'Umar
3. Jews
4. Sunni
5. imams
6. Sufi
7. Shi'ah
8. Moors

SECTION 3 ACTIVITIES
Organizing Information
China: textiles from silk, papermaking technique, an ancient system of mathematics;
Spain: fine leather goods, steel swords from Toledo;
Greece: ideas of philosophers, the astrolabe;
India: Arabic numerals

Classifying Information
1. T		4. F	
2. T		5. T	
3. F		6. F	

Understanding Main Ideas
1. b		4. c	
2. a		5. d	
3. a			

Chapter 12 (Modern Chapter 3)

SECTION 1 ACTIVITIES
Organizing Information
Sui Dynasty—defeated by invading Turks in 615; built the Grand Canal, unable to conquer southern Manchuria and northern Korea.
Tang—Buddhism reached its peak, high point in Chinese literature, brought back Confucianism.
Sung—more people lived in cities than ever before, prevented cheating on civil service tests, new type of rice helped farmers grow more crops.

Evaluating Information
1. T		6. T	
2. T		7. T	
3. T		8. T	
4. F		9. F	
5. F		10. T	

Reviewing Facts
1. Tang
2. Empress Wu
3. ruling
4. porcelain
5. gunpowder

SECTION 2 ACTIVITIES
Organizing Information
1. Genghis Khan and Mongols captured Beijing and renamed it Khanbalik.
2. Batu invades Europe around 1240.
3. Kublai Khan got the title of Great Khan.
4. Kublai Khan began the Yuan dynasty.
5. Yuan forces defeated the Sung dynasty.
6. The Yuan dynasty was overthrown.

Evaluating Information
1. F		5. F	
2. T		6. T	
3. F		7. T	
4. T		8. T	

Reviewing Facts
1. Golden Horde
2. Kublai Khan
3. Marco Polo
4. cavalry
5. Batu
6. Genghis Khan

SECTION 3 ACTIVITIES
Organizing Information
A. Chinese Buddhism—Japan, Korea, Vietnam
B. Confucian traditions and ideas—Japan, Korea, Vietnam
C. Chinese writing—Japan, Korea, Vietnam
D. Hindu and Indian beliefs—Non-Vietnam Southeast Asia
E. metalworking techniques—Korea
F. Chinese model of government—Japan, Korea, Vietnam
G. Sanskrit language—Non-Vietnam Southeast Asia

Evaluating Information

1. F   4. F
2. T   5. T
3. T   6. T

Understanding Main Ideas

1. c   3. a
2. a   4. b

Chapter 13 (Modern Chapter 4)

SECTION 1 ACTIVITIES
Organizing Information
The Rise of the Franks

1. Clovis became ruler of the Frankish tribes.
3. Pépin II and his successors united the Frankish kingdoms.
4. Charles Martel defeated the Spanish Moors.
5. Pépin III crowned; Carolingian rule began.
6. The Papal states were created.

Evaluating Information

1. T   6. F
2. T   7. F
3. T   8. F
4. F   9. F
5. T   10. T

Reviewing Facts

1. Middle Ages
2. Carolingians
3. Papal States
4. France
5. *missi dominici*

SECTION 2 ACTIVITIES
Organizing Information

lord—one who grants land to others
knight—warrior and protector of the castle
squire—teenager who serves as knight's attendant
serf—peasant who works the land
vassal—one who receives a fief or land grant
page—young boy who serves as knight's helper

Evaluating Information

1. T   4. T
2. T   5. F
3. F   6. F

Reviewing Facts

1. feudalism
2. fief
3. primogeniture
4. chain mail
5. compurgation
6. domain
7. serf
8. moat
9. keep
10. coat of arms

SECTION 3 ACTIVITIES
Organizing Information

1. pope
2. cardinals
3. archbishops
4. bishops
5. parish priests

Evaluating Information

1. T   5. F
2. F   6. F
3. T   7. T
4. T   8. F

Matching

1. d   6. j
2. g   7. b
3. e   8. j
4. a   9. h
5. f   10. c

SECTION 4 ACTIVITIES
Organizing Information

1. Alfred the Great made peace with the Danes.
3. Henry I sent traveling judges throughout the country.
4. King John was forced to accept the Magna Carta.
5. Simon de Montfort built middle class support for nobles.

Classifying Information

1. E	**5.** F
2. F	**6.** F
3. E	**7.** F
4. E	**8.** E

Understanding Main Ideas

1. c	**3.** b
2. c	**4.** d

SECTION 5 ACTIVITIES
Organizing Information
Popes

1. Placed England under interdiction.
2. Had the great power of excommunication.
3. Believed that people's souls were more important than their bodies.

European Rulers

4. Thought that kings should be able to choose bishops.
5. Chose four popes during the 1000s.
6. Thought of the church as a branch of the imperial government.

Evaluating Information

1. F	**5.** F
2. F	**6.** T
3. T	**7.** F
4. T	**8.** F

Reviewing Facts

1. Otto I
2. lay investiture
3. Henry III
4. Concordat of Worms
5. Lombardy
6. Italy

Chapter 14 (Modern Chapter 5)

SECTION 1 ACTIVITIES
Organizing Information

The First Crusade—Leaders: French and Italian lords; Outcome: Crusaders capture the Holy Land.

The Second Crusade—Leaders : Louis VII and Conrad III; Outcome: Crusaders return in disgrace.

The Third Crusade—Leaders: Frederick Barbarrosa, Philip II and Richard III; Outcome: Richard forges pact with the Muslims.

The Fourth Crusade—Leaders: French knights; Outcome: Crusaders attack Constantinople.

Evaluating Information

1. F	**6.** T
2. F	**7.** T
3. T	**8.** F
4. T	**9.** T
5. F	**10.** T

Reviewing Facts

1. Holy Land
2. Byzantine emperor
3. Asia Minor
4. 100
5. 60
6. Acre
7. crossbow
8. catapult
9. feudalism
10. southwest Asia

SECTION 2 ACTIVITIES
Organizing Information

Italy—Trading cities: **C.** Genoa, Pisa and Venice; Traded goods: **E.** Asian goods carried by ships from Palestine

Northern Europe—Trading cities: **A.** Kiev and Flanders; Traded goods: **F.** goods from Constantinople, fine wool

Baltic and North Seas—Trading cities: **B.** Bremen, Hamburg and Lubeck; Traded goods: **D.** Baltic goods like fish, fur, timber

Evaluating Information

1. T	**6.** T
2. F	**7.** F
3. T	**8.** T
4. F	**9.** T
5. T	**10.** T

Understanding Main Ideas

1. a	**3.** d
2. a	**4.** a

SECTION 3 ACTIVITIES
Organizing Information
Steps to becoming a master in a guild
1. Parents bring a boy to a master.
2. He is taken as an apprentice.
3. Parents pay the master to house, feed, and clothe him.
4. He trains for nine years.
5. A young man becomes a journeyman.
6. The young man receives wages.
7. The guild approves the young man's masterpiece.
8. The young man opens his shop.

Evaluating Information
1.	T	6.	T
2.	F	7.	T
3.	T	8.	F
4.	F	9.	T
5.	F	10.	T

Understanding Main Ideas
1.	a	3.	a
2.	a	4.	a

SECTION 4 ACTIVITIES
Organizing Information
1. Long poem or epic—*Song of Roland*
2. Romance—*King Arthur and the Knights of the Round Table*
3. Animal story or fable—"Reynard the Fox"
4. Miracle or morality plays—*Noah's Flood*

Evaluating Information
1.	T	6.	T
2.	F	7.	T
3.	F	8.	T
4.	T	9.	T
5.	F	10.	T

Reviewing Facts
1. Dante Alighieri
2. Geoffrey Chaucer
3. Peter Abelard
4. Thomas Aquinas

SECTION 5 ACTIVITIES
Organizing Information
The Hundred Years' War
Cause—Edward III claimed French throne;
Effect—New weapons of war used, Parliament gained power over king

The War of the Roses
Cause—English royalty, using the rose as badge, fought over throne;
Effect—Henry Tudor began strong English monarchy

War in the House of Burgundy and Orleans
Cause—French House of Burgundy took English side;
Effect—Charles the VII of Orleans won, was crowned king, and drove English out

War against the Moors
Cause—Ferdinand and Isabella wanted an all-catholic Spain;
Effect—Muslims' last stronghold captured, Spain united

Evaluating Information
1.	F	6.	F
2.	F	7.	T
3.	T	8.	T
4.	F	9.	F
5.	T	10.	F

Reviewing Facts
1. monarchy
2. freedom
3. nations
4. Holy Roman Empire

SECTION 6 ACTIVITIES
Organizing Information
Events that Led to the Decline of Church Power
1. Boniface decreed that popes had power over worldly affairs.
2. Popes were kept in Avignon during the Babylonian Captivity.
3. The Great Schism: church was divided into opposing groups.
4. The Council of Constance ended the Great Schism.
5. John Wycliffe attacked the wealth of the church.
6. Jan Hus angered the clergy and was burned at the stake.

Evaluating Information
1.	T	6.	F
2.	T	7.	F
3.	F	8.	T
4.	T	9.	T
5.	T	10.	F

Reviewing Facts
1. Innocent III
2. practices
3. Avignon
4. *Defender of the Faith*
5. reforms

Chapter 15 (Modern Chapter 6)

SECTION 1 ACTIVITIES
Organizing Information
Art—Leonardo da Vinci, perspective;
Literature—Francesco Petrarch, Niccolo Machiavelli;
Thought—admiration for human achievement, humanities

Evaluating Information
1.	F	6.	F
2.	T	7.	F
3.	F	8.	T
4.	T	9.	T
5.	T	10.	F

Reviewing Facts
1. ancient world
2. Roman glory
3. Hebrew
4. meaningful life
5. classical
6. power
7. realistic
8. perspective

SECTION 2 ACTIVITIES
Organizing Information
Writers:
Desiderius Erasmus believed that scholars had made Christian faith less spiritual.
Thomas More imagined a society where everyone worked to support one another.
Painters:
Jan and Hubert van Eyck paid attention to detail, such as facial expressions.
Pieter Brueghel used art to criticize intolerance and cruelty.

Evaluating Information
1.	T	6.	F
2.	T	7.	T
3.	T	8.	T
4.	F	9.	T
5.	T	10.	F

Understanding Main Ideas
1.	c	3.	c
2.	c	4.	b

SECTION 3 ACTIVITIES
Matching
1.	m	7.	e
2.	d	8.	g
3.	i	9.	f
4.	a	10.	h
5.	l	11.	b
6.	c	12.	j

Evaluating Information
1.	F	6.	F
2.	F	7.	F
3.	T	8.	T
4.	T	9.	T
5.	T	10.	T

Interpreting Visual Images
1. The pro-Catholic soldiers are engaged in a bloody civil war. The victims of the massacre are the Huguenots. The Catholic French monarchs considered the Huguenots a threat to national security.
2. In 1598 King Henry IV issued the Edict of Nantes that ended the Catholic persecution of the Huguenots.

SECTION 4 ACTIVITIES
Organizing Information
Council of Trent—defined official church position on matters of doctrine, emphasized the need for ceremonies;
the Jesuits—produced educated supporters of the church, defined official church position on matters of doctrine

Evaluating Information
1.	F	6.	F
2.	T	7.	T
3.	F	8.	T
4.	T	9.	T
5.	T	10.	T

ANSWER KEY

Reviewing Facts

1. pope
2. Jesuits
3. Loyola
4. salvation
5. chastity
6. Erasmus
7. Protestantism
8. heresy

SECTION 5 ACTIVITIES
Organizing Information

Cause:

Villagers lived in close-knit communities.

People needed time to relax.

Farming was time consuming.

Effect:

Anyone who upset village traditions was
   treated harshly.

Villagers played games and celebrated
   holidays.

Raising food used up all the daylight hours.

Evaluating Information

1. F		6. T
2. T		7. F
3. T		8. T
4. F		9. T
5. F		10. F

Reviewing Facts

1. preachers
2. inflation
3. wise person
4. almanac
5. exorcise
6. peddlers
7. Black Death
8. priests

Chapter 16 (Modern Chapter 7)

SECTION 1 ACTIVITIES
Organizing Information

Astronomy: Copernicus, Kepler, Galileo,
   Newton;

Chemistry: Boyle, Priestley, Lavoisier;

Anatomy: Harvey, Vesalius

Evaluating Information

1. T		6. T
2. T		7. F
3. T		8. T
4. F		9. F
5. T		10. T

Reviewing Facts

1. circulation
2. alchemists
3. anatomy
4. Galileo
5. natural philosophers
6. motion
7. geocentric
8. Kepler

SECTION 2 ACTIVITIES
Organizing Information

Technological Advances: invention of the
   compass/allowed explorers to know their
   location better and explore more accurately

Economic Conditions: banks could lend
   large sums of money to explorers and
   governments/banks began printing more
   money

Mercantilism: government efforts to
   obtain more wealth from rival nations/
   governments began to pursue riches from
   the territories it claimed

Social Changes: desire for religious freedom
   and greater curiousity about the
   world/many more people were willing to
   leave Europe

Evaluating Information

1. T		6. T
2. F		7. T
3. T		8. T
4. T		9. T
5. T		10. T

Reviewing Facts

1. precious metals
2. galleys
3. ducat
4. compass
5. discovery

SECTION 3 ACTIVITIES
Organizing Information
Spain: Asia and the East Indies, New World, Philippines;

Portugal: Brazil, Central and South America, eastern and western coasts of Africa

Evaluating Information
1. T	**6.** T
2. F	**7.** T
3. T	**8.** F
4. T	**9.** T
5. T	**10.** F

Classifying Information
1. b	**7.** k
2. f	**8.** d
3. i	**9.** g
4. l	**10.** E
5. c	**11.** A
6. j	**12.** h

SECTION 4 ACTIVITIES
Organizing Information
Economics of Spain: Spain was a consumer nation because it lacked a functioning middle class

Actions of the Colonists: large profits from the colonies drove inflation up

Actions of Charles V: fought continuous religious holy wars for Spain and the Holy Roman Empire

Actions of Philip II: lost possession of the Netherlands

Evaluating Information
1. F	**6.** T
2. T	**7.** F
3. T	**8.** F
4. F	**9.** T
5. T	**10.** T

Understanding Main Ideas
1. d	**3.** d
2. c	**4.** b

Chapter 17 (Modern Chapter 8)

SECTION 1 ACTIVITIES
Organizing Information
1. Scholar-gentry—These people read books and were the staff of the royal government.
2. Farmers—These people produced food and paid taxes that supported the empire.
3. Artisans—These people made beautiful and useful objects.
4. Merchants—These people sold objects that peasants and artisans had made or produced.

Classifying Information
1. M (Ming)	**4.** M
2. Q (Qing)	**5.** Q
3. Q	**6.** Q

Reviewing Facts
1. junks
2. queue
3. family
4. sweet potato
5. philology
6. White Lotus Rebellion

SECTION 2 ACTIVITIES
Organizing Information
1. Jesuit missionaries become advisors to the Qing emperor.
2. British begin shipping opium to China.
3. Chinese ask Britain to stop bringing opium to China.
4. Chinese and British fight the Opium War.
5. Opium War ends, China gives Hongkong to the British in the Treaty of Nanjing.

Evaluating Information
1. T	**5.** F
2. F	**6.** F
3. T	**7.** F
4. T	**8.** F

Matching
1. d	**5.** e
2. a	**6.** h
3. g	**7.** c
4. b	**8.** f

SECTION 3 ACTIVITIES
Organizing Information
1. shogun
2. daimyo
3. samurai
4. peasants
5. artisans
6. merchants

Evaluating Information
1. T
2. T
3. T
4. F
5. T
6. F
7. F
8. T

Understanding Main Ideas
1. d
2. a
3. b
4. a

Chapter 18 (Modern Chapter 9)

SECTION 1 ACTIVITIES
Organizing Information
A. 1526; **B.** 1336; **C.** 1520; **D.** 1444; **E.** 1453; **F.** 1396

Evaluating Information
1. T
2. F
3. F
4. T
5. T
6. F
7. T
8. F
9. T
10. F

Reviewing Facts
1. Osman
2. Genghis Kahn
3. Murad II
4. the Lawgiver
5. Turkey

SECTION 2 ACTIVITIES
Organizing Information
1. Shi'ah became the religion of the Safavid Empire.
2. Rulers after 'Abbās were inept.
3. Persians killed or imprisoned many Safavids.
4. 'Abbās wanted to defeat the Ottomans and Uzbeks.

Evaluating Information
1. T
2. T
3. T
4. F
5. T
6. T
7. F
8. T

Matching
1. a
2. c
3. f
4. e
5. d
6. b

SECTION 3 ACTIVITIES
Organizing Information
Akbar: tolerant of all religions; known as the greatest Mughal emperor

Shah Jahān: increased taxes to support wars in Persia; built the Taj Mahal

Aurangzeb: demanded strict following of Islamic law; revolts and economic problems weakened his empire

Evaluating Information
1. T
2. F
3. F
4. F
5. T
6. F
7. F
8. T

Understanding Main Ideas
1. c
2. a
3. c
4. d
5. b

Chapter 19 (Modern Chapter 10)

SECTION 1 ACTIVITIES
Organizing Information
Henry IV: converted to Catholicism to help bring peace and unity to France; wanted to protect the rights of Protestants

Cardinal Richelieu: led military attacks on towns held by Huguenots; made the intendants, or king's officials, more powerful

Louis XIV: caused Protestants to flee France by doing away with the Edict of Nantes; controlled the nobles by having them live at his palace

Evaluating Information

1.	F	5.	F
2.	F	6.	T
3.	T	7.	T
4.	F	8.	F

Reviewing Facts

1. Treaty of Westphalia
2. Versailles
3. intendants
4. Jean-Baptiste Colbert
5. balance of power
6. Treaty of Utrecht

SECTION 2 ACTIVITIES
Organizing Information

Peter the Great: built a new capital in St. Petersburg; modernized and Westernized Russia; created a new class of nobles based on "service nobility"

Catherine the Great: extended Russian borders into central Europe; opened access to Siberia; gained control of most of the northern shore of the Black Sea

Evaluating Information

1.	F	5.	T
2.	F	6.	F
3.	T	7.	T
4.	F	8.	T

Understanding Main Ideas

1.	d	3.	a
2.	b	4.	a

SECTION 3 ACTIVITIES
Organizing Information

1. War of the Austrian Succession: Austria allied with Great Britain, Russia and the Netherlands while Prussia allied with Bavaria, Spain, and France.
2. Diplomatic Revolution: Austria allied with France and Russia while Prussia allied with Great Britain.
3. Seven Years' War: Austria and France joined forces while Russia made peace with Prussia.

Evaluating Information

1.	F	5.	T
2.	T	6.	F
3.	F	7.	T
4.	T	8.	F

Understanding Main Ideas

1.	b	3.	a
2.	d	4.	c

SECTION 4 ACTIVITIES
Organizing Information

Mary I: was determined to restore Catholicism in England; persecuted Protestants and caused rebellion

Elizabeth I: had more tolerant religious policies; managed Parliament successfully

James I: approved a new translation of the Bible; believed in the divine right of kings

Evaluating Information

1.	T	5.	T
2.	F	6.	T
3.	F	7.	F
4.	F	8.	T

Understanding Main Ideas

1.	c	3.	c
2.	b	4.	c

Chapter 20 (Modern Chapter 11)

SECTION 1 ACTIVITIES
Organizing Information

1. Parliament passed Petition of Right.
3. Long Parliament began.
4. Civil war broke out.
5. Cromwell had Charles I killed.
6. Cromwell ruled as lord protector.
7. Cromwell failed to set up a constitution.

Evaluating Information

1.	F	5.	F
2.	T	6.	F
3.	T	7.	T
4.	T	8.	F

Matching

1.	g	5.	d
2.	c	6.	a
3.	h	7.	e
4.	f	8.	b

SECTION 2 ACTIVITIES
Organizing Information
Thomas Hobbes: People make a social contract with leaders; People act only from self-interest; Only the strong survive in the natural world.

John Locke: People need a government; Individual rights are more important than laws; A tyrant can be justly overthrown.

Evaluating Information
1. T
2. F
3. T
4. T
5. F
6. T
7. T
8. F

Reviewing Facts
1. Tories
2. English Bill of Rights
3. Toleration Act
4. Restoration
5. Whigs
6. cabinet
7. Habeas Corpus Act
8. prime minister

SECTION 3 ACTIVITIES
Organizing Information
John Cabot: gave England its first claim in America; Venetian sea captain who explored the coasts of Newfoundland and Nova Scotia

Sir Francis Drake: helped to defeat the Spanish Armada; plundered foreign ships, particularly those of Spain

Henry Hudson: searched for the Northwest Passage in northern North America; explored the bay in northern Canada that now has his name

Evaluating Information
1. F
2. T
3. T
4. F
5. F
6. F
7. T
8. F

Reviewing Facts
1. British East India Company
2. sea dogs
3. John Cabot
4. Henry Hudson
5. mercantilism
6. Sir Francis Drake

SECTION 4 ACTIVITIES
Organizing Information
Voltaire—freedom of speech
Wollstonecraft—women's rights
Montesquieu—checks and balances
Rousseau—popular sovereignty

Evaluating Information
1. T
2. F
3. F
4. T
5. T
6. T
7. T
8. F

Understanding Main Ideas
1. c
2. a
3. a
4. c

SECTION 5 ACTIVITIES
Organizing Information
Articles of Confederation: one-house Congress in which each state had one vote; Congress could not vote for taxes of coin money; individual states had all the power; very weak central government

Constitution: government divided into legislative, executive, and judicial branches; federal government could declare war, raise armies, and make treaties; set up executive branch headed by the president and enforced laws

Evaluating Information
1. T
2. T
3. F
4. F
5. F
6. T
7. F
8. T

Matching
1. c
2. f
3. b
4. h
5. d
6. a
7. e
8. g

Chapter 21 (Modern Chapter 12)

SECTION 1 ACTIVITIES
Organizing Information
First Estate—**A, E**; Second Estate—**D, F**; Third Estate—**B, C.**

Evaluating Information
1. T		**5.** F	
2. T		**6.** F	
3. F		**7.** T	
4. F		**8.** T	

Understanding Main Ideas
1. a		**3.** a	
2. b		**4.** a	

SECTION 2 ACTIVITIES
Organizing Information
Events of the French Revolution
1. The people of Paris loot and destroy the Bastille prison.
2. National Assembly creates the Declaration of the Rights of Man.
3. Constitution of 1791 is written.
4. Legislative Assembly meets for the first time.
5. France declares war on Austria in 1792.
6. The office of king is suspended, and Louis XVI is put in prison.

Evaluating Information
1. F		**5.** F	
2. T		**6.** F	
3. T		**7.** T	
4. T		**8.** T	

Reviewing Facts
1. Great Fear
2. Olympe de Gouges
3. émigrés
4. departments
5. Civil Constitution of the Clergy
6. radicals
7. moderates
8. conservatives

SECTION 3 ACTIVITIES
Organizing Information
French Government: National Convention—set up the Committee of Public Safety, abolished slavery in France's colonies;

The Directory—had five leaders who ran the government; neither the radicals nor the conservatives liked this government;

Napoléon—said that the crown of France was lying on the ground waiting to be picked up, seized power in a *coup d'état*

Classifying Information
1. T		**5.** T	
2. F		**6.** T	
3. T		**7.** T	
4. F		**8.** F	

Matching
1. g		**5.** h	
2. e		**6.** a	
3. b		**7.** d	
4. f		**8.** c	

SECTION 4 ACTIVITIES
Organizing Information
B. 1799, the Consulate is formed with Napoléon as First Consul;

G. 1804, Napoléon crowns himself emperor of the French Empire;

D. 1808, beginning of the Peninsular War;

F. 1811, Napoléon's son, Napoléon II, is born;

C. 1814, Napoléon is beaten and the Bourbon monarchy was restored;

A. 1815, Napoléon loses the Battle of Waterloo;

E. 1821, Napoléon dies in exile on the island of St. Helena.

Evaluating Information
1. T		**5.** T	
2. T		**6.** F	
3. T		**7.** F	
4. F		**8.** F	

Understanding Main Ideas
1. a		**3.** c	
2. d		**4.** a	

SECTION 5 ACTIVITIES
Organizing Information
Reactionaries—Holy Alliance, believed in absolutism, said that former ruling families should be restored to their power;

Liberals—ideas that came out during the American and French revolutions, individual rights were very important, supported freedom of speech and press.

Evaluating Information
1. T
2. T
3. F
4. F
5. T
6. F
7. T
8. F

Matching
1. f
2. f
3. a
4. b
5. h
6. e
7. d
8. g

Chapter 22 (Modern Chapter 13)

SECTION 1 ACTIVITIES
Organizing Information
Agriculture—seed drill, iron plow, replaceable plow blades;

Manufacturing—water-powered loom, cotton gin, steam engine;

Transportation—the *Clermont*, steam locomotive, canals with locks

Evaluating Information
1. T
2. F
3. T
4. F
5. T
6. F
7. F
8. F
9. T
10. F

Reviewing Facts
1. "Turnip" Townshend
2. farm workers
3. factory system
4. cotton gin
5. water power
6. steam engine

7. dots and dashes
8. battery
9. Great Britain
10. tariffs

SECTION 2 ACTIVITIES
Organizing Information
Factory System—employed women and children, did only part of a job, workers fined for being late, paid for hours worked;

Domestic System—workers paid for items completed, employed skilled workers, worked on complete products, workers decided when to work.

Evaluating Information
1. F
2. T
3. T
4. T
5. F
6. F
7. F
8. F
9. T
10. F

Understanding Main Ideas
1. c
2. a
3. b
4. d

SECTION 3 ACTIVITIES
Organizing Information
Eli Whitney—interchangeable parts for guns;
Henry Ford—assembly line;
J. P. Morgan—United States Steel Company

Classifying Information
1. F
2. T
3. F
4. T
5. T
6. F
7. T
8. T
9. F
10. T

Understanding Main Ideas
1. c
2. d
3. c
4. a

SECTION 4 ACTIVITIES
Organizing Information
The iron law of wages—David Ricardo;

A government should work for the good of all its citizens—John Stuart Mill;

The law of supply and demand and the law of competition—Adam Smith;

The connection between poverty and population growth—Thomas Malthus

Evaluating Information

1.	T	6.	T
2.	T	7.	F
3.	F	8.	T
4.	T	9.	F
5.	F	10.	F

Reviewing Facts

1. mercantilism
2. supply and demand
3. inevitable
4. leave things alone
5. laws
6. John Stuart Mill
7. enforce
8. unions

SECTION 5 ACTIVITIES
Organizing Information

Socialism—Government owns the means of production; private property allowed

Both—redistribution of wealth

Communism—The people own the means of production; dictatorship of the proletariat; classless society; "From each according to his abilities; to each according to his needs."

Evaluating Information

1.	F	5.	T
2.	F	6.	T
3.	T	7.	F
4.	T	8.	T

Understanding Main Ideas

1.	c	3.	d
2.	a		

Chapter 23 (Modern Chapter 14)

SECTION 1 ACTIVITIES
Organizing Information

Electricity—dams, dynamo, lightbulb;

Communications—radio, wireless telegraph, telephone;

Transportation— internal combustion engine, balloons.

Evaluating Information

1.	F	7.	F
2.	T	8.	T
3.	T	9.	T
4.	F	10.	F
5.	F	11.	T
6.	T	12.	F

Reviewing Facts

1. Michael Faraday
2. magnetism
3. water power
4. electric current
5. hydroelectric
6. wires
7. ship-to-shore
8. outside
9. fuel
10. Kitty Hawk

SECTION 2 ACTIVITIES
Organizing Information

Biology—Schleiden and Swann, Rudolf Virchow, Jean-Baptiste Lamarck, Charles Darwin, Gregor Mendel;

Medicine—Edward Jenner, Louis Pasteur, Joseph Lister, Robert Koch, Alexander Fleming;

Physics and Chemistry—Dmitry Mendeleyev, Wilhelm C. Röntgen, Pierre and Marie Curie, Max Planck, Albert Einstein

Evaluating Information

1.	F	5.	F
2.	T	6.	T
3.	F	7.	T
4.	T	8.	F

Understanding Main Ideas

1.	d	3.	a
2.	c	4.	d

SECTION 3 ACTIVITIES

Organizing Information

Archaeology—study of human culture through its artifacts, cave paintings in France;

Anthropology—study of past and present societies, Taylor, Frazer;

Sociology—study of human relationships, Spencer, Comte;

Psychology—study of the mind and human behavior, Pavlov, Freud.

Classifying Information

1.	T	6.	T
2.	F	7.	F
3.	F	8.	T
4.	T	9.	T
5.	T	10.	F

Understanding Main Ideas

1.	a	3.	c
2.	d	4.	b

SECTION 4 ACTIVITIES

Organizing Information

Connected to Population Growth—
  A. immigrants fleeing poverty;
  E. immigrants fleeing oppression;
  F. improvements in sanitation;
Connected to Growth of Cities—
  D. population shift from rural areas;
  B. decline in jobs on farms;
  C. factories located there.

Evaluating Information

1.	T	6.	T
2.	F	7.	F
3.	F	8.	T
4.	F	9.	T
5.	T	10.	F

Reviewing Facts

1. sewers
2. Jane Addams
3. refrigerated
4. public transportation
5. life expectancy
6. lower class
7. newspapers
8. public parks

SECTION 5 ACTIVITIES

Organizing Information

Connected to Music—Tchaikovsky, Verdi, Beethoven, Schubert;

Connected to Poetry and Drama—Keats, Byron, *Faust;*

Connected to Stories—*Legend of Sleepy Hollow* (Washington Irving), Grimm Brothers's fairy tales, *Ivanhoe*

Evaluating Information

1.	T	5.	T
2.	F	6.	F
3.	T	7.	T
4.	F	8.	F

Understanding Main Ideas

1.	d	3.	c
2.	a	4.	b

Chapter 24 (Modern Chapter 15)

SECTION 1 ACTIVITIES

Organizing Information

Pre-reform—Only property owners vote. No secret ballot. Only Anglicans hold office. Power is in the countryside.

Reform—People with less property can vote. Catholics, Jews, and non-Anglicans can vote. Power shifted to cities.

Unchanged—Only males vote.

Evaluating Information

1.	F	6.	F
2.	T	7.	F
3.	T	8.	T
4.	F	9.	F
5.	T	10.	T

Reviewing Facts

1. secret ballot
2. Emmeline Pankhurst
3. suffragettes
4. self-government
5. Canadian Pacific Railroad
6. convicts
7. aborigines
8. New Zealand

SECTION 2 ACTIVITIES
Organizing Information

The time line should be in this order:
Northwest Territory, 1787; Louisiana Purchase, 1803; Florida Cession, 1819; Texas Annexation, 1845; Oregon Country, 1846; Gadsden Purchase, 1853; Alaska Purchase, 1867; Annexation of Hawaii, 1898.

Evaluating Information

1. T	**6.** T
2. F	**7.** T
3. F	**8.** F
4. F	**9.** T
5. F	**10.** T

Understanding Main Ideas

1. c	**3.** d
2. a	**4.** c

SECTION 3 ACTIVITIES
Organizing Information

Louis Philippe—"Citizen King," Restricted free speech, Replaced by the Second Republic, Abdicated the throne

Louis-Napoléon—Elected by the people, Staged a coup d'état, Forced France to create a new constitution, Later elected and ruled as Emperor Napoléon III

Classifying Information

1. T	**6.** T
2. F	**7.** T
3. T	**8.** F
4. T	**9.** T
5. T	**10.** F

Understanding Main Ideas

1. c	**3.** d
2. b	**4.** c

SECTION 4 ACTIVITIES
Organizing Information

Simón Bolívar—Gran Colombia
Bernardo O'Higgins—Chile
José Francisco de San Martín—Peru
Toussaint-Louverture—Haiti
Agustín de Iturbide—Mexico

Evaluating Information

1. T	**5.** T
2. T	**6.** F
3. F	**7.** F
4. F	**8.** T

Reviewing Facts

1. Haiti
2. creoles
3. Gran Colombia
4. Monroe Doctrine
5. slavery
6. *caudillos*

Chapter 25 (Modern Chapter 16)

SECTION 1 ACTIVITIES
Organizing Information

Mazzini—**C, F**
Garibaldi—**A, G**
Victor Emmanuel—**B**
Cavour—**H, D, E**

Evaluating Information

1. T	**6.** T
2. T	**7.** T
3. F	**8.** F
4. T	**9.** F
5. T	**10.** F

Reviewing Facts

1. French Revolution
2. neither pope nor king
3. liberals
4. Cavour
5. Austria
6. Italy
7. Garibaldi
8. Rome

SECTION 2 ACTIVITIES
Organizing Information

The Rise of Prussia: From defeat—Conquered by Napoléon I in 1806, Prussian troops forced to fight for the French, French seize Prussian territory;

To victory—Helps defeat the French at Leipzig in 1813, Helps defeat the French at Waterloo in 1815, Bismarck unites Germany under Prussia in 1871.

Evaluating Information

1. T	6. T
2. T	7. F
3. F	8. F
4. T	9. F
5. T	10. T

Understanding Main Ideas

1. d	3. a
2. c	

SECTION 3 ACTIVITIES
Organizing Information
Kulturkampf
- **C.** Broke relations with the Vatican;
- **G.** Church property confiscated;
- **D.** Laws controlled Catholic clergy and schools;
- **H.** Anti-Catholic;
- **E.** Ended in failure

Classifying Information

1. T	6. F
2. F	7. F
3. F	8. T
4. T	9. F
5. T	10. F

Understanding Main Ideas

1. c	3. b
2. c	4. a

SECTION 4 ACTIVITIES
Organizing Information
Modernizing Russia
- **A.** Power of secret police curtailed;
- **E.** More freedom of the press;
- **B.** Rural areas allowed to elect their own governments;
- **G.** Serfs freed;
- **D.** Court system reformed

Evaluating Information

1. T	6. T
2. F	7. F
3. F	8. T
4. T	9. T
5. F	10. T

Reviewing Facts

1. Emancipation Edict
2. poverty
3. nobles
4. Nihilists
5. terrorism
6. repression
7. Revolution of 1905
8. Duma

SECTION 5 ACTIVITIES
Organizing Information
Austria—Parliament in Vienna, A market for farm products, Strongly industrial;

Hungary—Parliament in Budapest, Mostly agricultural, A market for manufactured products;

Austria-Hungary—Francis Joseph I, Three ministries for empire's affairs

Evaluating Information

1. F	5. T
2. T	6. F
3. T	7. T
4. T	8. T

Understanding Main Ideas

1. c	3. a
2. d	4. d

Chapter 26
(Modern Chapter 17)

SECTION 1 ACTIVITIES
Organizing Information
Kinds of Colonies—Settlement colonies, Dependent colonies, Protectorates;

Motives for Colonization—Need for raw materials, Establish new markets, "The White Man's Burden"

Evaluating Information

1. F	6. T
2. F	7. T
3. T	8. F
4. T	9. T
5. T	10. T

Reviewing Facts
1. Australia
2. India
3. West Africa
4. raw materials
5. create new markets
6. immigrants
7. Rudyard Kipling
8. improving

SECTION 2 ACTIVITIES
Organizing Information
France—Morocco, Tunis, Algiers;
Great Britain—Egypt, Sudan; Italy—Libya

Evaluating Information
1.	T	6.	F
2.	F	7.	F
3.	T	8.	T
4.	F	9.	F
5.	T	10.	F

Understanding Main Ideas
1.	c	4.	b
2.	b	5.	a
3.	c		

SECTION 3 ACTIVITIES
Organizing Information
West Africa: Colonizers—French, British;
Opponents—Samory Touré, Ashanti.
Central and East Africa: Colonizers—
King Leopold II, Belgium.
Southern Africa: Colonizers—Boers, British;
Opponents—Shaka, Zulu.

Classifying Information
1.	T	6.	T
2.	T	7.	T
3.	F	8.	F
4.	F	9.	T
5.	F	10.	F

Understanding Main Ideas
1.	b	4.	c
2.	d	5.	c
3.	a		

SECTION 4 ACTIVITIES
Organizing Information
Great Britain in India: As rulers—Built
bridges, roads, and railroads, Improved
schools, Treated Muslims and Hindus
equally, Did not ease religious hatreds,
Principle of "divide and rule";
Socially—Felt themselves a superior race,
Made India their permanent home,
No social contact with Indian people.

Evaluating Information
1.	T	6.	T
2.	F	7.	T
3.	F	8.	F
4.	F	9.	T
5.	T	10.	F

Reviewing Facts
1. imperialists
2. Korea
3. win
4. major world power
5. French Indochina
6. Siam
7. coaling stations
8. Lilioukalani

SECTION 5 ACTIVITIES
Organizing Information
Cuba: Spanish-American War—**F.** Explosion
of battleship *Maine*, **E.** A fight for Cuban
Independence, **D.** Rough Riders, **H.** Spanish
fleet defeated in the Philippines;
Treaty of Paris—**A.** Ended the war, **G.** New
Cuban constitution, **B.** Platt Amendment,
C. Spain gave up claims to Cuba.

Evaluating Information
1.	F	5.	T
2.	T	6.	T
3.	F	7.	T
4.	T	8.	F

Understanding Main Ideas
1.	c	3.	a
2.	b		

Chapter 27 (Modern Chapter 18)

SECTION 1 ACTIVITIES
Organizing Information
Alliances: Triple Alliance—Germany, Austria-Hungary, Italy;

Triple Entente—Great Britain, France, Russia, + Secret understanding with Italy.

Evaluating Information
1.	T	6.	F
2.	F	7.	F
3.	T	8.	T
4.	F	9.	T
5.	T	10.	F

Reviewing Facts
1. Pan-Slavism
2. Gavrilo Princep
3. France
4. Belgium
5. Great Britain
6. Italy
7. Dardanelles
8. Bulgaria

SECTION 2 ACTIVITIES
Organizing Information
Total War: Weapons—**A.** Machine guns, **E.** U-boats, **C.** Tanks, **G.** Long-range artillery, **D.** Airplanes;

Style of Fighting—**B.** Trench warfare;

Participants—**F.** Drafted civilians, **H.** War industry at home.

Evaluating Information
1.	T	6.	T
2.	F	7.	T
3.	F	8.	T
4.	F	9.	F
5.	F	10.	F

Understanding Main Ideas
1.	d	3.	d
2.	b	4.	c

SECTION 3 ACTIVITIES
Organizing Information
The Russian Revolution:
1. Strikes and demonstrations in Petrograd
2. Duma demands reforms
3. czar abdicates the throne
4. czar's family imprisoned
5. Petrograd Soviet formed
6. Menshevik-Bolshevik quarrels
7. October Revolution
8. Formation of Communist Party

Evaluating Information
1.	T	6.	T
2.	T	7.	F
3.	F	8.	T
4.	T	9.	T
5.	T	10.	T

Understanding Main Ideas
1.	c	4.	b
2.	d	5.	a
3.	a		

SECTION 4 ACTIVITIES
Organizing Information
Allied Demands: France—Border moved to Rhine River, Return of Alsace-Lorraine, Coal-rich Saar valley;

Italy—Tirol, Cities of Fiume and Trieste;

Great Britain—Germany's colonies in Africa, Destruction of the German navy;

Japan—Germany's Pacific colonies.

Evaluating Information
1.	T	6.	F
2.	F	7.	T
3.	T	8.	T
4.	F	9.	T
5.	T	10.	F

Understanding Main Ideas
1.	b	3.	a
2.	d	4.	b

SECTION 5 ACTIVITIES
Organizing Information
The Treaty of Versailles—Germany was forced to do all items on the list, except all but destroy all its crops and destroy all its factories

Evaluating Information

1. T		6. F	
2. T		7. F	
3. T		8. T	
4. T		9. F	
5. T		10. T	

Understanding Main Ideas

1. d	3. a
2. c	

Chapter 28 (Modern Chapter 19)

SECTION 1 ACTIVITIES
Organizing Information

Literature—Gertrude Stein, F. Scott Fitzgerald, Franz Kafka, Marcel Proust, Ernest Hemingway;

Music—Igor Stravinsky, Louis Armstrong;

Architecture—Louis Sullivan, Frank Lloyd Wright;

Painting—Georges Braque, Salvador Dali, Pablo Picasso, Piet Mondrian, Wasilly Kandinsky.

Evaluating Information

1. F	6. T
2. F	7. F
3. T	8. T
4. T	9. F
5. F	10. F

Reviewing Facts

1. pandemic
2. unconscious
3. Gertrude Stein
4. twelve-tone scale
5. World Cup
6. money and prestige
7. credit
8. prohibition

SECTION 2 ACTIVITIES
Organizing Information

The Great Depression: Causes— protectionism, speculation, overvalued stock, sudden sell-off;

Effects—poverty amid productivity, no jobs, breadlines, New Deal

Evaluating Information

1. F	6. T
2. T	7. T
3. T	8. F
4. T	9. T
5. F	10. F

Understanding Main Ideas

1. c	3. a
2. d	4. b

SECTION 3 ACTIVITIES
Organizing Information

Post-War France: Military Security— **B.** Maginot Line; **E.** 200 miles long, **H.** along border with Germany and Luxembourg;

Treaties and Alliances—**A.** Czechoslovakia, **C.** Romania, **F.** Poland, **G.** Yugoslavia; **D.** fear of Germany.

Evaluating Information

1. F	6. T
2. F	7. T
3. F	8. T
4. T	9. F
5. T	10. T

Understanding Main Ideas

1. c	3. a
2. d	4. b

SECTION 4 ACTIVITIES
Organizing Information

Fascism—appealed to the upper and middle classes, relied on dictatorship and totalitarianism, name chosen by Benito Mussolini of Italy, made Italy into a police state, won support in Germany during the Great Depression.

Evaluating Information

1. F	6. T
2. F	7. T
3. F	8. T
4. T	9. F
5. F	10. F

Reviewing Facts
1. nationalistic and militaristic
2. figurehead
3. Treaty of Versailles
4. Nazi party
5. master race
6. der Führer
7. Third Reich
8. Rome-Berlin Axis

SECTION 5 ACTIVITIES
Organizing Information
The Soviet Union: Names—Vladimir Lenin,
  Joseph Stalin, Leon Trotsky;
Economic Policies—nationalized industries,
  collective farms, new economic policy,
  Five-Year Plans;
Lifestyle—divorce easier, women's pay
  lower than men's, no emphasis on basic
  education.

Evaluating Information
1.	F	6.	T
2.	F	7.	F
3.	F	8.	F
4.	T	9.	F
5.	F	10.	F

Understanding Main Ideas
1.	d	3.	c
2.	a	4.	b

Chapter 29 (Modern Chapter 20)

SECTION 1 ACTIVITIES
Organizing Information
Egyptian Independence: Year—1922;
How Won—by declaration of British
  government;
Terms—Britain may station soldiers in Egypt,
  controls Sudan, oversees Egyptian foreign
  policy.
Year—1936; How Won—by Anglo-Egyptian
  Treaty;
Terms—Britain controls Suez for 20 years,
  sponsors Egypt in League of Nations, gets
  support in case of Mideast war.

Evaluating Information
1.	T	6.	T
2.	F	7.	F
3.	F	8.	T
4.	T	9.	F
5.	T	10.	T

Reviewing Facts
1. Wafd Party
2. troops
3. Zionism
4. Balfour Declaration
5. Nazi
6. autonomy

SECTION 2 ACTIVITIES
Organizing Information
Turkey: Founder—Mustafa Kemal; New
  Name—Kemal Atatürk
Accomplishments—imposed civil and social
  reforms, secularized society, forced adoption
  of Western ways, gave women the vote
Persia: Founder—Reza Khan; New Name—
  Reza Shah Pahlavi
Accomplishments—modernized country,
  renamed the nation Iran, held most of the
  power, sought ties with Germany

Evaluating Information
1.	T	6.	F
2.	F	7.	T
3.	T	8.	T
4.	T	9.	F
5.	T	10.	T

Understanding Main Ideas
1.	b	3.	d
2.	d	4.	c

SECTION 3 ACTIVITIES
Organizing Information
Empress Dowager Tz'u-hsi—imprisoned
  Emperor Qing, encouraged Boxer Rebellion,
  left China under foreign domination;
Sun Yixian—once studied medicine, wanted
  constitutional government, wanted China to
  be industrialized;
Chiang Kai-shek—led Nationalist Party,
  fought the warlords, attacked Communists.

Evaluating Information

1. T	**6.** T
2. T	**7.** F
3. T	**8.** F
4. F	**9.** T
5. T	**10.** T

Understanding Main Ideas

1. a	**3.** b
2. c	**4.** d

SECTION 4 ACTIVITIES

Organizing Information

Japan Against Russia—feared Russian presence in Manchuria, signed an alliance with Great Britain in 1902 to protect their mutual interests, attacked the Russian fleet at Port Arthur, destroyed the Russian Baltic fleet at Tsushima, Treaty of Portsmouth ended Russian competition in Manchuria.

Evaluating Information

1. F	**6.** T
2. T	**7.** T
3. T	**8.** T
4. F	**9.** F
5. T	**10.** F

Reviewing Facts

1. fleet
2. Treaty of Portsmouth
3. fifty years
4. tariffs
5. militarism
6. Monroe Doctrine

SECTION 5 ACTIVITIES

Organizing Information

Latin America:
Argentina—Rafael Trujillo Molina;
Mexico—Lázaro Cárdenas;
Nicaragua—Anastasio Somoza;
Cuba—Gerardo Machado, Fulgencio Batista

Evaluating Information

1. T	**6.** T
2. T	**7.** T
3. T	**8.** T
4. T	**9.** T
5. T	**10.** F

Understanding Main Ideas

1. c	**3.** b
2. b	**4.** c

Chapter 30 (Modern Chapter 21)

SECTION 1 ACTIVITIES

Organizing Information

Japan—**H, C**
Italy—**A, B, I**
Spain—**B, D, E, F, G, J**

Evaluating Information

1. F	**6.** T
2. T	**7.** F
3. F	**8.** T
4. T	**9.** F
5. F	**10.** F

Reviewing Facts

1. Osachi Hamaguchi
2. Manchuria
3. League of Nations
4. dictator
5. Ethiopia
6. another war
7. Nationalists
8. fascist

SECTION 2 ACTIVITIES

Organizing Information

World War II: Austria—annexed in 1938, violation of Treaty of Versailles, League of Nations did nothing;

Sudetenland—strong local Nazi party, German riots led to invasion, Czechoslovakia left defenseless;

Poland—nonaggression pact gave it to Germany, Germans live in Polish Corridor, invasion on September 1, 1939.

Evaluating Information

1. T	**6.** T
2. F	**7.** T
3. F	**8.** T
4. F	**9.** F
5. F	**10.** T

ANSWER KEY

Understanding Main Ideas
1. b   3. c
2. d   4. a

SECTION 3 ACTIVITIES
Organizing Information
Great Britain—blockades German ports, lands soldiers in France, evacuates its forces from Dunkirk;

Soviet Union—invades eastern Poland, captures Estonia, Latvia, and Lithuania, captures Finland;

Nazi Germany—invades Denmark and Norway, invades Netherlands and Belgium, outflanks the Maginot Line, captures France.

Evaluating Information
1. T   6. T
2. T   7. F
3. T   8. F
4. F   9. T
5. F   10. T

Understanding Main Ideas
1. a   3. a
2. c   4. c

SECTION 4 ACTIVITIES
Organizing Information
Attack on Pearl Harbor (December 7, 1941):

Before—cuts British sea route to Hong Kong and Singapore, makes Netherlands East Indies a protectorate, makes Indochina a protectorate, joins Germany and Italy as an Axis power;

After—captures Guam, attacks Philippines, captures Burma, Thailand, and Malaya, captures New Guinea and Solomon Islands.

Evaluating Information
1. T   6. F
2. F   7. T
3. T   8. T
4. T   9. F
5. F   10. T

Reviewing Facts
1. Ethiopia
2. El Alamein
3. Russia
4. Stalingrad
5. Guam
6. battleships

SECTION 5 ACTIVITIES
Organizing Information
Hitler's New Order: Beliefs—**B.** superiority of Aryan race, **K.** anti-Semitism, **E.** racial inferiority of Slavs;

Plans and Planners—**H.** Wannsee Conference, **D.** Heinrich Himmler;

Rescuers—**G.** Danes, **C.** Raoul Wallenberg, **J.** Oskar Schindler;

Concentration Camps—**A.** Dachau, **I.** Treblinka, **F.** Buchenwald, **L.** Auschwitz.

Evaluating Information
1. T   6. F
2. T   7. T
3. F   8. T
4. T   9. F
5. T   10. T

Understanding Main Ideas
1. d   3. a
2. b   4. c

SECTION 6 ACTIVITIES
Organizing Information
Allied Victory:

Major German/Italian Defeats—Stalingrad, Tunisia, Sicily, D-Day and France, Battle of the Bulge;

Major Japanese Defeats—Battle of the Coral Sea, Battle of Midway, Guadalcanal, Battle of Leyte Gulf, bombing of Hiroshima and Nagasaki.

Evaluating Information
1. T   5. T
2. F   6. T
3. F   7. F
4. F   8. T

Understanding Main Ideas
1. b   3. c
2. a   4. c

Chapter 31 (Modern Chapter 22)

SECTION 1 ACTIVITIES

Organizing Information

"Big Three" meeting in Tehran, 1943—defeat Germany by attacking it from two fronts;

Meeting at the Black Sea resort in Yalta, 1945—divide Austria and Germany into zones of military occupation;

Meeting of allied leaders in Potsdam, 1945—demilitarize Germany and outlaw the Nazi party;

Meeting of 51 nations in San Francisco, 1945—establish the United Nations.

Evaluating Information

1. F
2. T
3. T
4. F
5. T
6. T
7. F
8. F

Reviewing Facts

1. Big Three
2. Yalta
3. Harry Truman
4. Sudeten
5. concentration camps
6. three
7. East and West Germany
8. Eleanor Roosevelt
9. China
10. veto power

SECTION 2 ACTIVITIES

Organizing Information

Events that Led to the Cold War: 1. The alliance between the Soviet and the Western allies dissolved; [2. The Soviets created a buffer zone of communist nations]; 3. The Truman Doctrine considered the spread of communism a threat to democracy; 4. The Marshall Plan put Europe on the road to prosperity; 5. The Soviets established the Cominform to oppose the Marshall Plan, [6. The Soviets blockaded the East German border].

Evaluating Information

1. T
2. T
3. F
4. T
5. F
6. T
7. T
8. F

Understanding Main Ideas

1. c
2. b
3. c
4. d

SECTION 3 ACTIVITIES

Organizing Information

Two Economies:

Great Britain—won the war, economic downturn, too reliant on coal reserves, slow industrial growth, lost overseas colonies, outdated factories;

West Germany—lost the war, economic rise, technical innovaton, few labor troubles;

In Common—anti-communist, anti-Soviet.

Classifying Information

1. T
2. T
3. F
4. F
5. T
6. F
7. F
8. T
9. F
10. T

Reviewing Facts

1. Konrad Adenauer
2. Fifth Republic
3. Common Market
4. Prague Spring

SECTION 4 ACTIVITIES

Organizing Information

Postwar United States:

Problem—Eisenhower faces spread of communism in Southeast Asia;

Solution—Creates Southeast Asian Treaty Organization (SEATO).

Problem—Joseph McCarthy leads anti-communist hysteria;

Solution—Senate Committee investigation finds claims groundless.

Problem—Martin Luther King Jr. leads civil rights movement;

Solution—U.S. Supreme Court orders integration in schools.

Evaluating Information

1.	T	6.	F
2.	T	7.	F
3.	F	8.	T
4.	F	9.	T
5.	T	10.	F

Reviewing Facts

1. Fidel Castro
2. missiles
3. Chicago
4. refugees
5. Quebecois
6. Kurds

Chapter 32 (Modern Chapter 23)

SECTION 1 ACTIVITIES

Organizing Information

[National Congress resigns, calls for self-rule]; Britain sends Sir Stafford Cripps; Mohandas Gandhi starts "Quit India;" Gandhi and Jinnah fail to resolve differences; [Riots break out]; Lord Louis Mountbatten sets deadline for independence; [Independence declared, borders defined]; India and Pakistan are born.

Evaluating Information

1.	T	6.	T
2.	F	7.	F
3.	T	8.	F
4.	F	9.	T
5.	F	10.	F

Reviewing Facts

1. Sikhs
2. two percent
3. Dalai Lama
4. three-quarters
5. Bangladesh
6. Khalida Zia
7. Benazir Bhutto

SECTION 2 ACTIVITIES

Organizing Information

Cultural Revolution—Violent attempt at social change;
Four Modernizations—A shift toward an open society;
Great Leap Forward—Five-Year Plan for economic growth.

Evaluating Information

1.	T	6.	T
2.	T	7.	F
3.	F	8.	T
4.	F	9.	F
5.	F	10.	F

Understanding Main Ideas

1.	c	3.	a
2.	c	4.	b

SECTION 3 ACTIVITIES

Organizing Information

Cause: more factories
Effect: pollution and less land for housing
Cause: break up of zaibatsu
Effect: focus on highly skilled workers
Cause: land reform
Effect: land for small farmers
Cause: higher standard of living
Effect: longer working hours
Cause: women in workforce
Effect: family no longer center of Japanese life

Classifying Information

1.	T	5.	T
2.	T	6.	F
3.	F	7.	T
4.	F	8.	F

Understanding Main Ideas

1.	c	3.	c
2.	a	4.	b

SECTION 4 ACTIVITIES
Organizing Information

Turmoil in Southeast Asia after Independence:

Vietnam—**D.** 1950s: Guerrilla leader built a communist zone after the French freed his country;

Philippines—**B.** 1974: President placed country under martial for 12 years;

Cambodia—**E.** 1975: Guerrilla leader set up a government that enforced a brutal plan;

Indonesia—**A.** 1960s: Dictator created own parliament;

Myanmar—**C.** 1962: Leader took control of the economy and almost destroyed it.

Evaluating Information

1.	F	6.	F
2.	T	7.	F
3.	F	8.	F
4.	T	9.	F
5.	T	10.	F

Reviewing Facts

1. Myanmar
2. domino theory
3. Tet Offensive
4. Paris Peace Accords
5. boat people
6. Saigon
7. Khmer Rouge
8. Pol Pot

SECTION 5 ACTIVITIES
Organizing Information

Problems—Solutions: 1. desire for rapid economic growth—government control at the expense of rights; 2. continuing internal conflicts between ethnic groups—army and police forces to control citizens; 3. worries about national security—unrestrained anti-communist violence

Evaluating Information

1.	T	5.	F
2.	T	6.	T
3.	T	7.	F
4.	F	8.	T

Understanding Main Ideas

1.	c	4.	d
2.	a	5.	c
3.	b		

Chapter 33 (Modern Chapter 24)

SECTION 1 ACTIVITIES
Organizing Information

African Independence:

Ghana—Movement: began a campaign of civil disobedience; Leader: Kwame Nkrumah;

Kenya—Movement: Mau Mau organization, fought a four-year guerrilla campaign; Leader: Jomo Kenyatta;

Zimbabwe—Movement: voted to withdraw from federation of multi-racial state; Leader: Robert Mugabe.

Evaluating Information

1.	T	5.	F
2.	F	6.	T
3.	T	7.	F
4.	F	8.	T

Reviewing Facts

1. Kwame Nkrumah
2. Ghana
3. Prime Minister Ian Smith
4. Portugal
5. Jomo Kenyatta
6. France
7. Congo
8. Nelson Mandela

SECTION 2 ACTIVITIES
Organizing Information

Effect of Colonial Economics—Ghana, Nigeria

Effect of Cold War—Angola, Somalia

Effect of Cultural Differences—Nigeria, Rwanda, Zaire, Somalia

Evaluating Information

1.	T	6.	F
2.	T	7.	T
3.	F	8.	T
4.	T	9.	F
5.	F	10.	T

Understanding Main Ideas

1.	b	3.	a
2.	d	4.	c

SECTION 3 ACTIVITIES
Organizing Information
Parade of Leaders:
Iran—Reza Shah Pahlavi, Mohammad Reza
Pahlavi, Mohammad Mosaddeq,
Mohammad Reza Pahlavi;
Egypt—King Farouk, Gamal Abdel Nasser;
Turkey—Mustafa Kemal, Ismet İnönü.

Evaluating Information
1.	T	6.	F
2.	T	7.	T
3.	F	8.	T
4.	T	9.	F
5.	F	10.	T

Finding Facts
1.	l	8.	h
2.	k	9.	e
3.	m	10.	c
4.	f	11.	j
5.	i	12.	b
6.	a	13.	g
7.	d		

SECTION 4 ACTIVITIES
Organizing Information
Arab-Israeli Disputes—Six-Day War, bombing
of Lebanon, OPEC cuts off the United
States from oil;
Islam in the Arab World—Iran seizes
American embassy;
Inter-Arab Aggressions—Iran-Iraq War,
Gulf War

Evaluating Information
1.	T	6.	T
2.	F	7.	T
3.	T	8.	T
4.	T	9.	F
5.	F	10.	T

Reviewing Facts
1. Yasir Arafat
2. Syria
3. Tehran
4. Ariel Sharon
5. Kuwait
6. Saddam Hussein
7. Mohammad Reza Pahlavi
8. OPEC
9. Iraq
10. Arab Fundamentalism

Chapter 34
(Modern Chapter 25)

SECTION 1 ACTIVITIES
Organizing Information
Problems Facing Latin America—
monoculture, population growth,
environment/toxins/disease, inflation, debt;
Efforts to Combat Problems—NAFTA,
develop national industry, import
substitution, brought in multinationals

Evaluating Information
1.	T	6.	T
2.	T	7.	T
3.	F	8.	T
4.	F	9.	F
5.	F	10.	F

Understanding Main Ideas
1.	c	3.	d
2.	c		

SECTION 2 ACTIVITIES
Organizing Information
Country—Nicaragua; Left-wing group—
Sandinistas; Right-wing group—Contras;
Country—El Salvador; Left-wing group—
FMLN; Right-wing group—death squads

Reviewing Facts
1. Mexico City
2. NAFTA
3. PEMEX
4. Sandanistas
5. contras
6. the Panama Canal
7. Manuel Noriega
8. the FMLN
9. the Contadora Principles

Evaluating Information
1.	T	6.	F
2.	T	7.	T
3.	F	8.	F
4.	F	9.	T
5.	F	10.	F

SECTION 3 ACTIVITIES
Organizing Information
Cuba—Fulgencio Batista, Fidel Castro, Che Guevara;

Puerto Rico—Luis Muñoz Marín;

Dominican Republic—Rafael Trujillo, Juan Bosch;

Haiti—François Duvalier, Jean-Claude Duvalier, Jean-Bertrand Aristide, René Préval.

Evaluating Information
1.	F	6.	F
2.	T	7.	T
3.	T	8.	T
4.	T	9.	T
5.	T	10.	T

Matching
1.	f	8.	k
2.	h	9.	e
3.	c	10.	g
4.	a	11.	j
5.	b	12.	l
6.	m	13.	i
7.	d		

SECTION 4 ACTIVITIES
Organizing Information
Argentina—Falkland Islands, dirty war

Peru—Shining Path guerrillas, MRTA guerrillas

Chile—Salvador Allende, Augusto Pinochet

Columbia—Medellín drug cartel, "The Violence"

Evaluating Information
1.	T	6.	F
2.	F	7.	F
3.	T	8.	T
4.	T	9.	F
5.	T	10.	T

Understanding Main Ideas
1.	c	3.	d
2.	a	4.	b

Chapter 35 (Modern Chapter 26)

SECTION 1 ACTIVITIES
Organizing Information
Nixon—Watergate Scandal, Vietnam;

Carter—Iran hostage situation in Tehran, doctrine opposing Soviet control of Middle East;

Reagan—Iran-contra, increased military spending;

Bush—U.S. recession, Gulf War;

Clinton—sex scandal, lied to grand jury.

Evaluating Information
1.	T	6.	T
2.	F	7.	T
3.	T	8.	F
4.	F	9.	T
5.	T	10.	F

Reviewing Facts
1. Separatism
2. détente
3. Kim Campbell
4. NAFTA
5. Carter Doctrine
6. Tiananmen Square
7. Official Languages Act
8. Meech Lake Accord

SECTION 2 ACTIVITIES
Organizing Information
Great Britain—North Sea oilfields, Falkland Islands War, Margaret Thatcher, Tony Blair, Northern Ireland;

France—Georges Pompidou, nuclear weapons tests, Arab immigration problems, François Mitterand, Jacques Chirac;

Germany—Willy Brandt, Ostpolitik, Helmut Kohl, fall of Berlin Wall, German reunification.

Evaluating Information
1.	F	5.	F
2.	T	6.	F
3.	F	7.	T
4.	T	8.	F

Finding Facts

1. d
2. e
3. c
4. k
5. m
6. b
7. a
8. l
9. j
10. i
11. h
12. f
13. g

SECTION 3 ACTIVITIES

Organizing Information

Soviet Union—communist, Yuri Andropov,
Mikhail Gorbachev, *glasnost, perestroika,*
coup attempt by hard liners;

Federation of Russia—post-communist,
privatized industry, black market goods,
organized crime, war in Chechnya;

In Common—Boris Yeltsin.

Evaluating Information

1. F
2. T
3. F
4. T
5. T
6. F
7. F
8. T

Reviewing Facts

1. Afghanistan
2. Brezhnev Doctrine
3. perestroika
4. Yeltsin
5. Solidarity
6. Velvet Revolution
7. Yugoslavia
8. Dayton Accord

SECTION 4 ACTIVITIES

Organizing Information

8:45—An American Airlines passenger jet
crashed into the World Trade Center
north tower; United Airlines Flight 93
crashed southeast of Pennsylvania.

9:00—United Airlines Flight 175 slammed into
the World Trade Center south tower.

9:40—American Airlines Flight 77 hit the west
side of the Pentagon.

10:00—The south tower of the World Trade
Center collapsed.

10:30—World Trade Center north tower
collapsed.

Evaluating Information

1. F
2. F
3. T
4. T
5. F
6. T
7. T
8. T
9. F
10. T

Reviewing Facts

1. Rudolph Giuliani
2. Tony Blair
3. "the Base"
4. fundamentalist
5. Office of Homeland Security
6. Article 5

Chapter 36 (Modern Chapter 27)

SECTION 1 ACTIVITIES

Organizing Information

Painters: Andy Warhol, Jackson Pollock
Musicians: The Beatles, John Cage
Writers: Toni Morrison, Naguib Mahfouz

Evaluating Information

1. T
2. F
3. F
4. F
5. F
6. F
7. T
8. T
9. T
10. F

Reviewing Facts

1. experimentation
2. op art
3. conceptual artists
4. engineering
5. Beatles
6. New Wave
7. visual effects
8. modern
9. technology
10. cultural

SECTION 2 ACTIVITIES

Organizing Information

Human Genome Project: mapping of DNA
Roslin Institute: first successful cloning
Blaise Pascal: penicillin
Alexander Fleming: first automatic calculator

Evaluating Information

1. F	**5.** T
2. F	**6.** T
3. T	**7.** T
4. F	**8.** F

Understanding Main Ideas

1. a	**4.** a
2. b	**5.** c
3. d	**6.** b

SECTION 3 ACTIVITIES
Organizing Information

Philippines: Autocratic rule by Marcos ended.
South Africa: Black majority elected Nelson Mandela.
Indonesia: President Suharto left office.
Latin America: Many countries moved to a more democratic system.

Evaluating Information

1. F	**6.** F
2. T	**7.** T
3. F	**8.** F
4. T	**9.** T
5. F	**10.** F

Interpreting Visual Images

1. 1992
2. decreased

Epilogue

SECTION 1 ACTIVITIES
Organizing Information

1. British colonizers establish Jamestown;
2. Settlers found Plymouth; 3. Americans take to heart Rousseau's ideas; 4. Americans stage uprisings against taxes; 5. British troops seize guns in Boston; 6. America gains independence; 7. Confederate states adopt federal system.

Evaluating Information

1. T	**5.** T
2. F	**6.** T
3. F	**7.** F
4. F	**8.** T

Reviewing Facts

1. Articles of Confederation
2. guillotine
3. Waterloo
4. electricity
5. internal combustion engine
6. communism

SECTION 2 ACTIVITIES
Organizing Information

Italy: Benito Mussolini; fascism
Germany: Adolf Hitler; Nazism
Soviet Union: Josef Stalin; communism

Evaluating Information

1. T	**6.** T
2. T	**7.** T
3. F	**8.** F
4. F	**9.** T
5. T	**10.** F

Understanding Main Ideas

1. d	**3.** c
2. b	**4.** a

SECTION 3 ACTIVITIES
Organizing Information

The United States and Allies: restricted spread of communism, assisted in rebuilding the European economy, planned to unify Germany, formed NATO;
The Soviet Union: blockaded the East German border, expanded the influence of communism, established the German Democratic Republic, combined troop strength in the Warsaw Pact

Classifying Information

1. T	**6.** T
2. F	**7.** F
3. F	**8.** F
4. T	**9.** T
5. F	**10.** T

Reviewing Facts

1. a	**3.** d
2. c	**4.** b

SECTION 4 ACTIVITIES

Organizing Information

1. Douglas MacArthur
2. Mao Zedong
3. Corazon Aquino
4. Ho Chi Minh
5. Jawaharlal Nehru
6. Nelson Mandela

Evaluating Information

1.	T	6.	T
2.	T	7.	T
3.	F	8.	T
4.	F	9.	F
5.	F	10.	F

Understanding Main Ideas

1.	c	3.	c
2.	d	4.	a

SECTION 5 ACTIVITIES

Organizing Information

Faster, more reliable transportation led to easier movement and migrations;
Medical advances led to longer lives and population growth;
Industrialization led to large-scale production, and pollution and damage to the ozone layer.

Understanding Main Ideas

1.	a	3.	b
2.	d	4.	c

Matching

1.	h	6.	d
2.	g	7.	e
3.	i	8.	b
4.	f	9.	c
5.	j	10.	a

SECTION 6 ACTIVITIES

Organizing Information

8:45—An American Airlines passenger jet crashed into the World Trade Center north tower; United Airlines Flight 93 crashed southeast of Pennsylvania.

9:00—United Airlines Flight 175 slammed into the World Trade Center south tower.

9:40—American Airlines Flight 77 hit the west side of the Pentagon.

10:00—The south tower of the World Trade Center collapsed.

10:30—World Trade Center north tower collapsed.

Evaluating Information

1.	F	6.	T
2.	F	7.	T
3.	T	8.	T
4.	T	9.	F
5.	F	10.	T

Reviewing Facts

1. Rudolph Giuliani
2. Tony Blair
3. "the Base"
4. fundamentalist
5. Office of Homeland Security
6. Article 5

Prologue

SECTION 1 ACTIVITIES

Organizing Information

Egyptians—Nile Valley, strong believers in polytheism;
Sumerians—Tigris-Euphrates Valley, developed cuneiform;
Lydians—Asia Minor, first people to use coined money;
Hebrews—Canaan, worshiped Yahweh as creator

Evaluating Information

1.	F	6.	T
2.	T	7.	T
3.	F	8.	F
4.	T	9.	F
5.	F	10.	T

Reviewing Facts
1. prehistory
2. Neolithic Revolution
3. Menes
4. monotheism
5. Sumerians
6. Hammurabi
7. coined money
8. Judaism

SECTION 2 ACTIVITIES
Organizing Information
Indian Civilization—Hinduism and
   Buddhism, Gupta dynasty, began in the
   Indus River valley;
Chinese Civilization—Daoism and Legalism,
   Gobi Desert, began along the Huang River.

Evaluating Information

1. T	8. T
2. F	9. T
3. F	10. T
4. T	11. T
5. T	12. F
6. T	13. F
7. F	14. T

Understanding Main Ideas

1. a	3. d
2. a	4. a

SECTION 3 ACTIVITIES
Organizing Information
Greek—impressive works of art, logical
   explanations for natural events;
Hellenistic—blend of different cultures, spread
   of Greek ideas to the world;
Roman—a republic government, engineering
   marvels.

Evaluating Information

1. T	6. F
2. F	7. F
3. T	8. T
4. F	9. T
5. T	10. F

Classifying Information

1. j	6. b
2. e	7. d
3. f	8. h
4. a	9. i
5. g	10. c

SECTION 4 ACTIVITIES
Organizing Information
D. African city-states—merged African,
   Arabic and Persian elements;
A. Maya—invented the only writing system
   in the Americas;
B. Aztec—developed a calendar and used
   mathematics;
C. Inca—advanced in the practice of medi-
   cine, using anesthetic

Understanding Main Ideas

1. c	3. d
2. a	4. b

Reviewing Facts
1. Egypt
2. King 'Ezānā
3. coastal trade
4. Swahili
5. Mali
6. gold
7. Aztec
8. Andes Mountains